Rotherham Primary Care Trust
Oak House
Moorhead Way
Bramley
Rotherham S66 1YY
Tel. No. 01709 302096

Adolescence, Risk and Resilience

'm on or before the ⸱

Adolescence, Risk and Resilience

Against the Odds

edited by

John Coleman

and

Ann Hagell

BICENTENNIAL
1807
WILEY
2007
BICENTENNIAL

John Wiley & Sons, Ltd

Other Wiley Editorial Offices

John Wiley & Sons Inc., 111 River Street, Hoboken, NJ 07030, USA

Jossey-Bass, 989 Market Street, San Francisco, CA 94103-1741, USA

Wiley-VCH Verlag GmbH, Boschstr. 12, D-69469 Weinheim, Germany

John Wiley & Sons Australia Ltd, 42 McDougall Street, Milton, Queensland 4064, Australia

John Wiley & Sons (Asia) Pte Ltd, 2 Clementi Loop #02-01, Jin Xing Distripark, Singapore 129809

John Wiley & Sons Canada Ltd, 6045 Freemont Blvd, Mississauga, ONT, L5R 4J3

Wiley also publishes its books in a variety of electronic formats. Some content that appears in print may not be
available in electronic books.

Anniversary logo design: Richard J. Pacifico

Library of Congress Cataloging-in-Publication Data

Adolescence, risk and resilience : against the odds / edited by John
Coleman and Ann Hagell.
     p. cm.
  Includes bibliographical references and index.
  ISBN 978-0-470-02502-4 (cloth : alk. paper) — ISBN 978-0-470-02503-1
(pbk. : alk. paper)
1. Adolescent psychology.   2. Risk-taking (Psychology) in adolescence.   I.
Coleman, John. II. Hagell, Ann.
  BF724.2.A36 2007
  155.5'1824—dc22   2007019143

British Library Cataloguing in Publication Data

A catalogue record for this book is available from the British Library

ISBN 978-0-470-02502-4 (HB) 978-0-470-02503-1 (PB)

Typeset in 10/12 pt Times by Thomson Digital
Printed and bound in Great Britain by Scotprint, East Lothian
This book is printed on acid-free paper responsibly manufactured from sustainable forestry
in which at least two trees are planted for each one used for paper production.

Contents

Chapter 1

The Nature of Risk and Resilience in Adolescence

John Coleman

Senior Research Fellow, University of Oxford

Ann Hagell

Programme Director Adolescent Mental Health, Nuffield Foundation;
Editor, Journal of Adolescence

- ◼ Introduction
- ◼ Adolescence as a stage of development
- ◼ Risk factors
- ◼ Risk or risky behaviour
- ◼ Young people at risk, and the role of protective factors
- ◼ Resilience
- ◼ Conclusion

Learning Objectives

Once you have read this chapter you should be able to:

1 Understand the vulnerabilities that apply to the adolescent stage of development.
2 Be aware of the different ways that the concept of risk is applied to young people.
3 Understand resilience and the role of protective factors in adolescence.
4 Have some knowledge of strategies for the promotion of resilience.

Adolescence, Risk and Resilience: *Against the odds.* John Coleman and Ann Hagell (eds.).
Published in 2007 by John Wiley & Sons, Ltd

Introduction

Adolescence is often portrayed as an age of particular risk, in other words a potentially problematic age. However, the concept of risk has many definitions and can be used to mean different things about young people, not all of them negative. It is also a concept that has overlap with other ideas which are applied to children and young people, such as social exclusion, adversity, stress and vulnerability, as well as coping and resilience. It will be our intention in this book to explore the concept of risk and to outline the different ways in which it is used in the context of adolescence.

Because the term 'risk' has a predominantly negative connotation, we have chosen a title that gives a more balanced picture. The topics we have included represent some of the major challenges that more vulnerable young people are likely to face. We have given this book the subtitle 'Against the odds' because we want to highlight and discuss the nature of these challenges. In addition, however, we also want to recognize that many young people overcome the challenges and go on to make a positive adjustment in adulthood.

It may be helpful at this stage to state briefly some of the ways in which the concept of risk can be applied to young people. We will note four possible uses of the term.

- *Risk factors*: the term that usually refers to the factors that might contribute to poor outcomes for young people, such as poverty, deprivation, illness or dysfunctional family background.
- *Risk behaviour, or risky behaviour*: this term applies to potentially harmful behaviour that young people might engage in, such as having unsafe sex, abusing substances such as alcohol or illegal drugs, or taking part in anti-social activities.
- *Young people at risk*: this term is used to refer to those who are potentially vulnerable, such as those who are socially excluded, those who are subject to abuse or neglect, and those who are in custody or in care.
- *Young people who pose a risk to society*: this concept is used to apply to those who engage in anti-social behaviour or who in other ways pose a threat to their communities.

In later sections of this chapter we will be exploring these terms in greater detail, and showing how some elements of risk behaviour can be reframed and cast in a more positive light. We will also show how society's notions of risk contribute to the negative stereotype of young people that is both pervasive and unhelpful. As we have said, we want this book to present a balanced view of young people, and it is for that reason, as well as exploring risk, that we also want to highlight the concept of resilience. In the words of Luthar (2003), resilience "refers to patterns of positive adjustment in the context of significant risk or adversity" (p. 4). Luthar makes the point that for resilience to apply two fundamental judgements have to be made. First, that the individual is coping adequately, or in everyday language is 'doing okay'. Second, that there is now, or has been, significant risk or adversity to overcome.

It will be obvious from a cursory glance at the title page of this book that the themes covered here constitute significant adversity. We will be looking at families and the risks they pose for young people, at mental ill-health, at offending behaviour, at sexual risk, at disability, at being looked after, and at social exclusion. It is our intention to show how these adversities affect young people, and to look at how it is possible in the face of such circumstances to develop resilience. The focus of the book is on how to better understand the challenges that face those adolescents who are most 'at risk', and to assess the protective factors that can facilitate positive adjustment.

Adolescence as a Stage of Development

As part of the introduction to this book it will be as well to say something about the particular stage of development involved here. Throughout history the period of life which starts with puberty, and continues through the teenage years, has been seen by many as problematic. Textbooks like to quote Plato or Shakespeare who, centuries ago, saw youth as a difficult stage. More recently the notion of 'storm and stress' has had wide currency, and many of the early scientific studies of adolescence, particularly those which took place in the 1960s and 1970s, tried to establish whether this phenomenon was a fact or a fiction (e.g., Douvan and Adelson, 1966; Rutter *et al.*, 1976).

By and large, the empirical research has concluded that most adolescents navigate this stage of life with relatively little major trauma. Yes, there are struggles and challenges to overcome, and relationships with parents are not always sweetness and light, but on the whole the majority manage to cope relatively well (Coleman and Hendry, 1999; Jackson and Goossens, 2006). There is of course a group who do experience serious difficulty, but these young people are in the minority, rather then being the general rule where adolescence is concerned.

For all individuals, however, adolescence is a stage that requires considerable adjustment, and we should not underestimate the degree of change experienced during these years. One of the most helpful ways of understanding adolescence is to think about it as one of life's major transitions. Here are some of the characteristics of transitions:

- A feeling of anticipation for what is ahead.
- A sense of regret for the stage that has been lost.
- Anxiety about the future.
- A major psychological readjustment.
- A degree of ambiguity of status during the transition.

All of these characteristics are strikingly true of adolescence. Adulthood beckons, with its associated freedoms and opportunities, all of which appear very attractive at the age of 15 or 16. On the other hand, there is sadness about one's disappearing childhood and the loss of dependence and safety associated with it. One of the reasons that adolescents seem so contradictory in their behaviour is that inside every teenage individual is both a child and an adult. Young people worry about the future, perhaps more so today than ever before. Exams, long periods of economic dependence and the uncertainty of the job market all contribute to this anxiety.

In addition to all this, no one disputes that a series of major psychological adjustments have to be negotiated during adolescence, and these include shifts in relationships with family, friends, the peer group and the wider world. Lastly, the adolescent period carries with it a sense of uncertainty about status and role. The teenage question 'When am I grown up?' is one that any parent will find difficult to answer. With longer and longer periods of education and training, and yet with mature social and sexual behaviours being manifested at younger and younger ages, how can we provide clarity about the dilemma of the adolescent's status in society? What are the rights and responsibilities of someone who is 16, or 17? Parents, teachers, lawyers, doctors, the police, politicians – all might give slightly different answers, thus increasing the confusion over the status of young people in our society.

We referred briefly above to the uncertainties of the job market. Over the last 20 years there have been a number of major social changes that have had a particular impact on adolescents. Here we pick out two such changes – the transformation of the employment situation and alterations in family structure. Taking employment first, since the mid-1980s there has been a dramatic shift in the way young people experience entry into the labour market. Now hardly any 16-year-olds go into a full-time job, yet this was the most common option at the beginning of the 1980s.

Today almost everyone spends the years between 16 and 18 in some form of education or training, and only a minority find stable work at the end of this period. Roughly 45% of young Britons now go on to university, compared with 15% in 1980. The labour market for the 18- to 25-year age group has shrunk, so that there are fewer jobs available and entry into full-time employment takes substantially longer than it did for previous generations. It is perhaps worth noting that such changes have the greatest impact on those who are most vulnerable. Not surprisingly, where jobs become scarcer it is the individuals with the greatest number of adversities who are most affected by social change of this sort (see Figure 1.1).

The second social change that has had a serious impact on children and young people has been the alteration in family structure which has taken place over roughly the same historical period. During the 1960s and 1970s the rate of divorce in the UK increased substantially, leading to a period when new family types were being seen, especially those involving step-parents and non-residential parents. The divorce rate has become more stable since the mid-1980s, but equally important, the number of families headed by a lone parent has shown a significant increase. As can be seen in Figure 1.2, the number of such families has risen from 13% of all families with dependent children in 1981, to 26% of such families in 2002. The implication of this social change cannot be overemphasized, not least because families headed by a lone parent are three times more likely to be in poverty than couple families.

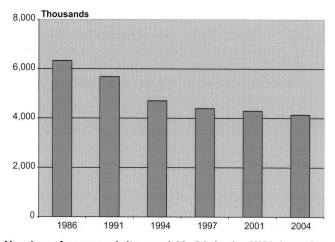

Figure 1.1   Number of young adults aged 16–24, in the UK labour force, 1986–2004
Source: Coleman, J. and Schofield, J., Key data on Adolescence, 2005. Trust for the study of Adolescence

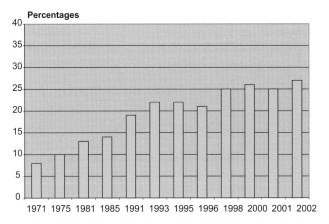

Figure 1.2   Proportion of families with dependent children headed by a lone parent in Britain, 1971–2002
Source: General Household Survey, Living in Britain, 2004, ONS.

There will be more discussion of the changing nature of the family in Chapter 2, but for the present we think it right to identify the increase in lone parents as one of the major social changes that has affected children and young people in Britain today.

As we can see, therefore, the adolescent stage carries with it a series of developmental tasks, as well as a variety of potential challenges. The empirical evidence tells us that within the general population the majority manage to cope with these tasks and challenges relatively well. However, there are, of course, a group who find this stage more difficult, and we will turn now to a consideration of this minority. How can we identify this minority?

One way to do so is to select particular groups that are vulnerable, such as those with a disability, those in custody, or those in care. Many of these groups will be the subject of various chapters in this book. Another way to consider the minority who are most vulnerable is to use a measure, such as one that relates to mental ill-health, and determine the proportion of the adolescent population experiencing such difficulty. If we were to do this, we might note that one of the most recent studies (Green *et al.*, 2005) showed that approximately 10% of young people in England and Wales have a psychiatric disorder.

Other studies, however, particularly those looking at stress or depression, do show higher rates of difficulty. In a study by West and Sweeting (2003), investigating young people in Scotland, it was reported that 33% of 15-year-old girls in 1999 were experiencing anxiety or depression. Interestingly this figure had increased substantially since the 1980s, as can be seen in Figure 1.3. There are two striking things about the results from this study. First, there are substantial gender differences in levels of anxiety and depression but second, there appears to have been a marked increase for girls in this measure over a 12-year period. Is this another important social change that is affecting adolescents today? (See Discussion Question 1 at the end of this chapter.)

Of course, using a measure of mental health is not the only way of identifying those who find the adolescent period a difficult one. There are many different ways in which the

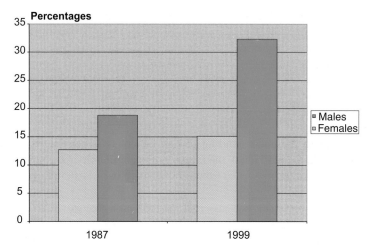

Figure 1.3   Psychological distress among 15-year-olds in Scotland, by gender, 1987 and 1999
Source: West and Sweeting (2003).

experience of difficulty is expressed, as, for example, through poor educational attainment, engaging in risky sexual behaviour, excessive use of substances and so on. In the same way, there are many reasons why young people struggle during this stage of their lives. The topics covered by the authors of this book will enable us to look at some of the most pervasive adversities experienced by adolescents, and to understand the factors that contribute to resilience in the face of such adversity. It is now time to turn to a more detailed examination of the notion of risk in adolescent development.

Risk Factors

As we have already indicated, there are a wide range of possible risk factors that may impinge on an individual's development, some of which we will be considering in this book. Landmark studies of risk and resilience have considered the impact of poverty, war, natural disasters, long-term family disadvantage, health problems of all types, abuse and maltreatment, and so on. These experiences represent some but not all of the established risk factors which are known to predict negative outcomes for children and young people. Early studies of risk factors tended to focus on one factor only, such as poverty for example, but later studies have recognized that risk factors tend to cluster or co-occur. Thus parents living in poverty are likely to have higher rates of depression and other mental disorders, as well as being less effective in their parenting behaviour. In such circumstances adult depression, parenting behaviour and financial hardship all impact on the child or young person in a cumulative fashion.

In this way the impact of risk can multiply, and later studies have tended to look at what is known as cumulative risk, where risk indicators have been aggregated together (Masten and Powell, 2003). All writers in this field agree that, in general, the more risks the individual is exposed to, or the greater the risk gradient, the greater the likelihood of a poor outcome (Appleyard *et al.*, 2005).

It is also important to distinguish between what may be called independent and non-independent risk factors. Thus events outside the control of the individual are known as independent events, and may include the death of a parent, a natural disaster and so on. On the other hand, non-independent events are those related to an individual's own behaviour, and may include relationship difficulties, taking health risks and other similar behaviours. The incidence of non-independent stressful events increases with age (Gest *et al.*, 1999), and this is perhaps not surprising in that adolescents have a greater degree of freedom as they move through the teenage years.

Another approach to the understanding of risk factors is to consider them in terms of whether they are within the individual, the family or the community. Of course not all factors can be identified in this way, but some of the following are useful examples.

- *Individual factors*: anxious temperament, low intelligence, poor health, hyperactivity, limited attention span, low frustration tolerance.
- *Family factors*: parental ill-health, parental conflict, parental involvement in crime, harsh or inconsistent discipline, loss of a parent due to death or divorce, disruptive siblings.
- *Community factors*: economic disadvantage, poor housing, quality of schooling and other services, crime rate, level of substance misuse, lack of community role models.

An alternative approach to the understanding of risk factors is that which originates from the clinical literature, particularly that dealing with the study of stress. The term 'stressor' deals with variables that are very similar to those described by other writers as risk factors. One important contributor to this literature is Bruce Compas (Compas *et al.*, 1993; Compas, 1995). He notes that stress will vary along a number of dimensions, including whether it is normative or atypical, large or small in magnitude, and chronic or acute in nature. Compas goes on to distinguish three broad categories of stressor, the categories being generic or normative stress, acute stress and chronic stress. As can be imagined, all young people experience some degree of stress as they move through adolescence. Such things will include changes of school, the loss of friends, daily hassles with adults, and so on. This is what is known as normative stress.

Compas, however, points out that some young people will experience more serious stressors, including such things as injury or accident, the death of a parent, and so on (acute stress). Alternatively, an adolescent may grow up in poverty, or will experience racism, parental conflict, bullying or other long-standing difficulty (chronic stress). These distinctions are helpful, and yet there are other factors needing to be taken into account as well if we are to understand a young person's adaptation to such adversities. Two key factors include the timing of events, and the number of stressors experienced by the young person at the same time.

Looking first at the number of stressors, it will be clear that the more difficulties any young person experiences, the more resources will be needed to deal with these. This is particularly true during adolescence, when there may be both normative and non-normative stressors to manage. Thus, for example, if an adolescent has to deal with moving school, going through puberty, losing friends, as well as having an acute problem to deal with at home (for example, parental illness), then this is going to be very different from someone who only has one stressor to deal with. This notion is similar to that of a risk gradient,

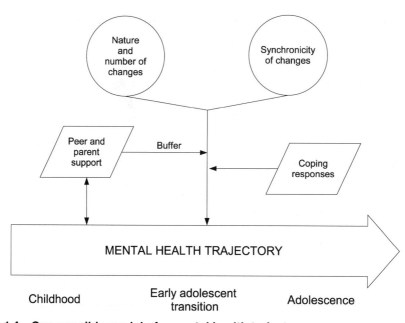

Figure 1.4   One possible model of a mental health trajectory
Source: J. Coleman and L. Hendry, *The Nature of Adolescence*, 3rd edn. Routledge, 1999, p. 211.

mentioned above, where we gave the example of poverty interacting with parental depression and parenting behaviour.

The number of events is also linked to the question of timing. The way normative and non-normative events cluster together is a key factor in determining the ability of the individual to cope. If difficulties impinge on the individual all at the same time, this will obviously make things more difficult than if stressors occur one at a time. An interesting model of a mental health trajectory is shown in Figure 1.4, where it can be seen that both timing and the number of stressful events are shown as contributing to the trajectory. This model also identifies a number of protective factors, including parent and peer support, coping responses, and so on. We will look in more detail at these protective factors in a later section of this chapter.

Risk or Risky Behaviour

(*Note*: To the adult ear the term 'risky' sounds somewhat more dangerous than the word 'risk', but we will use the latter term in this chapter, recognizing that there is little difference between the two.) Up to this point we have been considering risk factors but, as we have noted above, this concept differs in many respects from the idea of risk behaviour. While risk factors are the variables that may contribute to poor outcomes, risk behaviour concerns those activities, engaged in by the majority of adolescents, that are potentially harmful. Included here are such things as drinking, smoking, substance use, various types of anti-social behaviour and what might be called risky sexual behaviour. A challenging question arises when we consider these behaviours:

- Is the engagement in risk behaviour a normative feature of adolescence? Do adolescents need to take risks in order to grow and develop, or is risk behaviour a threat to health and to social order?

To take a more concrete example, is 'Just say NO to drugs' the right message to use with young people? Alternatively, should parents and teachers be emphasizing the 'harm minimization' or 'harm reduction' approach, thus recognizing that exploration and experimentation is probable, although not of course inevitable, in this age group?

There is no easy answer to this question. For some commentators a degree of risk behaviour is commonplace, and indeed beneficial, for young people. In this model adolescents, for example, have to learn how to drink alcohol without exposing themselves to serious danger. As for drugs, research shows that somewhere between 30% and 40% of those aged 16 have experimented with cannabis, so that it makes little sense to describe cannabis use as seriously harmful behaviour. On the other hand, there has to be a degree of moderation. While we might encourage young people to learn how to handle alcohol, and develop strategies to keep themselves safe, no sensible adult is going to endorse binge drinking or drinking in unsafe environments.

One of the particular problems with the concept of risk behaviour is that it gives currency to a negative stereotype of young people. Thus we can see that, if adolescents are perceived as sexually promiscuous, drug-taking and engaging in other 'unsafe' behaviours, then this allows adults to feel critical – even threatened – by this age group. This is a serious concern, and gets to the heart of the mutual misunderstanding that can be a feature of inter-generational attitudes and opinions. It is very important to underline two facts:

- Not all adolescents engage in risk behaviours.
- Many of those who do engage in such behaviours only do so at a minimal, non-harmful level.

It is also essential to be clear about the differences between risk factors and risk behaviour. There may be some situations where they overlap, so, for example, those in custody or in care may be more likely to have problems with substance misuse than those in the general population. However, those who do engage in risk behaviours will not necessarily be those who have experienced a high number of risk factors in their development. Many examples of risk behaviour can be seen in the population as a whole, and indeed those who have risk factors in their background do not necessarily engage in risk behaviour. It is important to recognize that the two notions of risk are conceptually distinct.

Another interesting question regarding risk behaviour is how young people understand the concept of risk. In a recent study, Rodham *et al.* (2006) asked adolescents how they defined risk, and how they made decisions about engaging in risk behaviours. First, how do young people see risk?

I think it is something you do, hoping that the outcome will be beneficial to you, but also knowing that it could have negative effects, so it's kind of taking a chance. (Male, 17)

I see risk as something you can't control the outcome of. It could be bad, but when you do it you're not sure what the outcome will be. (Male, 17)

A risk is something that if you don't do well, then it will harm you in some way. (Female, 18)

(Rodham *et al.*, 2006, p. 266)

It can be seen from these statements that, for young people, risk either involves a degree of chance, or it involves potential harm if precautions are not taken. The main theme which emerges from the responses to questions about engagement in risk behaviour is that of personal responsibility.

If you don't, if you kind of don't want to do it, you don't, and there is nothing that is going to make you…(Male, 17)

There's so much, and the sex education as well…It's all drummed into you from an early age. And then I think it is just up to them. No-one can blame not knowing that drugs can damage you and stuff. It's just whether you want to take the risk or not. I think people do know. I think they can't not know, if you know what I mean. (Female, 17)

(Rodham *et al.*, 2006, p. 268)

There is a strong argument for a change of terminology in relation to risk behaviour, as Michaud (2006) believes. In his view, it would be best if terms such as 'exploratory' or 'experimental' were used to describe behaviours that are common in adolescence, but which do not necessarily lead to harm or danger. Examples of such behaviours would include moderate alcohol use, moderate smoking, protected sex with a known and trusted partner, and so on. However, there still remain many uncertainties and issues for debate. Would it be right to include substance use in this category? And if so, how would you define what is experimental and what is harmful? We have to recognize that, where adolescent risk behaviour is concerned, adults struggle with issues of protection, the need to keep young people safe from harm, and uncertainty about the long-term consequences of many risk behaviours. (Further questions for discussion can be found at the end of this chapter.)

Young People at Risk, and the Role of Protective Factors

We turn now to a different use of the term 'risk' – that is, those young people who may be said to be 'at risk'. By and large these young people are likely to be those who have a high number of risk factors in their background.

Studies show that such young people are significantly more likely than others to have poorer outcomes and restricted life chances. However, it is not always the case that those with a high number of risk factors in their background do badly. The major studies of risk and resilience (e.g., Werner and Smith, 1992; Fergusson and Horwood, 2003) point out that there are some who, despite being exposed to major adversity, appear to cope well and to show remarkable resilience in the face of huge odds. Why should this be so?

The key lies in the presence of protective factors. As John Bynner puts it:

Protective factors work on the more malleable components of development, reflecting the differ-ent kinds of resources that may help the child to resist adversity. They comprise the emotional,

educational, social and economic influences on the child's life, operating singly, or more usually,
in interaction with each other.

(Bynner, 2001, p. 286)

What are these protective factors? Many writers believe that it is helpful to draw the distinction, as we have already done with risk factors, between those which are individual attributes, those which originate from within the family, and those that depend on resources in the neighbourhood or community. This distinction was first described by two of the major writers in this field, Michael Rutter and Norman Garmezy (Garmezy and Rutter, 1983). In this paradigm, the following are some of the most common attributes described.

- *Individual attributes*: good intellectual skills, positive temperament, positive views of the self.
- *Family attributes*: high warmth, cohesion, high expectations, parental involvement.
- *Community attributes*: good schools, neighbourhood resources, strong social networks.

Readers will be aware that these categories are the same as those we have used to describe risk factors, and the relationship between risk and protective factors is one that inspires continuing debate. Two key questions arise (see Luthar and Zelazo, 2003). Firstly, do the factors that contribute to protection, and those that contribute to risk and vulnerability, essentially lie on the same continuum, or are they qualitatively different? The second question is one of the most hotly debated in all the literature. This is whether protective factors are factors that contribute to competence in general, so that they will help everyone (both those who have and those who have not experienced serious adversity), or whether there are specific protective factors that are directly relevant to adversity only? We will consider these questions in turn.

In relation to the first question, we can certainly suggest variables that are protective at one extreme yet create vulnerability at the other. Luthar (2003) argues that intelligence provides just such an example, being a protective factor at one end of the scale and engendering vulnerability at the other end. However, not all variables which are modifiers of risk fall into this pattern. Poverty is certainly a factor that leads to increased vulnerability, yet extreme wealth may not necessarily lead to a positive outcome either. Rutter (1985) has proposed the notion that some variables are most effective in modifying risk when they are at the mid-point along the continuum. He suggests that closeness to parents is one such factor. A lack of closeness to parents is obviously potentially damaging, but then being too close, and experiencing over-protection, is also an unhealthy circumstance. The same argument might be applied to attachment, which is normally thought of as a positive benefit. However, a too secure attachment may not allow the child or young person to develop skills to deal with the inevitable disappointments that are part of any relationship.

As for the second question, there are many writers in this field who believe that protective factors do need to be differentiated between those that enhance competence for all, and those that are specific to particular risk experiences. Thus reasonable economic advantage, parental warmth (as long as it is not taken to an extreme degree), above average intelligence and high self-esteem are all generally considered to be protective factors that will benefit everyone, not only those suffering adversity. However, we can also suggest protective factors that have a particular role in certain circumstances. Parental strictness is often given as one such example. By and large strictness, or an authoritarian parenting style, is considered to be detrimental for children and young people. Nonetheless, some studies have shown that strictness can be beneficial for inner-city children growing up in disadvantaged environments (Cauce *et al.*, 2003).

Let us return now to the major studies of risk and resilience mentioned earlier. One of the most interesting challenges for social scientists working in this field has been to try to understand how it is that, even in situations where there is a high level of adversity, some children and young people manage to cope well, and to overcome the extreme risks to which they are exposed. Two landmark studies are often quoted when considering this question. The first is one carried out in Hawaii during the 1980s by Werner and colleagues (Werner and Smith, 1982, 1992). In this study the researchers managed to track down over 500 individuals at age 30 who had been studied as part of a large cohort when they were children. They found that, out of the sample who had experienced major risk factors (chronic poverty, parents lacking education, troubled family environment), two-thirds had developed serious problems by the age of 18. However, approximately one-third appeared to have survived well, and to be functioning effectively as adults.

This group was distinguished by high levels of achievement orientation, as well as by having alternative care-takers during middle childhood. Other factors that were prominent included sociability, good communication skills, a supportive neighbourhood and good peer relationships. Of considerable importance also was the presence of additional stress factors experienced later on, especially in adolescence. Thus those who were exposed to a high number of risk factors in childhood, and who also experienced further stress as teenagers, did worst of all. Thus, as we noted earlier, when the risk gradient becomes steeper, the individual is at the greatest level of disadvantage.

The second study is that known as the Christchurch Health and Development Study, carried out in New Zealand over the last 25 years. The lead researcher on this study is David Fergusson, although many other individuals have worked with him and contributed to the scientific excellence of the research. In essence this is a longitudinal study of an unselected sample of 1200 children born in 1977. The cohort was studied at a number of points between birth and 21 years, and a particular focus of the research was to identify those children exposed to major risk factors, such as parental ill-health, substance misuse, placement in custody, chronic family conflict and so on. The study shows that, as with the Hawaii research, some who experience such risk environments do survive and overcome adversity. Fergusson and others (Fergusson and Lynskey, 1996; Fergusson and Horwood, 2003) report that, with increasing exposure to childhood adversities, there were marked increases in mental health problems in adolescence. Yet not all individuals developed such disorders. Some showed a capacity to overcome the risk environment, and most of the protective factors we have already mentioned were present in those individuals who could be described as resilient.

In recent discussions of the interplay between risk and protective factors (e.g., Olsson *et al.*, 2003; Rutter, 2003, 2006a) there is a strong emphasis on the importance of considering dynamic processes, rather than considering a catalogue of static factors acting in a summative fashion. Rutter is particularly keen to emphasize the role of gene–environment interactions, as well as the importance of biological factors such as the neuroendocrine system and brain structures. He argues that the psychological variables such as personal agency, coping mechanisms and so on interact with the genetic and physiological characteristics of an individual, and that all these variables contribute to an ongoing dynamic process of adaptation to adverse environmental circumstances.

One final point while we are considering questions of risk. This is to do with the preeminence of early childhood experiences in determining outcomes for vulnerable young people. Are risk factors in childhood more powerful than those that occur at later ages? Is it the case that, as Bynner (2001) puts it, "The earlier the disadvantage occurred, and the longer it has persisted, the lower the likelihood that these factors (protective factors) would counter it"? This is an assumption that is generally accepted by social scientists and policy makers, and many of the results of the longitudinal studies on resilience mentioned above do appear to support this conclusion.

However, the evidence is not entirely clear-cut, and it may be that there are some exceptions to the rule that the earlier the exposure to risk factors, the more difficult it is to alter the course of development. It would appear that, even for those who have suffered high levels of adversity at an early age, there are some protective factors that operate in adolescence and early adulthood. Studies of young offenders, as well as of those who have been brought up in care, have shown that changes in relationships in adulthood, especially marriage to a stable partner, can act as a powerful protective factor (Sampson and Laub, 1993; Rutter *et al.*, 1997b). There is also evidence that, during the adolescent years, involvement with positive peer groups, as well as the impact of a caring and supportive adult, can act to counter early exposure to risk factors (Luthar, 2003). One of our favourite articles in the scientific literature on this subject is entitled: "I met this wife of mine, and things got on a better track" (Ronka *et al.*, 2002).

Up to this point we have been considering the nature of risk, and the role played by protective factors in modifying experiences of adversity. We have explored various questions to do with risk and protective factors, including whether they lie along the same continuum, or are qualitatively different. We have considered whether protective factors are beneficial for all, or whether there are some factors which impact in specific risk circumstances. We have looked at the results of major studies of resilience, and seen that some young people do overcome serious adversity in their early development. Finally, we have asked whether there are protective factors that can be effective in adolescence and in early adulthood, despite early disadvantage. During the course of the chapter we have mentioned resilience at various times, and it is now appropriate to turn to a closer examination of this concept.

Resilience

As we noted at the beginning of the chapter, two things have to be in place for the concept of resilience to apply. One is that the individual is experiencing, or has experienced, major adversity, and the second is that the individual is now functioning well, that 'things are okay'. In an important paper by Olsson *et al.* (2003), the authors make a distinction between resilience as an outcome and resilience as a process. Where outcomes are concerned, researchers are likely to emphasize the effective functioning of young people who have been exposed to risk. Studies that take this perspective focus on variables such as self-esteem, good mental health and social competence. From this standpoint a young person could be showing a degree of emotion or stress as a result of negative experiences, but may still be showing resilience in the management of everyday tasks and responsibilities. On the other hand, studies looking at resilience as a process are more interested in the mechanisms that act to modify the impact of risk. Understanding the process of adaptation to risk involves taking account of both the individual's reaction to adversity, as well as the protective factors that may mitigate the impact of risk. Many of these processes will be explored in the chapters that make up this book, and we will return to a more detailed consideration of resilience in the concluding chapter.

For the present it is important to note here some of the things we have not yet covered.

- There is strong evidence from longitudinal studies that, where protective factors are present, most children and young people do recover from short-term adversity. In this sense we can say that the majority of children and young people have the capacity for resilience so long as the risk factors are limited, and protective factors are in place.
- Where risk factors are continuous and severe, only a minority manage to cope. The more serious the adversity, the stronger the protective factors need to be. Thus, under conditions of major risk, resilience is only apparent among a minority who can draw on the strengths gained from protective factors.
- The major risk factors for children tend to lie within chronic and transitional events, rather than in the acute risks. Thus children show greater resilience when faced with acute adversities such as bereavement, or short-term illness, and less resilience when exposed to chronic risks such as continuing family conflict, long-term poverty, and multiple changes of home and school.
- Resilience can only develop through exposure to risk or to stress. Resilience develops through gradual exposure to difficulties at a manageable level of intensity, and at points in the lifecycle where protective factors can operate. Rutter (1985) calls these "steeling experiences".

To conclude this exploration of risk and resilience we draw on the work of Newman and his colleagues (Newman *et al.*, 2004), who suggest a number of strategies for promoting resilience in children and young people. *The first strategy* is to reduce the child's exposure to risk. This sounds obvious, but is often difficult to achieve. One example given by Newman concerns the role of the school environment in combating poor nutrition, by providing school meals, and in offering homework clubs and after-school activities to those who would otherwise have nowhere to study and would be playing on the streets.

A second strategy is to find ways of interrupting the chain reaction of negative events. As we have noted, the presence of one risk factor increases the likelihood that others will be present. As a result, if one risk factor can be diminished or reduced, then it may follow that other positive consequences will follow. The provision of safe places for children to meet with their non-residential parent following divorce or separation is one good example here. Many non-residential parents find it hard to keep up regular contact with children if they live at a distance, or if there is nowhere for them to come together with their sons or daughters. Innovative schemes which provide meeting places make it possible for relationships to flourish despite adversity, and thus may act to reduce the accumulation of negative experiences following parental separation.

The third strategy of note is to offer the child or young person positive experiences in order to enhance the strength of potential protective factors. Finding ways for young people to discover their strengths, to enhance self-esteem or to develop positive relationships with significant adults can all contribute to the individual's capacity to overcome adversity. Looking again at the issue of divorce, we can envisage situations where the absence of a parent can

offer adolescents opportunities to take on new roles, or to carry out tasks that would normally be done by adults. Research indicates that such experiences, as long as they are not too onerous, can give young people confidence and assist them to develop new skills, thus bolstering protective factors.

Conclusion

In this chapter we have explored the ways in which the concepts of risk and resilience can be applied to adolescents in today's society. We have looked at different meanings of the term 'risk', and noted that there are at least four ways in which this term is used in discussions about youth. We have considered adolescent development and seen how the social changes of the last two decades have had the potential to create increased risk for adolescents. We have noted the views of some commentators who believe that the use of terms such as risk or risky behaviour as applied to adolescence has the unwanted effect of increasing negative stereotypes of the young. Such commentators would prefer the use of words like 'experimental' when applied to such things as smoking or drinking.

We have reviewed the major studies of risk and resilience, and seen how risk and protective factors can work together to enhance resilience. Studies of those who have experienced major adversity show that there are some who, despite being exposed to a range of risk factors, still manage to survive and do well as adolescents or adults. 'Vulnerable but invincible' was the title of one of the landmark studies in this field. We have considered two ways in which resilience can be studied, and we have ended the chapter by looking at suggestions for the promotion of resilience among vulnerable children and adolescents. It is our intention that this discussion of risk and resilience will form a background for a better understanding of the chapters that follow.

Further Reading

Coleman, J. and Hendry, L. (1999) *The nature of adolescence*, 3rd edn. Routledge: London.

Jackson, S. and Goossens, L. (2006) (Eds) *Handbook of adolescent development*. Psychology Press: Hove, Sussex.

Luthar, S. (2003) (Ed.) *Resilience and vulnerability*. Cambridge University Press: Cambridge.

Olsson, C. *et al*. (2003) Adolescent resilience: a concept analysis. *Journal of Adolescence* **26**: 1–11.

Discussion Questions

1. From your own experience, do you see evidence that there has been an increase in psychological distress among young people over the past 20 years or so?

2. Do adolescents understand the nature of risk differently from the way adults understand risk?

3. Do you agree that some experiment with risk behaviour is essential for positive adolescent development?

4. What do you think of the suggestions by Newman *et al*. (2004) for the promotion of resilience? Do you have other suggestions?

Chapter 2

The Role of the Family

Catherine O'Brien

Research Associate, Department of Sociology, University of Cambridge

Jacqueline Scott

Professor of Empirical Sociology, University of Cambridge

- ■ Beating the odds
- ■ The changing nature of families
- ■ How families facilitate adolescent resilience
- ■ How families contribute to adolescent risk
- ■ Policy implications
- ■ Conclusion
- ■ Discussion point

Learning Objectives

Once you have read this chapter you should be able to:

1 Understand what makes adolescence a particularly challenging time for families.

2 Reflect on parents' and adolescents' respective expectations and aspirations about families.

3 Describe some of the changes that have marked families in the last half-century. How do families form, reform, and juggle work, family roles and responsibilities?

Adolescence, Risk and Resilience: *Against the odds.* John Coleman and Ann Hagell (eds.).
Published in 2007 by John Wiley & Sons, Ltd

4 Determine how these changes influence the way families and adolescent children inter-relate. How has family change affected the form and quality of relationships between young people, their parents and kin?

5 Review evidence that links family structures and practices to adolescent risk and resilience. What family processes and characteristics impede and promote adolescent well-being?

6 Review major studies which have contributed to knowledge of the role of the family for adolescent children.

7 Draw together some policy implications for supporting families of adolescents.

Beating the Odds

In this chapter we will look at the role of families in adolescence and at some of the research which attempts to understand how families contribute to the constraints, setbacks, opportunities and successes experienced in adolescence.

The Peculiar Challenge of Adolescence for Families Today

With the approach of adolescence, family functioning changes. Parents of teenagers overwhelmingly agree that the teenage years are hardest for them to deal with. Conversely, adolescents often become increasingly dissatisfied with family life This is likely to be related to adolescents' growing awareness of dependence on family and their desire for freedom and autonomy, both psychological and structural (Bergman and Scott, 2001). The net result is that parent–child relationships may become more conflictual and distant. The amount of time spent with family declines and young adolescents express negative emotions when in family company. Psycho-social disorders that tend to rise or peak in frequency during the teenage years include crime, alcohol and drug abuse, depression, anorexia and bulimia, and suicide (Rutter and Smith, 1995). More adolescents, however, experience milder personal changes involving: self-concept, insecurity about self-appearance, hormonal changes, conflicts with parents, peer pressure, smoking, drinking alcohol, and other minor risk-taking or deviant behaviour.

There is some rather disturbing research suggesting that young people today are exhibiting more behavioural problems and greater psycho-social stress than was the case for previous generations. From national surveys undertaken in 1974, 1986 and 1999, Collishaw et al. (2004) analysed data on 15- to 16-year-olds, looking at trends in the same kinds of problems in UK adolescents over a 25-year period. The results showed a rise in adolescent mental health problems in the UK across this period. Teenagers in the 1990s were more likely to indicate depression, anxiety, lying, stealing, disobedience and other risky behaviour than teenagers in the 1970s, with correspondingly poorer outcomes in the later-cohort teenagers. Interestingly, the main cause did not appear to be changes over time in family structures, such as the growing number of single-parent families. Nor did the increase in problems obviously link to socio-economic status. Instead, Collishaw et al. attribute the increase to: changes in youth culture and differences in peer group dynamics; changes in parenting which manifest only in adolescence; and changing educational and occupational expectations. The changing nature of the labour market means that poor educational achievement, which represented no significant barriers to employment in the past, now predicts marginalization in the labour market and loss of status (Bynner, 2001).

There is evidence suggesting that increasing education is associated with rising expectations. Rutter and Smith (1995) present a comprehensive report by an international group of multi-disciplinary experts on changes in youth behaviour and culture (ages 12 to 26) in Europe in the past 50 years, focusing primarily on youth problems as opposed to youth successes. Other possible explanatory factors for the increase in adolescent problems include changes in living conditions, values and morals, the media and the developmental process. They also note that adolescence is increasingly likely to coincide with family structural changes. Parents are more likely to become ill, handicapped, separated or divorced, or die as their children get older. Such disruptions, instabilities and losses in adolescent lives increase their risk of depressive disorders later in life (Brown and Harris, 1989). An implication of these time trends in adolescent well-being is that different sets of factors may be expected to protect and harm adolescent well-being across different socio-historical contexts.

Popular explanations for the increase in adolescent psycho-social disorders:

- *The government* – not enough youth services, too many school examinations, not enough jobs or houses?
- *Society* – competitive, fast-moving and bewildering, due to too little attachment to institutions such as family and religion?
- *Family breakdown and serial parenting* – networks of security and love increasingly shattered by the fragmentation of family life?
- *Schools* – 'child-centred' educational theory which treats pupils as the equals of their teachers, leaving young people floundering in a sea of ignorance and too much responsibility and choice?
- *The law* – too paralysed to exert the authority and discipline that show children acting out their anger and distress that someone, somewhere, cares?
- *The moral and spiritual vacuum*?

Source: Summarized from Melanie Phillips, Childhood's lost idyll, *Daily Mail*, 14 September 2004.

The Expanding Boundaries of Adolescence

The family has particular significance for adolescents. Not only are families the crucible of identity-formation and the basis of children's shifts from dependent childhood into independent adulthood; they are also increasingly the main economic support of young people, often until young people are in their mid-twenties. New social policies in the UK, such as withdrawing and reducing benefits for certain age groups, have been particularly effective in making families more responsible for their offspring for longer periods (Morrow and Richards, 1996). Moreover, changes that affect parents' life-world, such as the long-work-hours culture or marital conflict, have far-reaching implications for their children (Morrow and Richards, 1996). Young people are staying on longer in further or higher education, acquiring independent identities and lifestyles later, entering the labour market later, marrying later and becoming parents later, while biological maturity is occurring at younger ages (Brannen, 1999). The net result of these different aspects of adulthood becoming increasingly disconnected from each other is the increasingly difficult transition to independent adulthood for many young people.

Interaction between Agency and Structure

Disadvantaged and advantaged circumstances undoubtedly affect young people's behaviour and achievements, but it is wrong to assume that children's lives are *determined by* household structures, family processes and economic circumstances (Scott, 2004a). Far from being passive objects of concern or remedy, young people are moral actors in their own lives and those of their family (Williams, 2004). Young people play a crucial role in realizing, failing to realize, or actively undermining the opportunities that family background and parenting support can offer. Conversely, parents may undermine or support children's positive actions. Thus agency is not individual but relational (Scott, 2004b). Similarly, resilience and vulnerability are not personal attributes, although individuals do vary in traits that make resilience and vulnerability in the face of psycho-social adversity more or less likely (Rutter and Smith, 1995). Resilience is a construct describing positive adaptation in the face of adversity (Schoon and Bynner, 2003), while vulnerability is described variously as an adaptational failure, maladjustment or lack of resistance to adversity (e.g., Bynner, 2001; Schoon and Parsons, 2002). Resilience may derive less from individual traits alone than from compensatory experiences, such as a good relationship with one parent. Vulnerability is similarly a dynamic interaction of personality characteristics (for example, low self-esteem and lack of confidence) and external factors (for example, an unsupportive teacher or low parental aspirations).

Schoon and Parsons' (2002) four-fold classification of young people captures the idea that background factors interact with individual characteristics in varying proportions to determine outcomes for young people. *Resilient youth* are those who grow up amid disadvantage and risk but who manage to 'beat the odds' by making a success of their lives. *Vulnerable youth* are those from disadvantaged backgrounds, such as low-income households or family disruption, who attain below-average academic and behavioural competences. *Underachievers* are individuals from socially advantaged backgrounds, such as high-income households or a harmonious family environment, who fail to attain the academic and behavioural competences one would expect from such advantage, while *multiple-advantaged* are those from advantaged backgrounds who attain above-average competences. Such variations imply that growing up in a socially disadvantaged family does not necessarily have lasting implications for psycho-social adjustment in adulthood.

Relationship between Risk Factors and Protective Factors

Protective factors can impede or ameliorate the process of one risk reinforcing another in a 'risk trajectory' (Bynner, 2001; Rutter, 1987; Schoon and Bynner, 2003). Less common in the literature is the corresponding idea that risk factors impede or halt the process of one protective factor reinforcing another in a 'success trajectory'. But it does emphasize that the potential for gaining capabilities lasts throughout the life course, therefore the targeting of appropriate assistance needs to occur "at every age, at every stage and in every place" with interventions determined by research evidence (Bynner, 2001, p. 297). Risk and protective factors are, broadly speaking, the negative and positive poles of the same concept, and not different concepts (Rutter, 1987).

Although there is some debate about what is to be counted as risk and protective factors, by and large, we can view protective mechanisms as those that build up resilience (or defuse risk) and promote healthy developmental pathways into adulthood, with increasing opportunities for participation in adult life. Risk factors build up vulnerability (or fail to build up resistance) and promote problematic pathways into adulthood, with restricted outcomes or social exclusion.

Family Expectations and Aspirations

Independence from parents, culminating in the establishment of an independent household, is a deeply held expectation for both parents and adolescents (Allatt and Yeandle, 1992). An unintended consequence of this norm may be a disappointed and frustrated generation whose expectations are not fulfilled (Morrow and Richards, 1996). This is because there is an increasing mismatch between young people's expectations and ambitions and the reality of their everyday experiences in their various transitions from school or higher education and training to the labour market, leaving home, social and sexual adulthood, and becoming parents. Although the nuclear family norm remains very powerful, expectations of relationships have changed, such that parents may tolerate their children being involved in relationships while they are still living at home. Alternatively, adolescent expectations and aspirations about families in the twenty-first century may differ from their parents' in ways that can fuel generational misunderstandings. Conversely, parents may desire greater individual freedom and family choice, which often clashes with their children's need for family stability.

Research also points to a convergence between young people's aspirations and those of their parents. There is evidence that parents' hopes and expectations strongly influence their children's aspirations (Heaven, 1994; Morrow and Richards, 1996; Schoon and Bynner, 2003). Parents' aspirations are in turn strongly associated with socio-economic status levels. Young people from less privileged backgrounds, for example, are less likely to want to continue education after the minimum school leaving age, or to aspire to a professional career.

Review of the Literature

Studies on the parenting of adolescents focus variously on processes within families and family structures that contribute towards positive or negative outcomes for young people. We first consider how family structures contribute to the risks and benefits encountered by young people, before turning to family practices – although structures and practices inevitably overlap to some extent. We present evidence from large-scale, robust studies on the effects of family on transition to adulthood mainly, but not exclusively, in the current UK context.

Summary

This section demonstrated the importance of exploring how family support and lack of support affect transitions to adulthood. Adolescents' actions and choices are particularly codependent on the lives of their family members. But they also actively shape their family environment through their actions, attitudes and aspirations. Thus family context is crucial for understanding adolescents' contemporary well-being and future pathways, particularly because a combination of government policies in recent years has delayed the integration of young people into the wider community. This makes the provision of support for families vital. Young people who have few family resources to draw on are more likely to be disadvantaged in a climate where family support is crucial to future outcomes. Before we look more closely at the nature of these outcomes, we discuss some of the ways in which families are transforming themselves, both as a cause and an effect of recent social and economic trends. Such trends pertain to globalization and market forces; labour markets and evolving employment patterns; financial, legal, technological and political change; social norms concerning what is right and proper; shifting gender relations and increasing options in sexual orientation.

The Changing Nature of Families

Marriage, how do we need thee? Let me count the ways: Marriage greatly benefits the poor and disadvantaged. Marriage benefits children. Children who live with their married parents enjoy better physical health than children in other family forms. Marriage decreases the chances children will tangle with the law and increases the likelihood they will graduate from high school, attend college and land a good job.

Source: Borgman, L (April 23, 2006) 'TomKat' thumb noses at reality and marriage. IndyStar. com Columnists. Available at: http://www.indystar.com/apps/pbcs.dll/article?AID=/20060423/ COLUMNISTS16/604230316/1049 (15 May 2006).

The Rise of Non-traditional Family Forms

Like the quote above from a newspaper column, most research to date suggests that children experiencing lone parenthood or family disruption, or both, have on average tougher lives, more limited options and less desirable outcomes than those who don't (Scott, 2004b). Associated with neo-conservative ideology, the heterosexual conjugal unit based on marriage and co-residence remains the most common form of family (Silva and Smart, 1999). Yet a diversity of living arrangements and family groups is increasingly the norm, notwithstanding the persistence of gender inequalities and other power imbalances. Changes include: an increase in cohabitation and divorce, often resulting in step-parents, step-siblings and half-siblings if there is re-marriage; more children born outside marriage; more lone parenting; decline of the male breadwinner; more dual-earner couples; more working mothers, with the rise of women's financial and social independence; declining fertility; fewer siblings; postponement of family formation; increased life expectancy; and the acceptance of a diversity of sexual lifestyles.

Rutter and Smith (1995) stress that research does not *demonstrate* that changes in family structure are a cause of the increase in psycho-social disorders. First, changes in family structures are inter-related with so many other social changes. Second, it is highly plausible that structure is linked to processes or family functioning. The various family forms will differ in terms of parental ability to be involved and provide stability, strong emotional support, emotional warmth, a sense of belonging to the family, and the required level of independence. For example, single working mothers generally have less time and energy to devote to their children than couples. It is in this sense that such structural changes have consequences for the culture of care, in which children are both recipients and providers (Scott, 2004b). Below, we consider the implications of single parents, working mothers, divorce and step-parents, and, briefly, same-sex parents and siblings, for the transmission of risks and benefits to the next generation.

Lone Mothers

The main risk that single-parent families are thought to pose for their adolescent offspring is poverty. Since the vast majority of single-parent families are headed by women, and therefore lack a male wage, lone-mother families are especially prone to poverty (Scott, 2004b; Williams, 2004). Using data from two large-scale surveys, the UK Family Expenditure Survey (since 1957) and the National Child Development Survey (since 1958), Gregg *et al.* (1999) found that being brought up in a lone-parent family does not seem to matter in the absence of family poverty. Whether a family is able to meet the material needs of its children depends more on whether it has income from work than directly on whether it has two parents (Golombok, 2000). But family economic resources are positively correlated with parental involvement in children's lives. Poorer, often lone, mothers are generally under great pressure and consequently tend to be less involved in their children's course work and assignments (Catan, 2004). Children of single parents have less time for interacting with their parents and for receiving emotional support, less access to male and female role models, and fewer opportunities for leisure and positive experiences outside the home (Rutter and Smith, 1995). The 1994–1999 British Household Panel Study revealed that 11- to 15-year-olds are more likely to report 'past worries' if they come from lone-parent households (Bergman and Scott, 2001). Reported smoking behaviour also tends to be higher among young people from such households than among those living with both biological parents. This suggests lower well-being, perhaps due to problematic parent–youth communication patterns and the upheavals associated with family change (Bergman and Scott, 2001). While psychological effects of the presence or absence of the father are difficult to isolate, Bergman and Scott (2001) found that the occupational status of the father (associated with social class and household income) has no discernible effect on adolescent *well-being* or *behaviour*. But family economic resources seem to matter far more than family structure in terms of children's *cognitive development* (Duncan and Brooks-Gunn, 1997; Joshi *et al.*, 1999). Financial hardship means fewer opportunities for the developing adolescent (Rutter and Smith, 1995). Such economic disadvantages can lead to economic and social difficulties in adulthood, and feed through to the next generation (Gregg *et al.*, 1999). Those least likely to escape from disadvantage more often come from single-parent families with severe material problems, often combined with acute problems in family relationships (Morrow and Richards, 1996; Pilling, 1990).

Working Mothers and the Changing Role of Fathers

The changing role of women in the economy has an important impact on the nature of family life and parent–child relations (Morrow and Richards, 1996). It is possible that the greater work-life choices for parents and equality gains for women that have come about since 1960 may be at the expense of their children (Scott, 2004a). Since women are more likely to move into relationships after already having had experience of working, earning and financial independence, they may have different expectations of relationships. They know they can leave unsatisfactory relationships because they will be able to support themselves or be (minimally) supported by state benefits (Morrow and Richards, 1996). This is likely to expose children to a greater risk of family disruption.

Ideas about the merits of the traditional family, the nature of motherhood and gender–role ideology are likely to remain contentious. One reason is that maternal employment is associated with both detrimental and protective consequences for young people. Like lone mothers, working mothers may pose a risk for children in terms of being less involved in their school work. Scott (2004a) found that children whose mothers worked full-time in their young adolescent years (ages 11–15) were significantly less likely to attain five or more GCSE passes at age 16 than those whose mothers stayed at home, whereas part-time work was not detrimental to children's educational attainment. Similarly, O'Brien and Jones (1999) found that teenagers from families where the mother had a part-time job had the best chance of good exam results. In contrast, full-time maternal employment in the early years of childhood has a small detrimental effect on educational attainment at GCSE and A-level (Ermisch and Francesconi, 2001; Joshi and Verropoulou, 2000). This suggests that time conflicts detract from maternal involvement in children's schooling.

On the positive side, there is some evidence that maternal employment benefits older children, especially girls (Kiernan, 1996). Career-minded mothers may enhance their daughter's own career ambitions, with girls benefiting at higher levels of educational attainment. Based on longitudinal data from two British birth cohorts born 12 years apart, Schoon and Parsons (2002) found that being born to a mother who postponed her child-bearing years until after age 30 years is a detrimental factor for disadvantaged children in the earlier (1958) cohort, in terms of an increased risk of educational and behaviour problems; while for privileged children in the later cohort (1970), it is a protective factor. This finding could indicate that advanced medical technology has reduced some of the risks associated

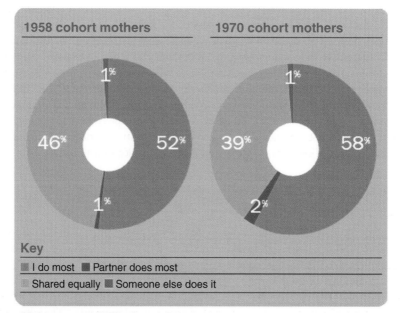

Figure 2.1   Main responsibility for childcare
Source: CLS Briefings, November 2005. Reproduced by Permission of Center for Longitudinal Studies, Institute of Education, University of London.

with late childbirth for the later-born cohort. But it could also indicate that children benefit from being born to a mother who delayed child-bearing in order to establish a career first. Apart from progressive gender–role attitudes, mothers who work may promote adolescent independence, although Hochschild (1997) cautions that this benefit is to be carefully weighed against adolescents being forced to 'grow up' prematurely.

As the numbers of women in employment have grown, have the roles of fathers changed to accommodate this? Figure 2.1 depicts the contrasting answers of 1958 and 1970 cohort mothers who were in their thirties when they were asked who had the main responsibility for looking after the children.

For both generations, the majority of mothers had the main responsibility for looking after the children (CLS Briefings, November 2005). It should be noted that a substantial proportion of mothers report that responsibility is shared equally between themselves and their partners. However, although the proportion of fathers taking the *main* responsibility had doubled from 1 to 2%, the number taking *equal* responsibility had dropped from 46 to 39%. Interestingly, fathers in both cohorts claimed shared responsibility more often than mothers, showing either different subjective perceptions of levels of care between genders (Ferri and Smith, 2003), or different impression-management agendas!

Fractured and Step-parent Families

The common perception that it is preferable for children to have married parents (Williams, 2004) is not unfounded. There are clear disparities in overall outcomes between children from two-parent intact families and those from other family types, including lone-parent or reconstituted families (Scott, 2004b). Based on US and Canadian longitudinal studies, Duncan and Brooks-Gunn (1997) conclude that poverty affects children's ability and achievement, but it is family breakdown that affects behaviour, mental health and physical health – and also educational attainments even when poverty is taken into account. Recomposition of family following parental break-up can also affect school achievement. Zimiles and Lee (1991) found that adolescents living in single-parent or step-families lag behind their peers from intact families on achievement test scores, and that there is a threefold increase in drop-out from school in non-intact families.

But there is evidence that the detrimental effects of divorce are not unequivocally due to family structure or disruption alone. Preceding family conflict tends to make families more prone to disruption and children more prone to unhappy outcomes (Scott, 2004a). Even if family disruption itself causes adverse outcomes for children, it could be for a variety of different reasons, including: a fall in economic status, loss of a father figure, erosion of social contacts and reduction in parental care. It is also likely that these factors matter differently for different children. Further evidence suggests that it is marital discord rather than separation that matters, and Block *et al.* (1986) found that children who were disturbed in the aftermath of divorce had behaviour problems before the divorce. The Collishaw *et al.* (2004) study identified chronic parental conflict and family separation as two primary family experiences which increase the degree of risk to which the young person is exposed.

As with lone parents, one of the main harms of divorce arises from poverty, due to the loss of potential source of support from one parent (Smart, 1999). Young people may be deprived of potential sources of financial, practical and/or emotional support as they make the transition to adulthood (Morrow and Richards, 1996). The poverty effects of divorce are likely to continue from childhood through to early adulthood (Morrow and Richards, 1996). For example, there is some evidence that the increase in divorce rates limits the availability of small, cheap housing available for single young people (Walker *et al.*, 1991). Divorced parents may simply not be able to afford to help their children when they leave home.

A protective factor that parental divorce may afford is the termination of parental conflict. Post-divorce parents may also decide to hide or live apart from a new partner to reduce the risk of exposing their children to further stress and conflict (Smart and Neale, 1999; Willams, 2004). Thus structural constraints are mediated through the particularities of the family environment and may be counterbalanced by practices within the family, which are indicative of the overall quality of family relationships (Catan, 2004). A key factor that impedes the 'risk trajectory' of family disruption is the quality of the parenting before the divorce. If children were treated with respect, and their views were listened to and recognized, then change is better negotiated by adults and children alike (Williams, 2004). The potential for rupture of a divorce, and associated loss of kinship networks and other resources, can be countered with attentiveness to others' needs; adaptability to new identities; maintaining relationships with extended family members; and a spirit of reparation (Smart and Neale, 1999).

If there is re-marriage, children may experience conflict with step-parents. An associated risk is youth homelessness (Jones, 1995; Kiernan, 1992). Although the large majority of boys and girls from both intact and disrupted families do not leave home by age 18, a higher proportion of those who do leave home before age 18 have experienced family breakdown and have a step-family (Ainley, 1991; Kiernan, 1992). Premature transitions reflect uninformed decision-making between the young person and their family, which can stifle young people's opportunities, including early school-leaving, leaving home early, teenage first partnership, early entry into parenthood and extra-marital childbirth (Bhrolcháin *et al.*, 2000). These findings were replicated in a longitudinal study of adolescents and young adults in the UK between 1998 and 2001 that was carried out as part of the Economic and Social Research Council's (ESRC) programme on Youth, Citizenship and Social Change (YCSC). Most at risk of homelessness were those who left home early after family quarrels, those living with a step-parent, young Afro-Caribbeans and a category which combined all these forms of disadvantage, 'frequent movers' (Catan, 2004).

Thus the main risks of family breakdown are structural, emotional and cognitive (Smart, 1999). Changes in family structure appear to make only a modest contribution to changes in adolescent well-being. The main risk factors are: socio-economic decline; declining parental responsibility due to division of responsibilities and/or personal antagonisms; and poor quality of parent–child communications. Disadvantaged outcomes include lower educational attainment, delinquency, homelessness and emotional difficulties.

Lesbian and Gay Parents

Lesbian and gay parents may provide different kinds of influences than heterosexual parents. One reason is the potentially greater diversity of homosexual parenting arrangements, such as biological or adoptive parents, non-biological co-parents, lovers and ex-lovers (Weeks *et al.*, 1999). Parents may identify as homosexual either before or after children are born, while a same-sex partner may or may not assume a step-parenting relationship to the children, and their children may or may not assume step-sibling relationships with one another (Patterson,

1996). A second reason is that many cultural anxieties surround such complex parenting arrangements. The main fears are that children of lesbian/gay parents will grow up to be homosexual; they will be more vulnerable to behavioural and emotional problems due to the lack of father/mother figure; and they will be more vulnerable to being bullied because of their unconventional background (Golombok, 2000). An associated risk factor for children is that if their parents separate, they do not live with their homosexual parent, since custody is usually awarded to heterosexual parents. There is a growing body of research that exposes such anxieties to be unfounded (e.g., Barrett and Tasker, 2001; Golombok and Tasker, 1996). Some of the literature claims that homosexual parenting is superior to heterosexual in various ways, for example, being more child-centred, more responsive, or having a more liberal outlook. But there is a possibility that some of these findings are a product of sampling bias, given the sensitivities that surround sexual identity.

Siblings

In sociological texts, siblings figure more from the perspective of parental resource allocation than from the perspective of children's family experience (Scott, 2004b). Children with many siblings are at an increased risk of impeded academic progress and behavioural problems than children with fewer siblings, although large family size may have a more detrimental effect on socially disadvantaged children than on socially advantaged children (Schoon and Parsons, 2002). Dunn and Plomin (1990) suggest that differential treatment by parents is more influential for children's development than the common characteristics of family environment. Children tend to notice and respond to differences in the way they are treated relative to their siblings.

Summary

The quote at the beginning of this section asserted that the riskiest form of family for young people's outcomes is single-parent families and that the strongest is two-parent, heterosexual families. But structural factors alone do not predict all outcomes for young people. This review showed that the socio-economic events and changes that structure young people's lives are mediated through families because young people's lives are co-dependent on parents and other family members. It is increasingly recognized that non-traditional family forms may have relationships that are just as strong as traditional forms (Leonard, 2005). Connectedness, reciprocity and the ethic of nurture and care are being carried out in more various ways, often independent of biological, inheritance or marriage ties (Williams, 2004). Even though non-traditional families are becoming increasingly common, there is surprisingly little evidence that family composition effects are weakening.

Interestingly, when adolescents are apparently doing well, like outperforming previous generations in educational qualification, families are rarely given credit. It is increasingly recognized that youth research needs to pay as much attention to the emergence of successful outcomes and advantage as to the emergence of poor outcomes and disadvantage (Schoon and Bynner, 2003). Of central interest to our discussion is not so much adaptational failure, which is the traditional focus of research on high-risk groups, as positive adaptational outcomes, including academic competences, feelings of confidence, connectedness and positive powers such as energy, adaptability and idealism. We shall therefore focus first on protective factors and processes within the family that can supply the foundations of resilience in young people during adolescence, and then move onto risk factors and processes.

How Families Facilitate Adolescent Resilience

Protective factors associated with positive adjustment include: academic attainment; behavioural adjustment; personality characteristics such as positive self-esteem and confidence; and external factors such as a supportive family environment (Schoon and Parsons, 2000). Morrow and Richards (1996) define family support widely to include: earlier socialization for adult life; social and emotional support during transitions; and financial and other material support. A useful framework for explaining the role of the family in adolescents' well-being is provided by the concepts of social/cultural and human capital (Catan, 2004). *Social capital* is reflected in the educational, cultural and social resources of the family which are built up over time due to positive relationships, supportive social networks and know-how. *Human capital* refers to parents' education and is closely linked with parents' educational aspirations for the child. Families reproduce advantage through financial, human, cultural and social capital (e.g., Bourdieu, 1986; Coleman, 1988; Furstenberg and Hughes, 1995; Sullivan, 2001). This transmission of advantage helps the younger generation to negotiate successfully the transition to adulthood (Scott, 2004b). Success, in conventional terms, refers to such factors as university entrance, good qualifications and upward mobility (Catan, 2004).

Human Capital and Financial Support

Human capital is reflected in parental emphasis on school, employment and other cultural activities, located in the family's values, relationships and practices, which directly shape young people's participation in education. It is also reflected in a wide range of financial support, occasionally in terms of regular cash payments but more commonly on an irregular, discretionary and negotiated basis (Catan, 2004). Young people use family social and cultural capital to benefit from education, building up human capital at the individual level, which in turn feeds back into the social/cultural capital of the family.

Parents' educational level influences the cultural environment in which children are raised, for example, by passing on values concerning the importance of learning to their children. Scott (2004a) found that family background strongly affects children's attainment. Children are advantaged if they come from 'intact' homes, from higher socio-economic backgrounds, and have parents with higher educational qualifications. Both Ermisch and Francesconi (2001) and O'Brien and Jones (1999) found that household income and housing tenure are important influences on children's educational attainment. Pilling (1990) studied a sample of 27-year-olds from the 1958 British Birth Cohort study who met the criteria for 'resilience'. That is, with disadvantaged childhoods but above-average educational achievement at age 16, as well as high incomes, high-status jobs and adult home-ownership. This sample was compared with disadvantaged children who had not succeeded in adult life. It was found that, despite parents' economic difficulties, the achievers experienced family cohesion, high parental aspirations and interest in their progress, and that their teachers had shown 'strong commitment' to them over an extended period of time. The earlier the disadvantage occurred, and the longer it had persisted, the lower the likelihood that these factors would counter it. This suggests that high parental aspirations are associated with a high quality of family life. While all forms of human capital matter, mother's education in particular has a beneficial effect on children's attainment. Scott (2004a) found that the mother exerts more interpersonal influence than the father over children's educational performance. Other research from the Youth, Citizenship and Social Change programme found that material and financial support ranged from offering a warm and supportive home to high levels of specialized academic or intellectual support – depending on parents' qualifications and values. In some families the level of involvement in, and supervision of, students' college attendance and progress is very high. Material resources affecting conditions for studying at home include: private study space or shared family spaces; personal use or shared computers; the presence or lack of books and other materials (Catan, 2004).

Apart from parental aspirations, parental involvement in children's education and support for school and college work, family advantage is transmitted through planning the future. Career planning (both education and training) tends to be the preserve of young people from well-resourced families (Catan, 2004). Families subsidise the search for work in a variety of ways such as fares to job centres and postage of application forms (Allatt and Yeandle, 1992). Parents of unemployed youth help to equalize the income of children out of work or use credit to subsidise their children's income (Hutson and Jenkins, 1989). Parental subsidy, in the form of board and lodging, continued for both those in education and training and for those in low-paid work, with a very mixed picture regarding parents' expectations of financial contributions from resident young children. Even when a relatively early transition out of the family home was possible, due to lower rents or attending a university course away from home, most young people remained dependent on their parents for help with housing costs. Ongoing material and financial support from families provides a general underpinning for young people's progress towards independent living in their twenties. A risk associated with young people's receiving financial help from their families, identified by White (1991), is family arguments and stresses. Those receiving material help from family also risk lower levels of psychological well-being (Morrow and Richards, 1996). Nonetheless, the above trends reinforce wider and deeper-rooted social inequalities associated with social class, parents' educational levels, and access to social and cultural capital, described below.

Social Capital: Build-up of Personal and Social Resources

Several studies from the YCSC research programme found that socio-economic factors are only indirectly predictive of many important aspects of youth transitions. Less tangible or measurable aspects of family life and relationships were found to be more directly influential. The family contributes to the build-up of personal and social resources in the school years, which decisively influences outcomes in early adulthood (Catan, 2004). Coleman (1988) conceives of social capital in families as strong relations between children and parents. Even if parents lack the appropriate social/cultural capital, and feel powerless to help in more practical ways, they attempt to preserve the young person's 'spirit' and prevent despondency from turning into despair (Allatt and Yeandle, 1992). Affectional ties within the family provide emotional support in times of stress (Werner, 1989). YCSC research identifies crucial resources in subtle and subjectively perceived aspects of family life such as family roles and relationships, communication between parents and children, and parenting practices. Good quality of family life and relationships is indicated by: a stable family environment; doing things together; family mealtimes; a father who undertakes domestic tasks and childcare; good parent–youth communication with few quarrels, especially with the mother, and supervision of adolescent TV viewing. Family-based protectors include cohesion, warmth and an absence of discord (Bynner, 2001).

Other crucial material and social/cultural resources coordinated by families include the social networks and contacts available through the family, often used in advice and job searches (Catan, 2004). There is evidence that businesses use kinship links as a recruitment strategy (Morrow and Richards, 1996) – making job acquisition more a matter of who you know than what you know (Allatt and Yeandle, 1992). Young people from middle-class families whose members are in employment or relatively affluent are advantaged in terms of practical use of family social networks for information and influence about local job opportunities (Morrow and Richards, 1996). While information can circulate within a group, and privileged access to (or inside information about) jobs or other valued positions may be offered merely by being an accepted member of a group, it is also important to know how to take initiative in these processes (Allatt, 1993). Parents can help nourish children's skills in using networks, by utilizing their own networks on their children's behalf (Allatt, 1993).

Summary

This section reviewed evidence of the importance of family for adolescents' positive adjustment in the face of adversity, or successful development of individual resources in the face of family advantage. The family makes two main contributions to adolescent resilience and success. First, through human capital including parents' educational aspirations and ongoing material and financial support. This provides the general underpinning for young people's progress towards independent living through their twenties (Catan, 2004). Second, through the supportive, positive quality of family relationships and the social networks to which families give their children access. This build-up of personal and social resources in the school years decisively influences outcomes in early adulthood. Research showed that families mobilize their educational and social resources vigorously to build up human capital in the next generation. Parents invest their time, qualifications and knowledge and call upon those of their wider family and social networks to support young people's progress through both academic and vocational courses and shape eventual outcomes. The importance of human and social capital for providing routes to resilience is evident from the plight of children whose key family relations are weak or absent. Young people 'without kin' who leave local authority care face a range of difficulties, financially, socially and psychologically (Stein and Carey, 1986). Children growing up in public care are most at risk, followed by children with absent parents, parents with alcohol or drug problems, and those with criminal records (Bynner, 2001).

How Families Contribute to Adolescent Risk

Having justified the credit due to families for the educational attainments and other positive adaptations of their children, this section provides an overview of the role of family in creating risk for young people. In most cases, risk derives less from any irreversible effect in early life than from continuing disadvantaged circumstances which reinforce the social relations identified with risk (Bynner, 2001). Early experiences of social risk can have long-term consequences, continuing into adulthood and into the next generation. The long-term effects of early disadvantage are typically given in terms of educational attainment, employment status and family formation or partnership. The risks of growing up in a socially disadvantaged family include the pressures of poverty, poor neighbourhoods and limited opportunity (Catan, 2004).

Parents' Own Social Exclusion

It is virtually a truism to say that those who end up less educated, less healthy and poor come mainly from families that themselves are socially disadvantaged and marginalized (Scott and Chaudhary, 2003). Many risk factors for children arise through difficulties in the parents' lives and their social exclusion paths (Bynner, 2001). The notion of social capital is central to the study of social exclusion – an absence of social capital as well as 'negative' social capital. Problem or risky behaviour is a product of the use of negative social capital. This has short-term social and emotional benefits which young people may be unwilling to relinquish. The long-term disadvantages include decisions to pull out of difficult college courses or to remain in a drug-using peer group (Catan, 2004).

Parents' own lack of education and lack of interest in and support for their children's education, as reported by teachers, is often coupled with low parental aspirations for the children, an incapacity to encourage and help their children with their school work, and a desire for them to leave school at the earliest age (Bynner, 2001; Huurre et al., 2006). Children of parents with low educational levels tend to lack those abilities normally transmitted by the family and valued and rewarded by schools (Bourdieu and Passeron, 1977). Fathers who are unemployed over the long term may unwittingly reinforce a role model that challenges the importance of educational and occupational achievement (Trommsdorff, 2000). Labour market problems brought about by poor educational achievement impel many young women into early pregnancy – especially those growing up in state care.

Apart from unemployment, other vulnerabilities within parents which pre-dispose adolescents to risk, and have a major impact on the young people, include: substance misuse, criminal conviction and illness, especially psychiatric illness (Robins and Rutter, 1990). YCSC studies found that many young people who used drugs had grown up in families with drug- or alcohol-addicted parents (Catan, 2004). Dependent drug and alcohol use in families of origin pushes young people into care, where children often continue to function poorly. Indeed, earlier, more regular and higher levels of use of both recreational and hard drugs are found among young people in care than in the general youth population. While psycho-social disorders and disability in parents can constitute risks of exclusion (Williams, 2004), poverty is the more obvious pathway to social exclusion.

Poverty

There is a clear overlap between social exclusion and poverty. A 1983–1999 Finnish longitudinal study of 16-year-olds found that parental socio-economic status is a strong predictor of children's educational career (Huurre *et al.*, 2006). Family socio-economic background influences educational outcome through various mechanisms, such as the economic resources available to children and the family's educational values. Socio-economic adversity generally refers to poor standard of rented accommodation, poor living conditions, over-crowding, low family income, children eligible for free school meals and lack of material resources (Bynner, 2001). In some circumstances, (unemployed) parents are dependent upon children's earnings – making poor families even poorer if young people cannot meet all their housing costs (Morrow and Richards, 1996). While the family's influence on young people's educational aspirations was shown above to be an important mechanism by which class advantage is transmitted across the generations, Scott (2004a) found that class and household material circumstances (such as income and tenure) matter for educational attainment, even controlling young people's aspirations. The detrimental effect of poverty on children's ability and achievement has been widely documented (e.g., Duncan and Brooks-Gunn, 1997; Gregg *et al.*,1999; Roker, 1998; Schoon and Parsons, 2002).

Parenting Styles

The tasks of parenting change in important ways as young people enter adolescence. Variations in parenting are strong and well-established risk factors for individual differences in vulnerability to mental health problems in adolescents (Hess, 1995). The most extensive and consistent links have been demonstrated in relation to anti-social behaviour, delinquency and other 'problem' behaviours (Loeber and Stouthamer-Loeber, 1986). This influential article identifies four broad areas of family risk, summarized in the table below.

Four broad areas of family risk:

- *Neglect*: low parent–child involvement and poor parental supervision.
- *Conflict*: hostile or coercive parent–child relationships and discipline.
- *Deviant behaviours and attitudes*: such as exposure to criminal behaviours or deviant attitudes in parents.
- *Disruption*: centring on marital conflict between parents and parental absence.

Family problems found to be correlated with adolescent problem behaviours include: parental under- or over-involvement with the adolescent; parental under- or over-control of the adolescent; poor quality of parent–adolescent communication; inconsistent or absent rules and consequences for adolescent behaviour; inadequate monitoring and management of the adolescent's activities with peers; poor adolescent bonding to family and poor family cohesiveness (Dishion and McMahon, 1998; Stattin and Kerr, 2000; Szapocznik and Coatsworth, 1999).

Adolescents require increased autonomy and often pressurize parents to be allowed more unsupervised time with their friends, and at earlier ages than in the past. Some parents reduce their attempts at supervision in the face of such demands for independence, resulting in a pattern of 'premature autonomy' among teenagers (Dishion *et al.*, 2000). On the other hand, there may be opposing pressures for parents to increase levels of supervision of children as they become more concerned about high levels of risk behaviours in the peer group, as well as other dangers in society, such as street violence. There are complex interactions between neighbourhood safety, characteristics of the young person, and parental culture and expectations, all of which may influence patterns and effects of parental supervision (Leventhal and Brooks-Gunn, 2000; Ingoldsby and Shaw, 2002; Pinderhughes *et al.*, 2001).

With adolescent–parent relationships facing increased (albeit temporary) levels of conflict, new demands are placed on parents and on parenting skills. There is no causal consistency in that some families inter-relate poorly before young people develop problem behaviours, whereas others develop problematic responses subsequent to their children's problem behaviour (Szapocznik and Coatsworth, 1999; Santisteban *et al.*, 2003). On a positive note, parental monitoring and supervision have been found to be open to successful modification in parenting intervention trials (Dishion *et al.*, 2003).

Marginalized Groups and Conflicts about Sexuality

It is important to recognize that young people do not constitute a homogenous category in their needs and transitions. Transitions from family of origin to family of procreation vary enormously with class and ethnic differences (Morrow and Richards, 1996). Moreover, while most poor children in the UK are white, the risk of child poverty is markedly higher in all minority ethnic groups, especially households of Bangladeshi or Pakistani origin (Bradshaw, 2002). Racism, lack of respect for religious or cultural differences, and material disadvantages continue to be part of daily life for ethnic minorities (Williams, 2004). Such disadvantages add to the difficulties young people face in making a successful transition to adult life.

Certain geographical locations such as the inner cities are likely to show higher-than-average concentrations of risk centred on poor housing, family poverty and low achieving in schools (Bynner, 2001). Variations in neighbourhood disadvantage and collective efficacy are associated with a broad spectrum of behavioural and health-related outcomes (Sampson and Laub, 1993). Parenting and neighbourhood processes such as informal social control and affiliation with delinquent peers may interact, such that parenting is supported in some neighbourhood contexts but more severely challenged in others. There are further marginalizing pressures if ethnic minority youth are gay/lesbian (Catan, 2004).

Gay and lesbian youth often face being thrown out of the family home or allowed to remain in it under persecutory conditions. They risk being permanently cut off from their families and experiencing homelessness following 'coming out'. Such lack of family support creates rapid pathways to social exclusion. Family disappointment and rejection were most acute for working class young people, where family aspirations focused more on marriage and children (Catan, 2004).

More generally, parental aspirations tend to militate against honesty in matters of sexuality. Constituting a further source of risk for young people is the relative absence of sexual education from parents (Holland *et al.*, 1993). Young people exacerbate their vulnerability through their attempts to protect their parents from knowledge of their social and sexual lives. Family culture variables, ethnicity and the nature of parent–child relationships are likely to influence whether young people have sex at home (Morrow and Richards, 1996).

Summary

This section demonstrated that educational and material disadvantage in the parents' own childhood are important factors in children's development, as they signify continuity of the social exclusion risk from one generation to the next. Persistent child poverty has a pronounced detrimental effect on educational attainment. A particularly salient factor that is predictive of anti-social behaviour in adolescence is parental monitoring and supervision (Dishion and McMahon, 1998; Stattin and Kerr, 2000). More proximal aspects of parenting, such as neglect, conflict and deviant behaviours, appear to mediate effects of family structure on behavioural outcomes (Sampson and Laub, 1993). Taken on its own, no single risk factor is likely to lead to social exclusion. It is in combination that their potency for impeding children's cognitive and behavioural development becomes apparent (Bynner, 2001).

But general statistics mask huge variations in how young people cope as individuals and differences in the resources and experiences of disadvantaged families (Scott and Chaudhary, 2003). Growing up in a socially disadvantaged family does not necessarily have lasting implications for psycho-social adjustment in adulthood. Studies of young people at risk of social exclusion showed that exclusion could be both resisted and overcome (Catan, 2004), although resilient individuals from disadvantaged backgrounds tend not to succeed to the same level as young people from privileged backgrounds in terms of obtaining degree-level qualifications (Schoon and Parsons, 2002). Privileged young people are more likely to reap all the knock-on advantages that a university education can bring in terms of job security and income in adult life.

Policy Implications

The family has a critical role, both as creator of the conditions for later social exclusion and the means by which it can be resisted (Trommsdorff, 2000). There are key turning points in a child's life when exclusion processes are most easily reversed (Bynner, 2001). Major transitions in the life course which occur in adolescence, such as leaving school, constitute 'sensitive periods' during which young people are particularly responsive to interventions (Schoon and Bynner, 2003). Knowledge about the protective factors and processes involved in positive adaptation, despite the experience of adversity, can bring a new impetus to the development of social policies aiming to promote the well-being of disadvantaged, high-risk adolescents. Rather than crisis intervention, Schoon and Bynner (2003) recommend primary prevention before serious maladjustment has already manifested itself. This involves a shift from preventing youth problems to the promotion of youth development and youth engagement in their communities and societies. Area-targeting and services which are too differentiated and specialized run the risk of missing families and children that are 'invisible' to policy or who are exposed to co-occurring, multiple or accumulating risks (Bynner, 2001). Intervention or prevention programmes should be based on a more holistic strategy, that is, integrated into the cultural context, the educational programme and personal behavioural repertoire of the developing individual (Schoon and Bynner, 2003). Specific education policies may entail strengthening parental aspirations through the medium of continuing teacher–parent interaction and direct reinforcement in the classroom for those children who are falling behind.

It is, however, sometimes quite hard to separate out claims that derive from evidence about families and adolescents and claims that derive from ideological convictions about what families should be. Silva and Smart (1999) point out that the increasing diversity of family forms, discussed above, should not be understood as a total democratization of choice. Institutional supports for family life and policy frameworks are as crucial as ever for enhancing autonomous choices in living arrangements. Moreover, young people's interests, family's interests and societal interests do not necessarily coincide (Scott, 2004b). Thus, government policies aimed at reducing poverty, for example, by raising family income through paid work may not necessarily be consistent with the desire to strengthen family ties or to prioritize parental care of young children. Since there is no single norm of mother/worker or father/worker identity, only "a plurality of balancing acts", policy may have to take into account people's own definitions of closeness and commitment (Williams, 2004, p. 60). Current policy has underestimated increasing demands on the family for material and financial provision for young people, care of the elderly and provision for parents' own retirement (Catan, 2004). The research discussed in this chapter presents a need to support families more adequately, by extending youth policy to cover the needs of the young person and the needs of the families themselves, in the light of their continuing support of young adult offspring.

Conclusion

This chapter looked at the role that families can play in helping to shape the experiences associated with adolescence. The studies reviewed confirm that young people's actions are closely bound up with the actions of their families and that 'parenting matters'. The majority of families, whatever the nature of the parents' own problems, provide the protection and the stimulus to positive development that children need. Many adolescents are doing well in terms of outperforming previous generations in educational qualification, upward mobility and keeping apace with rising expectations. We focused on the role that families play in helping young people survive and thrive in what is often a prolonged period of dependency. We considered the role of family in supporting young people as they move towards adulthood. Human and social capital, including parents' educational aspirations and social networks, were found to be assets that young people can draw on in the future as they move towards adulthood. But family capital, including wider kinship relations, can also support and give young people status in the present.

We noted the rather disturbing research suggesting that young people today may be exhibiting more behavioural problems and greater psycho-social stress than was the case for previous generations. Family types and practices that put children at risk of poorer outcomes included family disadvantage, family instability and lone parenthood. Although changes in family roles in the last half-century have influenced the way that families and adolescent children inter-relate, our focus on the interaction between structure and agency suggested that the experience of growing up in a socially disadvantaged family does not necessarily have lasting implications for psycho-social maladjustment in adulthood.

On balance, the literature suggests that extreme or clichéd assumptions about family and adolescent conflict need to be moderated. But it also suggests that we resist generalization and pay attention to whether research participants are reporting on youth and adults in general or their own relationships, and on rejection and rebellion or on small daily conflicts in an otherwise supportive relationship (Williams, 2004). Talking about risk in adolescence more generally, what the literature does *not* suggest is that the aim is to protect adolescents from *all* risk. Taking some risks can be an inherent part of the process of healthy transition to becoming an independent adult who, in due course, will form close family bonds of their own. The advantages and disadvantages that family bestows tend to cascade down the generations and thus effective policies supporting families and adolescents have a double benefit of helping both current and future families.

Discussion Point

The following case is an extreme and fortunately very rare example of the tragedy that can overtake young people's lives before they reach adulthood. The case does, however, illustrate many issues that are more commonly applicable to the role that families can play in exacerbating and reducing adolescent risk.

Pupil jailed for murder of boy, 11, with cystic fibrosis

An 11-year-old schoolboy who coped courageously with cystic fibrosis was murdered by another pupil who used their school's mentoring system to lure him to his death.

Joe Geeling was stabbed to death and buried in a tree-lined gully in Bury, Greater Manchester, by Michael Hamer, 15, who was sentenced to life in jail yesterday after admitting the crime. He will serve at least 12 years.

Hamer, who was 14 at the time of the murder, was being bullied at St Gabriel's RC High School by boys who were briefly excluded for taking his dinner money from him. A few months later, in part to reassert his own personality, he singled out Joe, who was the smallest boy in his class as a result of his illness.

Hamer wrote a fictitious letter to him, purporting to be from the deputy head and telling him that he was to go home with him as they had been paired under the school's system of older pupils mentoring younger ones.

"I have given the address to your mum and she will meet you at the house at 4.30pm tonight", Hamer wrote. "Sorry for the inconvenience. Do not discuss this with anyone else as this will cause confusion."

Hours before the murder, Joe's teacher saw the letter. She realised it was a hoax and told Joe to see the deputy head about it. But nothing was done to stop Joe going to Hamer's house, where he was beaten to death with a frying pan and stabbed 16 times.

The lives of Joe and his killer were very different. Despite a condition that required overnight hospital treatment for two weeks every three months and impaired his growth, Joe was always "100mph", Manchester Crown Court was told. He had been in his primary school choir, and was in the local Crusaders motorbike club with his father.

While in hospital, he would go to school as normal and in the evenings return to hospital. He never complained about his illness and enjoyed playing video games with other children on the ward.

By contrast, Hamer suffered from "infrequent and intermittent" contact with his father – a policeman, who left the child's mother before he was born.

He was affected by having heard his father tell his mother that he had no feelings for him and he struggled to integrate at school, where he was at the "low end of average" ability.

Hamer tended to associate with children three years below his own age group – his extra years giving him, for once, some respect. He made an "adolescent sexual approach" to Joe, which was rejected.

Soon after lunch on the day of his death, the fake letter – written in red ink after three earlier drafts in which Hamer honed his letter-writing technique – was being passed around. Joe went to the deputy head's office but by chance was intercepted there by Hamer.

Minutes later, and again by chance, the two teachers who first saw the note saw Joe and Hamer in the corridor. They questioned Joe, who looked to Hamer for approval as he answered their questions. The teachers were interrupted when a fire alarm was set off, and everyone filed out to the playground before returning to class.

Hamer's letter was discovered with Joe's body, stained with his blood, in the gully in Whitehead Park, Bury. Hamer told police he had beaten Joe with a pan because he had interfered with a photograph of his deceased step-brother. But Hamer had not even met the step-brother.

Joe's father, Tom, described how, despite his illness, Joe had no self-pity. "He understood those were the cards God had dealt to him and together we made the best of what we had", he said.

The couple's knowledge about how their son had suffered throughout his ordeal had been "enough to break any man, let alone a loving and devoted mother".

Source: Ian Herbert, *Independent Online Edition* > *Crime*, 17 October 2006. Available at: http://news. independent.co.uk/uk/crime/article1879416.ece (17 October 2006).

If we roll back to the time before the tragedy occurs, these two young people differ considerably in how well their lives are going. Joe is disabled, yet enjoys high parental involvement and an apparently caring and concerned family. In contrast, Michael is being bullied and is reported to come from a broken home. Not only does Michael suffer from an absent father and lack of affection, but also from active paternal rejection. Joe appears to have good psycho-social adjustment, despite his disability, while Michael clearly has conduct and emotional problems.

Many teenagers in Britain today face similar problems to those of Joe and Michael, yet the outcome of murder and a life sentence is extremely rare. This case highlights more general issues. To what extent are the boys' differences in psycho-social adjustment attributable to 'disability' and 'being bullied' respectively, compared to the differing quality of their family lives? Does Michael's difficult family situation perhaps make him more vulnerable or in fact more 'disabled' than Joe? Could events have turned out differently if Michael's family had received some training in effective parenting? Was Michael's attitude and behaviour ultimately his own responsibility?

Further Reading

Catan, L. (2004) *Becoming adult: Changing youth transitions in the 21ˢᵗ century: A synthesis of findings from the ESRC Research Programmes.* Youth, Citizenship and Social Change 1998–2003. Trust for the Study of Adolescence: Brighton.

Jones, G. (2002) *The youth divide: Diverging paths to adulthood.* York Publishing Services for the Joseph Rowntree Foundation: York.

Scott, J., Treas, J. and Richards, M. (2004) (Eds) *The Blackwell companion to the sociology of families.* Blackwell: Oxford.

Williams, F. (2004) *Rethinking families.* ESCRC CAVA Research Group. Calouste Gulbenkian Foundation: London.

Discussion Questions

1. What evidence do we have that families are of immense importance to young people?
2. Do those who end up less educated, less healthy and poor invariably come from families that themselves are socially disadvantaged and marginalized?
3. Why do some young people do well in their lives despite disadvantaged circumstances?
4. How important are young people's experiences with parents relative to the young person's own attitudes and aspirations in overcoming family disadvantage?
5. Under what circumstances do positive family relations *not* counterbalance otherwise disadvantaged circumstances?
6. How can government best combat the exclusion of young people from the poorest sectors of society?
7. Is it always best to encourage and support poor and lone parents to enter or return to the labour market?
8. Are liberal democratic countries becoming less family-centred and more individualistic?

Chapter 3

Growing Up in Substitute Care: Risk and Resilience Factors for Looked-after Young People and Care Leavers

Sue Mills

Independent Social Work Consultant and Part-Time Tutor (child welfare)
Centre for Life Long Learning, University of Leeds

Nick Frost

Professor of Social Work, Faculty of Health, Leeds Metropolitan University

Be optimistic when your young person is in trouble to get them back on their feet. Tell them not to give up and to remember that a fighter always achieves their goal.
(A care leaver's message to social workers, staff and carers,
as part of a consultation process on strategic development)

- Introduction
- The demographic profile of looked-after young people
- The routes into public care
- Looked-after young people as the 'other'
- The view from the centre
- Residential care
- Foster care
- Leaving care
- Direct work with young people
- Conclusion

Adolescence, Risk and Resilience: Against the odds. John Coleman and Ann Hagell (eds.).
Published in 2007 by John Wiley & Sons, Ltd

Learning Objectives

Once you have read this chapter you should be able to:

1 Understand the demographic profile of looked-after young people.
2 Understand routes into public care.
3 Describe the different types of public care.
4 Analyse the connections between wider social factors and how they influence looked-after young people.
5 Understand the issues involved in promoting resilience with young people in substitute care.

Summary of Key Points

Young people in the public care system are often viewed as somehow 'pathological'. This is neither accurate nor helpful in understanding the risk factors they face and their resilience in responding to these factors.

General theories of youth are helpful in understanding the experience of looked-after young people, but specific theories of their experience are also required.

Services for looked-after young people need to be contextualized in a wider understanding of the organization and management of services.

Direct practice with looked-after young people, and those leaving care, needs to build upon sound organizational practice.

The five outcomes outlined in Every Child Matters form a useful framework for promoting good practice and building on the resilience of young people.

Successful outcomes for looked-after young people can be promoted using the framework proposed in this chapter.

Introduction

In this chapter we will be exploring, from a social constructionist perspective, the ways in which looked-after young people, by the very fact of being cared for within the public care arena, are placed in a precarious and vulnerable position. In taking a wide-angled view on risk and resilience factors for looked-after young people, we bring societal and organizational issues into sharp focus. It is our contention that in order to effect positive and enduring change for the whole looked-after population, organizations must be aware of and responsive to the wider theoretical landscape of childhood.

The organizations that deliver services for looked-after young people (young people for whom the local authority shares or has exclusive parental responsibility) require an awareness both of childhood as a social construct, and of the consequences for looked-after young people resulting from these constructs. These organizations can then take the lead in developing coherent, strategic and holistic responses that can help to positively re-position looked-after young people. Importantly, it is through the very process of both unpicking what it means to be a looked-after young person within contemporary life and positively re-positioning them, that a space is opened up from which to explore the risks and resilience factors with looked-after young people. We would argue, as we have elsewhere, that the route to the empowerment of looked-after young people has to be via the empowerment of staff (Frost *et al.*, 1999) and foster carers. Clear and coherent signposting for staff and carers, underpinned by support, supervision and training, begin to build in the necessary infrastructure that enables them to work effectively with individuals, families and groups.

In taking a wider societal and organizational perspective, we hope this will provide the building blocks that can underpin existent work on addressing risk and resilience factors with individual looked-after young people, both when they are looked after and when they are in the process of leaving care (Daniel and Wassell, 2002; Gilligan, 2001).

Looked-after young people are not a homogenous group, and as with all young people, their lives represent rich and diverse childhoods. As such, the dimensions of gender, ethnicity, disability, sexuality and socio-economic status, alongside the particular and specific care experiences that help shape and inform young people's lives, will be woven into the fabric of this chapter. Thus, we hope to convey the uniqueness of every young person and to explore realistically and holistically some of the ways to minimize risk factors and promote their resilience.

The Demographic Profile of Looked-after Young People

Until recently, statistical information gathered by the government provided a limited picture of the looked-after population. *Looked-after young people are those in the public care system following an order made by the courts or by voluntary agreement between themselves or their parents and the local authority.* Since 2001, however, data collection has become increasingly responsive to the diverse, dynamic and complex picture of the public care system. As such, it is now possible for anyone wanting to find out more about the data to access this via the appropriate departmental website.

Available snapshot statistics for 31 March 2003 reveal that for England, 43% of the total care population (26 500) were aged between 10 and 15 years and 16% (10 400) were aged 16 and over. The majority of these young people are cared for within foster care (around 68%), but group care remains significant with 13% living in children's homes and residential schools. A further 10% of the looked-after population who are on care orders are cared for at home under specific regulation under the Children Act 1989. Residential care generally looks after an older population, with over 70% living in children's homes aged 13 years and over. This chapter will also explore the position for the 6500 or so young people who leave care each year aged 16 years and over within England.

Gender

Overall, boys make up 55% of the care population and this figure rises to 57% for the 10–15 years age group, compared with 51% of boys within the general population of children under the age of 18 years. Gender has a significant impact on the experience of young people looked after in public care.

Ethnicity

80% (48 800) of children looked after on 31 March 2004 were white, 8% (4800) were of mixed racial background, 2% (1500) were Asian or Asian British, 8% (4900) were black or black British and 2% (1200) were from other ethnic groups. These figures therefore reveal that 20% of the care population are from minority ethnic backgrounds. Whilst these figures reveal a significant over-representation of ethnic minority young people, they nevertheless remain a minority numerically to their white counterparts within the looked-after system. The challenge is therefore to ensure that young people from ethnic minority backgrounds are not further marginalized by the looked-after system. The need to promote a positive identity for all young people should focus attention on the specific needs that arise, for example, in relation to culture, language and religion.

Unaccompanied Asylum-Seeking Children

There were 2400 unaccompanied asylum-seeking children, looked after within England, as of 31 March 2003. An overwhelming majority (76%) were boys, with girls making up the remaining 24%.

The statistics highlight gender and ethnicity, alongside citizenship as deeply relevant for these young people. Furthermore, whilst the particular and profound issues that asylum-seeking children face cannot be specifically responded to within this chapter, the experiences they bring serve to further underline and emphasize the way in which there are indeed multiple and diverse childhoods.

Disability

Statistics relating to the looked-after population throughout 2002–3 reveal that 12 000 (13%) children and young people became looked after because they had a disability. It is, however, difficult to build up an accurate numerical picture because, unless disability is the principle reason why a child or young person becomes looked after, there is no requirement to record that a child or young person is disabled. Whilst we are not suggesting that such invisibility within data collection leads to invisibility for disabled young people within their care contexts, nevertheless, the way in which statistics are gathered does raise an issue for government to address. Chapter 6 of this volume is devoted to the topic of challenges faced by disabled adolescents, and discusses further the particular issues faced by them in a range of contexts.

Lesbian and Gay Sexual Identities

Clearly there is no legal requirement to gather statistics discerning sexual identities of young people. Furthermore, the precarious legal position for young men under the age of 18, alongside a prevailing view of homosexuality as abnormal, means gay and lesbian young people would not necessarily be comfortable with identifying their sexuality. The presumption of heterosexuality, hence an invisibility that accompanies this, is a particular consequence of homophobia (Logan *et al.*, 1996) and this further explains the lack of statistics for young people who identify as lesbian or gay or whose lives are touched by their parents' or carers' sexual identity (Frost *et al.*, 1999).

The whole area of sexual identity for all young people needs to be addressed in positive and proactive ways. The lead for developing appropriate, safe and empowering policies and practices should take place from the centre of the organization. A clear lead is then able to provide sufficient safety and guidance from which to dare to 'speak the name' of teenage sexuality, including lesbian and gay identities.

The Routes into Public Care

There are many reasons why a young person enters the looked-after system. The following provide the reasons (as defined in England and Wales by the 'children in need' codes) for children who started to be looked after in 2003. We include them in order to provide readers with a sense of why and how someone becomes looked after: they include abuse or neglect (45%), family dysfunction (13%), family in acute stress (11%), absent parenting (10%), parental illness (8%), socially unacceptable behaviour (7%), disability (3%) and low income (1%).

Whatever the reason for being looked after, it is important to note that the Welfare Principle of the Children Act 1989 applies. That is: "*The welfare of the child is paramount*", which means that they are in care for their safety and welfare and not because they are in any way 'bad'.

Equally diverse are the trajectories in and out of care, including the length of stay, as well as the type and variety of placements. So, for instance, it is not unusual for a young person to have experienced several care episodes, punctuated by returns to their family, as this account testifies: "I might be only 13 years old, but I have been in and out of care for 8 years, 7 months and 14 days" (Shaw, 1998, p. 26). Family life, too, will reflect change and diversity, including a range of possible combinations of birth and step-family members (Department of Health, 1998). Furthermore, it is highly likely that a looked-after young person will have experienced at least one, if not several, placement moves or breakdowns. The looked-after and leaving care systems and experiences are therefore multi-dimensional, complex and dynamic in a way that statistics cannot possibly portray.

Key Messages

Looked-after young people are in care for their safety and welfare and should not be perceived as 'pathological'.

Looked-after young people's lives represent rich, multiple and diverse childhoods in which the dimensions of ethnicity, gender, disability, sexuality and class intersect with both the experiences that prompted the care episode, as well as the experiences whilst in care.

The looked-after system and experience is multi-dimensional, diverse, dynamic and complex.

Looked-after Young People as the 'Other'

> *...contemporary parents perceive their own children to be innocent and vulnerable (angels) whilst simultaneously representing other people's children as out of control in public space and a threat to moral order (devils)*
>
> (Valentine, 1996, pp. 581–582)

Looked-after young people's lives are lived in the public arena, they are always someone else's child, residing outside the sanctity and anonymity of their families, they are always positioned as the 'other'. And, whilst all young people tend to have a negative press, "Youth is present only when its presence is a problem" (Hebdige, 1979, cited in Hebdige, 1988, p. 12), for looked-after young people they are constantly in the public gaze, as this account testifies:

> *We're the ones who have to live there, to always look different when we're at school or summat, 'cos y'know, we're in a kid's home*
>
> (Young person living in a residential setting: Mills, 1998)

This is the first potential risk factor that we wish to highlight here because, not only are looked-after young people always someone else's child, but they are also positioned as 'problematic' and often viewed as 'bad'. This is a view frequently supported by accounts from young people, for instance when a young person told us that her school friend's mother had been incredulous that she lived in a children's home because she was "too nice" and "too good" (cited in Frost *et al.*, 1999). Accounts from staff also provide witness to this unfavourable positioning of looked-after young people. The following is just one of many examples we could draw upon: a member of staff who answered the door to an irate neighbour, holding a struggling young person whom he wrongly assumed must live at the children's home because he had been throwing stones (cited in Frost *et al.*, 1999). The impact on young people's self-esteem, as a result of being viewed in this negative way, needs no further development here but it raises the question of where such a view comes from and crucially, what can be done about it?

Universal Childhood

The problem, in part at least, lies with the wholesale adoption of Western notions of an idealized and universal child in which childhood is situated along a pathway to becoming fully human. This view of children as 'human becomings' positions children as innocent, weak, vulnerable and dependent (James *et al.*, 1998; Valentine, 1996). Universal notions are disrupted, however, when we investigate childhood over time (Gittens, 1998), place (Holloway and Valentine, 2001) and culture (James *et al.*, 1998).

When we cast historical glances at childhood we see a landscape that shifts and changes. Indeed, there are points at which childhood was not separated from adulthood. In earlier generations, children worked, dressed and socialized in the same manner as their adult counterparts (Aries, 1962). When we view childhood in other parts of the world we also see differences that further contest and disrupt the universal notions in which biology predominates. Consider, for example, life as a child living on the streets in Brazil (Ennew, 2002), or life as an only child, enforced by the authorities in China (West, 2002). And finally, a consideration of the cultural, economic and personal circumstances within our own society also disrupts universal notions. The experience of childhood for a child born into poverty and deprivation clearly is not the same as for a child born into affluence. Certainly poverty and deprivation is an overwhelming feature of the lives of looked-after young people and their families (Bebbington and Miles, 1989; Department of Health, 1998). And once we weave in other dimensions of age, gender, ethnicity, culture, disability and sexuality it becomes plain to see that there are indeed many childhoods.

But perhaps even more important is to reveal the way in which universal has become equated with the notion of 'normal' hence 'superior' childhood. Thus, a deviation from the norm becomes viewed as less than, deficient and in need of remedy or adaptation, a view that will therefore always position looked-after young people unfavourably.

Universal Family and Parenthood

It is not possible to unravel notions of universal childhood without also considering notions of the family and parenthood. If childhood is idealized within a universal gaze, then so too is parenthood. What it means to be a universal child cannot be separated from what it means to be a universal parent (Valentine, 1996). Despite a growing recognition of the diversity in family life (Smart and Neale, 1999; Williams, 2004), nevertheless the family formation of two married biological parents living together with their child or children remains an idealized notion. As with idealized childhood, so too idealized parenthood becomes the 'norm' from which all other forms are judged. Not only does this present

difficulties for looked-after young people and their parents who fall outside this idealized norm, but also for staff and carers who look after young people in public care. They too are positioned at odds, to be treated either with suspicion or to be glorified as saints. Either way, if these norms remain unchallenged, the space for the exploration of new ways of caring can so easily be closed off.

Parents also have huge expectations placed upon them to provide a childhood that not only fits the family norm referred to above, but also one that is somehow untainted by the real world: a childhood bathed in innocence provided by a parenthood that is wholly protective. What consequences then for young people and their parents when the idealized family has failed?

In the above we have begun to tease out some of the problems, so what are the solutions? First, we would argue that it is crucial for children to be seen as people in their own right, as fully human, with diverse and rich experiences and having their own agency (James *et al.*, 1998). So, whilst child development theory has its place and relevance, we argue for this to be considered within an overall social context that enables a space to be opened up from which to allow young people's voices to be heard. Similarly, we are not denying the importance of a social investment in children as 'the future', which is very much evident within current child-care policy (Fawcett *et al.*, 2004). However, we would stress the importance of balancing the notion of children as the future with ways that enable them to also have value and agency in the present.

Second, opening up and validating diverse forms of family life and caring for children (Featherstone, 2004; Williams, 2004) would enable an opening up to different and diverse lenses on both childhood and parenthood. In relation to looked-after young people, we would begin at the very centre of the organization.

Key Messages

It is important to explore and unpick notions of universal child and parent in order to open up space for exploration of all kinds of ways of caring for young people.

Looked-after young people need to be freed from negative labels that position them as the 'other', as 'inferior' and often 'pathological'.

The View from the Centre

In this section, we argue that it is contingent on senior managers and local politicians, who manage the looked-after and leaving care systems, to take a lead in valuing multiple childhoods thus helping to position looked-after young people outside the box that tends to only view them as 'problematic'. Furthermore, those at the centre need to provide a clear lead on routes to empowerment, hence a focus on strengths and resilience, by the way in which legislation, policy and practice are enacted upon and developed. We will draw upon some best practice models in order to provide concrete examples of the way in which organizations can make a difference.

'Good Enough for your Child?'

Local authorities and their partner agencies in health and the voluntary sector have a duty to act as 'corporate parents'. Indeed, all local councillors, once elected, and this is not negotiable, take on the role of a corporate parent. Frank Dobson, when Minister for Health in 1998, gave a clear direction to Local Councils, including local politicians, when planning services for all children and young people he said they should ask "Would this be good enough for my child?" Following the death of Victoria Climbié in 2000, this message was further underlined and strengthened.

Best Practice Example

Wakefield Council has a Corporate Parenting Panel, named by looked-after young people as 'U 'n' Us', which uses the formal, local political committee process to bring together:

- looked-after young people;
- local councillors (all of whom take on, when elected, the role of corporate parent);
- senior managers of key services for looked-after young people and care leavers.

The role is to debate and decide on some of the key areas of the looked-after system.

Importantly, this was also the place to steer the corporate parenting strategy through the various processes.

Not only do such forums have obvious benefits in terms of inclusive decision-making, but they also challenge preconceived, negative notions.

Looked-after Young People at the Heart of the Process

In responding to and developing policies and strategies, young people must be placed at the heart of the process from the outset. Invariably, there will be a need for negotiation between the pressing timescales that focus the adult professional agenda 'to get the job done' and the young people's need to learn about and trust the process before coming on board. A champion for looked-after young people who also understands the professional agenda but crucially sits outside each arena can be invaluable in helping the organization navigate a way through some of the tricky parts of the process. In placing young people at the centre, one of the first tasks will be to discover what young people feel and think.

Examples of Ways to Consult with Looked-after Young People

- Choose a venue that young people feel comfortable meeting in and that can offer fun activities as well as a place to consult from, i.e. sports centres, youth centres, libraries (council-run venues can be persuaded to meet some of their corporate parenting responsibilities by providing facilities free of charge).
- Schedule events to take place in school holidays, weekends and evenings.
- Consult at young people's pace and to help with this:
  - Build activities and fun events into the consultation process.
  - Draw on popular culture and creative methods of consultation – Big Brother Diary Rooms, Online Messaging, Music, Art and Drama.
  - Train and support young people to take on research roles.
  - Feedback results, check for accuracy and agree and involve young people in the way forward.

The next section will consider residential care and foster care, as the two primary manners in which looked-after young people are cared for.

Residential Care

The residential childcare landscape has witnessed considerable change over the last 20 years. As noted earlier, not only is the residential population much smaller, it is generally older, with 70% of the population aged 13 years and above. With some rare exceptions, most local authorities have childcare policies about not placing young people under 12 years of age in children's homes. The explicit reason behind such policy is that family life is seen as superior to other forms of living, particularly for the younger child. Bradford Metropolitan District Council, Social Services Department represents one exception to this policy, in that they use residential care purposely for some younger children. They operate a specialized resource for children under 11 years of age, with the aim of helping children recover from traumatic family experiences before either being placed with foster families or returned to their families of origin.

Whilst further discussion of this policy is beyond the scope of this chapter, it is important to note that such policies do raise identity issues for those young people placed in residential care. It may automatically place them in a negative position because the message is that family life is always preferable. Invariably, because many young people living in residential care have also lived in foster care, they are faced with not only carrying the burden of their own family failure but also the failure within the substitute family. Alternatively, young people who ask for foster care often receive the message that there are no foster carers willing or able to look after them. This is due to a lack of adequate foster care resource, which we will discus further in the next section.

Interestingly, however, some young people have consistently made residential care a positive placement choice. At the first ever 'Who Cares?' conference in 1976, young people confidently expressed the view that if they could not live with their own family, residential care was, for a number of reasons, preferable for them (Page and Clarke, 1976).

Furthermore, despite the scandals of abuse in residential care coinciding with the implementation of the Children Act 1989 in England and Wales, residential care was positively reframed by the Utting Report of 1991 (Utting, 1991). When William Utting was asked to preside over 'People Like Us' in 1997, which reviewed the measures that had been put in place to help safeguard children living away from home, he reiterated support for residential care as a placement choice and warned about the need to "keep deterministic pessimism about residential care in check" (Utting, 1997, p. 22).

The case for residential care as a necessary part of the placement provision was also inadvertently made when Warwickshire County Council, Social Services Department abandoned its residential childcare provision in the mid-1980s. The commissioned research to assess the impact of this decision overwhelmingly reported that not only was the decision financially more costly, but there was also a negative impact on young people's care careers. For example, not only were there more placement breakdowns, but more young people were being placed many miles away from their families and communities of origin (Cliffe and Berridge, 1991).

It is also important to understand the case for and against residential care if we are to work in ways to reduce risk and build upon young people's resilience. In the first instance, we have mapped out some of the ways in which young people are stigmatized for living in residential care. The organization needs to address this and work in ways that reduce the risk factors for young people resulting from stigmatization. There are a number of ways that we would suggest. These include: involving young people at all levels of the decision-making processes and fully endorsing and resourcing Total Respect Training, developed by CROA (the Children's Rights Organization).

Creativity is the key; for instance, a group of looked-after young people in Australia successfully carried out an advertising campaign on national television that challenged the negative stereotype of looked-after young people. At an individual children's home level, it is also contingent on the staff team to be proactive with the local community in which the home is located, becoming as involved as possible with local community activities, groups and events, such as youth clubs, after-school clubs, sports teams, guides, scouts, using local shops and libraries.

The risk involved for young people when they carry the negative self-image that comes from being looked after in residential care is difficult to quantify. What we do know, however, is that there are negative consequences which result from low self-esteem and these can impact on all areas of a young person's life (Gilligan, 2001; Jackson, 2001; Social Care Institute for Excellence, 2005). Furthermore, the promotion of positive self-esteem is one of the building blocks of resilience (Social Care Institute for Excellence, 2005). It is therefore crucial that the factors that impact negatively on young people's self-esteem from the wider societal and organizational levels are addressed, alongside any individual work to help build positive self-esteem.

Understanding the reasons why residential care remains a positive choice for some young people is also central to tapping into their resourcefulness and resilience. Young people have commented that they choose residential care because they enjoy living with groups of young people of a similar age. They also say they enjoy having a number of adults to relate to in ways that are different from a parent. Related to this last point, they say they do not have to feel disloyal to their own parents if they become close to a member of staff because they are clearly not a parent substitute. Young people have also said that foster care can be too painful, it reminds them too much of how they have been hurt by family life (Frost *et al.*, 1999; Page and Clarke, 1976). Finally, some parents of young people also say they find it easier to visit their child in residential care because it is not the private domain of a family. Added to this, parents have reported that they do not automatically compare themselves unfavourably with staff. Crucially, the role of staff in residential care is seen as different from that of a parent, whether natural or substitute.

Informed practice that draws upon these messages from young people and their families is clearly the way forward. In so doing this will tap into and build upon young people's resilience, thus providing an empowering environment in which to care for some of the most vulnerable young people within society. We will consider ways of addressing and proactively responding to issues from an individual perspective in a separate section.

Best Practice Messages for Working with Young People in Residential Care

- Well-supported, trained, skilled and diverse staff teams with clear anti-oppressive value base, able to deliver a safe, empowering and appropriate balance of care and control.
- High-quality buildings inside and out, located within and as part of community life.
- Clear statements of purpose for appropriate mix and number of young people that map out what, how and who the children's home is for and how its aims will be achieved.
- Positive representation of difference and diversity within all aspects of the home.
- Young people involved in all aspects of residential life. This will include young people's interview panels for staff interviews, trained and supported by training units.
- Young people's group meetings which, if successfully developed, can contribute to the running of the home, address issues as they arise and be part of future developments.
- Clear, consistent and involved care planning, assessment and reviewing that works out with young people what, how, when, who and where each dimension of a young person's life will be addressed and responded to.

Foster Care

As noted earlier, foster care over recent years has become the prime site for looking after children and young people in England and Wales, with an average of 68% of the total care population being cared for within foster homes each year. The recruitment and retention of a sufficient number of carers for all age groups, but particularly for teenagers, is a huge challenge for organizations (Sinclair *et al.*, 2004a). Further to this is the need for carers from diverse backgrounds who can provide skilled care for vulnerable young people, many of whom present particularly challenging behaviour (Farmer *et al.*, 2004; Hayden *et al.*, 1999; Hill, 1999; Sinclair *et al.*, 2004b; Triseliotis *et al.*, 2000).

Sinclair *et al.* (2004a,b) argue that foster care, including both long- and short-term placements, is the most common way in which local authorities look after other people's children. They utilized questionnaire responses from over a thousand foster carers across seven different local authorities, and highlighted the importance of identifying and fulfilling appropriate kinds of care; the need to recruit and retain carers; and examined the ways that carers can be supported to reduce strain and turnover through, for example, housing and financial support, training and carers' groups.

Farmer *et al.* (2004) in their study argued that teenage young people are the most difficult group to foster and have the highest rates of placement breakdown. The study explored what helps to make their placements work. Key issues for this age group were explored, including peer relationships, sexual health and relationships, the impact of the young person themselves on the foster family and balancing their need for safety and autonomy. The authors consider which kinds of professional support at which stages make a difference, the foster carer parenting skills that are crucial and how foster carers can draw on professional support to manage a young person's behaviour, maintain their educational attainments and negotiate ongoing contact with their birth parents. They point out how strain on carers can be reduced, and emphasize the role foster carers' own children play in placement success or breakdown. Lessons are shared on how to contain the young people who are hardest to foster; implications are drawn out for training requirements for foster carers and the management of contact.

Agencies responsible for providing foster care need to utilize recent research, which is now beginning to address the previous dearth of research in this area. Furthermore, there are major childcare organizations such as the British Association for Adoption & Fostering (BAAF), Barnardo's, National Children's Bureau (NCB) and NCH, as well as government responses to fostering issues, all of which provide a wealth of resources that local agencies can access. Alongside accessing and responding to research findings and best practice models, agencies also need to mobilize local resources, such as the social responsibility agenda of major businesses and employers. This could involve asking for help with foster care recruitment drives by advertising in show rooms, staff rooms, refectories and on transport systems. Furthermore, major employers could be asked to host information days about fostering. By holding events in familiar places, such as work sites, this can help to bring in potential foster carers, willing to hear more from a known and non-threatening place. Information events that also include current carers and young people can not only provide a view from the heart of the task, but also help to engage and empower both carers and young people.

The role of foster care has not remained static and particular trends can be noted from the ways in which social work interventions with families have become more focused on helping families stay together. It follows, therefore, that when young people do need to be looked after, they are frequently very troubled and potentially present troublesome behaviour (Department of Health, 1998). Organizations must acknowledge the increasingly complex task of fostering, thereby rising to the complex challenge that results. As we have argued earlier, it is about opening space to explore all manner of possible solutions that lie beyond idealized notions of parenting and family life. The need for specialized, diverse and professional foster care, alongside mainstream provision, is ever more present (Sinclair *et al.*, 2004a,b).

It is well documented within the resilience literature that young people do best when they have positive caring relationships that value, respect and support them, thus helping to improve levels of self-esteem (Gilligan, 2001; Social Care Institute for Excellence, 2005). In order to assist foster carers to provide empowering relationships based on care, support and respect that bolster self-esteem, they too, just as we argued for residential staff, also need to be valued, supported and empowered. This will involve meeting a whole range of training needs, ranging from the most basic to specialist areas. Involving foster carers in training with other professionals not only provides an opportunity to share and exchange skills and knowledge, it also sends a message that foster care is valued. Some training also needs to involve young people. We mentioned earlier Total Respect training, but young people, as well as experienced foster carers, can also be involved in specific recruitment drives as well as training for new foster carers.

Valuing Both Foster Care and Residential Care as Complementary to One Another

These two primary sites for caring for young people, foster and residential care, have a great deal of experience, knowledge, skills and support to share and exchange with one another. Frequently, however, they are implicitly placed in opposition to one another. This opposition can be partly understood by unpicking idealized notions of childhood and parenthood that we discussed earlier. A particular consequence of idealized, universal notions is that childhood, parenthood and family life are viewed as 'natural' and therefore there is a tendency to view the task of foster caring as a natural-occurring event wrapped up in notions of maternal affection. Clearly this is not helpful because it can prevent conscious, dedicated and strategic service development that provides support and training to foster care. In other words, foster carers can lose out on much needed support because they are viewed as doing a job that is 'natural' and 'normal'.

Thus, we would argue that foster and residential care need to be valued for their differences and positioned as complementary, rather than in opposition to one another in the particular ways in which they care for young people. By not pitting them in opposition to each other, the way can be paved for resources between the two to be pooled and shared. For example, unlike residential staff, foster carers do not always have respite from the task of caring for vulnerable young people. It is an activity that takes place within their homes and usually on a 24-hour, 7-day a week basis. Organizations therefore need to respond in creative ways to provide carers with the necessary support and, when needed, respite from care. Linking foster care with residential care, as well as recruiting respite foster carers in order to share the care for some young people, signposts the way forward.

Crucially, however, shared care arrangements need to be planned with young people so that they are very much part of the decision-making process, thus helping them to feel in control of the ways in which care is provided. In this way young people are more likely to feel positive about shared care, as opposed to feeling they are unwanted, bothersome, too much trouble and so on, which only serves to feed into feelings of rejection, and hence adds to low self-esteem.

Key Messages

- Foster care has become an increasingly complex task that involves caring for young people who have often experienced considerable trauma and trouble in their short lives. Their behaviour often reflects this, hence it can be extremely challenging.
- Foster care and residential care need to be assisted to work together, to share care, to share and exchange skills and knowledge, and most importantly to support one another in the complex task of caring for young people.
- Organizations need to take on board recent key research messages and work in ways that enable proactive partnerships.

Leaving Care

Every year about 6500 young people over the age of 16 years leave care. The issue of leaving care barely appeared on the policy agenda before the publication of the ground-breaking study 'Leaving Care' (Stein and Carey, 1986) and agitation from young people themselves that this process was being undervalued. Recently we have seen advances in the attention paid to the leaving care issue – exemplified by the Children (Leaving Care) Act 2000.

The overwhelming problem facing young people leaving care has been that they are more likely than the rest of the youth population to face a number of risk factors and consequent poor outcomes. For example, they are likely to leave care earlier than other young people leave home, they are less likely to hold educational qualifications, more likely to be homeless and young women are more likely to be mothers (Biehal et al., 1995; Stein and Carey, 1986). A recent survey of almost 300 care leavers by A National Voice, a user-led organization of care leavers, found that despite recent advances, 45% said they often got lonely or depressed living on their own, a half said that housing professionals were not aware of their needs and around two-thirds of respondents said they were unhappy with the after-care support they had received (A National Voice, 2004). This depressing list acts as a major challenge for the whole looked-after system. Young people enter the looked-after system with disadvantage but the system seems unable to address this issue and instead the young people seem to 'accumulate disadvantage' as they pass through the system to the process of leaving care.

These facts – as we have seen previously – hide some complex trends. Certainly we do not want to paint a picture of the looked-after system as always failing young people – the need is rather to assess how policy and practice can be improved and how we can work with the undoubted resilience of young people striving for successful outcomes to their care careers.

It is helpful to see young people leaving care as falling into three groups. These have been identified by Stein as the 'moving on' group, the 'survivors' group and the 'victims' group (Action on Aftercare, 2004; Stein, 2005). It is worthwhile exploring each group in turn – as each has different risk and resilience factors that are relevant to the main thrust of this chapter.

The group most likely to have successful outcomes on leaving care – the moving on group – are those who have had a stable looked-after experience. They will have perhaps had one stable placement, had a settled educational experience and will have a relatively positive self-image. They are highly resilient and are able to make good use of any help and assistance that is offered to them. They form, perhaps, 20% of the leaving care population.

At the opposite end of the continuum are the victims group. The experience of this group contrasts strongly with the moving on group and again perhaps makes up 20% of the leaving care population. They have had a number of care placements, a disrupted education and may have a negative self-image. This group will struggle to utilize support that is offered and will experience many of the depressing list of outcomes that we have outlined above – perhaps ending up homeless, and involved in crime and substance abuse.

The group at the centre, the majority 'survivors', are a group where the nature of the outcomes they experience remains uncertain. They may have had more than one placement and experienced elements of a disrupted educational experience. For this group the nature of the support offered is crucial, it can help them develop their resilience and work towards successful outcomes.

Resilience will be promoted amongst care leavers only if the quality of their entire care experience is improved – providing them with stability, a positive sense of identity, a coherent educational experience and support on leaving care. Further, just as we have argued for increased integration between foster and residential care, leaving care needs to be a process that is integrated with the entire care process (Stein, 2005).

Direct Work with Young People

Having addressed the important structural and policy issues that have to be in place to support practice, we now move on to explore issues relating to direct practice with looked-after young people and those leaving care. The visual model utilized here is one of a tree, whereby its roots are crucial to its strength and survival over time. The structural, policy and procedural areas represent the roots. The trunk and branches are the staff, carers and other resources. When everything is in place, providing the care and nourishment, the tree will, even after the harshest of winters, burst into life and show signs of resilience. Direct work can help with this final flourish. In this last section we therefore want to highlight some of the ways in which direct work with young people can help to address potential risk factors and build upon young people's strengths and resilience.

The important and over-riding point to note is that staff, foster carers and leaving care workers within the looked-after children system are presented with tremendous opportunities to work in a truly holistic way and at a pace that the young person determines. The nature of the work and care arrangements means that appointments do not necessarily have to be made in advance to do the work. The flexibility of the work allows staff and carers plenty of opportunities to respond when young people are ready. This might be, for example, whilst watching a TV programme that provokes some discussion, driving in the car or doing the washing up. The starting point of course, as with all people work, is the quality of the core relationship. Within the demands and challenges of looking after young people the importance of the relationship can be lost, overlooked or minimized but if we listen to young people they will remind us how central the relationship is:

> . . . if you're attached to 'em [staff] and they tell you off, you feel hurt don't yer? You think yer letting 'em down

> (Young person living in residential care, cited in Mills, 1998)

As a result, attention must always be on building, developing and maintaining safe, positive, respectful and empowering relationships with young people. The relationship will then be the vehicle through which to explore with young people what is important to them and what concerns they may have. It may also include staff and carers naming issues, but in a way that opens up the possibility for young people to say what they think would work (and not work) in addressing the issues.

In the following section we will use the main themes and dimensions that 'Every Child Matters' (2003) first identified in consultation with children and young people, and which the Children Act 2004 carries forward. The themes, of course, are dynamic and interactive and it is the dynamic relationship between them that truly addresses the whole of a young person's life.

> The government, in writing the consultation document 'Every Child Matters' (Department for Education and Skills, 2003), agreed with children and young people the following main themes which the subsequent Children Act 2004 legislation incorporated:
>
> • Be Healthy
> • Keep Safe
> • Enjoy and Achieve
> • Make a Positive Contribution
> • Achieve Economic Well-being

We utilize the five outcomes in order to understand direct practice that can support and promote resilience amongst looked-after young people.

Be Healthy

This refers to the whole area of a young person's health and well-being and therefore includes physical, emotional, psychological as well as the social realms that also influence health and well-being.

Looked-after young people, besides the concern that many have missed out on routine health checks and immunisations, can respond to the statutory requirement for health checks in antagonistic ways. It is therefore important to address the underlying reasons why a young person is reluctant to engage with health professionals. The reasons could be many and varied, for instance, past experiences of abuse, shyness and awkwardness with the body and avoidance of detection by professionals of drug and/or alcohol use.

The adult, professional preoccupation with health issues is well placed, supported by the available research on health outcomes (Department of Health, 1998) but if not handled sensitively it can become an agenda that can get in the way of promoting young people's health and well-being. Careful and considerate attention is therefore needed of the ways to engage young people in the process. Helping looked-after young people to take charge of their own health promotion can both reduce risk factors and promote young people's resilience.

Group work with young people can be particularly productive. First, this is because the peer group is an important aspect of young people's lives and they can be very responsive to their peers in the training, supporting and/or mentoring role. Second, within residential contexts, young people live in groups. Third, talking in a group can present a less threatening way to address some of the issues such as smoking, alcohol and drug use and sexual health that young people face more generally within society. And finally, it can be an expedient use of health professional resources, for instance, involving health promotion workers in group work programmes. Individual work will also be an important part of the process, indeed it will be crucial for some young people.

CASE STUDY

An example from our own practice is a young woman whom we shall call Gillian, who had many and severe issues in her life including one around food. Gillian arrived at her new placement at a stage when the psychiatrist was threatening to hospitalize her if her weight fell any further.

The issue was identified with her, and because she lived in a group care context, boundaries were agreed with her that had as much to do with respecting the group as well as balancing her particular and acute issues. It was agreed, therefore, that whilst Gillian did not have to come to the table to eat, she must not disrupt mealtime for the other young people. It was agreed that she could eat when she felt able and could prepare food with staff. It was also agreed with her that she would not go to the toilet immediately after eating because this was when she would make herself sick.

In effect, Gillian was given as much control as possible but in a way that was not detrimental to herself or others. It was agreed that the other young people needed to know why, at mealtimes, Gillian was being treated differently from them. This was explained in broad terms and sent a message that each young person was an individual and all had their own issues to deal with. Each of the young people already had experience of being treated as an individual. The key elements as to why this approach began to work included:

- *Taking a holistic approach.* While the issue of food was critical, the approach was to ensure that Gillian was responded to as a whole person and not just as someone who had the label of 'anorexic'.
- *Naming the issue in a sensitive but direct manner.*
- *Negotiation.* Working out with Gillian what would help and constantly reviewing and evaluating with her how the plans were going.
- *Navigation.* Working with Gillian on which way to go, sometimes staff taking the lead but also allowing, within the previously negotiated safe boundaries, for Gillian to take the lead.
- *Flexibility.* Being open to try new ways, to always be responsive and to make sure nothing was set in tablets of stone.
- *Reviewing and Evaluating.* A constant need to review and evaluate the strategies with the young person at the heart of the process.

Keep Safe

This is another area that raises all manner of issues and concerns. Crucially, it is worth reiterating that, at the organizational level, measures must be in place to ensure as much as possible that young people are safe from perpetrators and abusive practices. With the necessary infrastructures in place staff and carers, alongside their colleagues within the organization and beyond, can begin to address with young people ways in which they can keep safe, both whilst looked after and having left care.

As with the previous theme, adult, professional agendas need to be balanced with a need to hear from young people what the issues are for them. Young people do not necessarily define risk in the same way as adults. Risk can often be viewed by young people as having fun, taking a chance, pushing adult boundaries:

> *I don't see it as taking risks, it's just having fun, in'it? Staff might think it's a risk but, and they'll tell you again and again that it is, but you don't see it like that, unless summat bad happens to you*
> (Mills, 1998)

For this young person, when asked if anything bad had ever happened to her, the response was:

> *No, I'm not stupid. I've been going out and stuff for a long time and I know how to look after myself*
> (ibid)

What this highlights is that it is important not only to allow young people to define what risk means, but also to allow their own agency to come to the fore in considering solutions. Looked-after young people have often experienced aspects of life that their adult carers have no direct experience of. For some they have had to take on 'adult' roles from a young age. For others they have experienced lifestyles that would be considered dangerous but they have survived. It is the survival aspects that are important to acknowledge, to take the positives from and to develop within new and different contexts where positive, caring and respectful relationships are key. Again, group work with young people can be particularly helpful in enabling them to work together and learn from one another.

For some young people their current behaviour may be so unsafe that there has to be an immediate response. Again we want to draw upon Gillian who, alongside her issues with food, was placing herself at risk outside her children's home. Gillian was highly addicted to nicotine at this stage and so much so that she was offering sex to strangers in exchange for a cigarette. As part of the whole group, Gillian received the consistent message that this was unsafe and that staff would, at all times, seek to ensure that she did not continue with this behaviour. The over-riding message was that she was worth caring for even when this meant having to exercise some control on her behaviour. Alongside this, her key worker, with whom she was already developing an excellent relationship, began to unpick with her what the issues involved were. What transpired was that besides her need for cigarettes, Gillian also said she had an overwhelming need for sex, so much so, it hurt. Gillian had been, prior to her becoming looked after aged 13 years, sexually abused over a number of years. Whilst staff were aware of this it was important that it was Gillian who named it and was able to explore what was behind her behaviour. What was important was that the sexual desire was separated from the potentially dangerous behaviour of approaching unknown men on the streets. What also emerged was that Gillian had little knowledge of her own body. Talking and learning about sex and sexuality in safe and appropriate ways began to empower Gillian to take control of her own desire. It was, however, highly sensitive ground for the staff team and it was crucially important that staff were supported in equally safe and appropriate ways. Gillian became an advocate of masturbation, she talked openly with other young women about not feeling ashamed of their bodies and that to explore their own sexuality was more than okay, alongside advice on why and how to keep safe.

Enjoy and Achieve

One image that we wish to promote of young people who are or have been looked after is that they have positive features which enable resilience and help to overcome risk factors. This is one way in which the five outcomes represent a major step forward in how we think about looked-after young people. In a sense it represents the final break with the politics of 'less eligibility' represented by the Poor Law that has cast a long shadow over residential care in particular (see Frost *et al.*, 1999). 'Less eligibility' was the Poor Law system that attempted to ensure that conditions inside the workhouse were not attractive to those living outside the workhouse, ensuring it did not attract 'undeserving residents'. All young people, whether looked after or not, can enjoy life and make positive achieve-ments. There are positive images of people who have left care – currently John Fashanu, the former footballer, and Kerry Katona, the pop singer are representatives of people who have built successful lives after care. Many young people speak positively about their care experiences as improving their life chances and giving them a chance to grow and develop.

To support achievement we need to build on educational achievement in particular. There are now many specific projects that exist to promote the positive engagement of looked-after young people with the education system and to support them through school, further education and higher education. This process has been enhanced by the emphasis on education contained in the Children (Leaving Care) Act 2000 and in subsequent government initiatives.

Make a Positive Contribution

Making a positive contribution again adds a welcome positive perspective in relation to young people being looked after. Looked-after young people have been able to organize both locally and nationally through A National Voice (see www.anationalvoice.org). They have contributed to planning and strategy for the looked-after system, participated in in-terview panels for professional staff, and have in many ways led the agenda for the rights of children more widely. Former and current looked-after young people now often actively participate in issues that were previously the preserve of professional staff, such as inspec-tion and training.

A recent survey of members of the public undertaken by the Prince's Trust optimistically found that 80% of the public agreed with the statement that 'young people in care have as much potential as their peers to succeed' (Prince's Trust, 2004).

Achieve Economic Well-being

Economic well-being rests at the centre of risk and resilience for looked-after young people and those leaving care. Looked-after young people are likely to have entered care from a poor background and in the past have been more likely to experience poverty once having left care. All the factors we have examined above have to rest on the bedrock of economic well-being. Here, once again, we require a holistic approach. Economic well-being can only be achieved by young people who have been well supported and well educated whilst being looked after, who experience leaving care as a supportive process and who are valued as making a positive contribution socially. In terms of leaving care again the developments since the implementation of the Children (Leaving Care) Act 2000 have been significant and there are reasons to be optimistic here (Action on Aftercare, 2004). Young people leaving care can receive leaving care grants and weekly allowances towards employment, education and training, all of which can enhance their life chances.

Conclusion

In this chapter we have aimed to explore the lives of young people looked after and leaving care. We have argued for a 'wide-angled' perspective that understands looked-after young people in the wider context of young people in general. We have identified risk factors that confront looked-after young people much more starkly than many other young people. We have argued that these risk factors can often be overcome where there is a comprehensive approach taken to understanding, supporting and caring for looked-after young people. We remain optimistic that we can build on resilience towards positive outcomes for looked-after young people, and the ideas and examples presented in this chapter help us to take steps forward in this direction.

Further Reading

Fawcett, B., Featherstone, B. and Goddard, J. (2004) *Contemporary child care policy and practice*. Palgrave Macmillan: Basingstoke. [An excellent overview of the 'New Labour' approach to childhood.]

James, A., Jenks, C. and Prout, A. (1998) *Theorising childhood*. Polity Press: Cambridge. [A key text in understanding the recent sociology of childhood and the social construction of childhood.]

Thomas, N. (2005) *Social work with young people in care: Looking after children in theory and practice*. Palgrave Macmillan: Basingstoke. [An up-to-date overview of many of the issues raised in this chapter.]

Websites

www.anationalvoice.org

[The website of the national organization that represents young people in care and those who have left care. A useful resource for young people and for those who want to know more about the issues confronting young people in care.]

www.thewhocarestrust.org.uk

[This website contained CareZone – a website designed to support and empower young people in care.]

Discussion Questions

1. How do wider social factors influence the make-up of the 'looked-after' young people population?
2. How can the separate elements of the 'looked-after children' services be encouraged to work together and learn from each other?
3. How can direct work with young people promote resilience?

Chapter 4

Sex and Risk

Jennifer J. Pearce

Professor of Young People and Public Policy, University of Bedfordshire

- Introduction
- Risk and resilience
- Sex, risk and sexual health
- Risky relationships
- Case studies: lessons for practice
- Conclusion

Learning Objectives

Once you have read this chapter you should be able to:

1 Identify risk factors that can impact on young people's sex and sexual relationships.
2 Identify protective factors that can support young people to be resilient when managing sex and sexual relationships.
3 Understand the relationship between risk and resilience.
4 Be aware of the potential problems and preoccupations of a society concerned with risk and with protecting young people from all harm.
5 Describe the risk of poor sexual health and of early conception rates amongst young people, particularly those under 16 years of age.
6 Explain the relationship between risky sex and risky violent interpersonal relationships as experienced by young people.

Adolescence, Risk and Resilience: *Against the odds.* John Coleman and Ann Hagell (eds.).
Published in 2007 by John Wiley & Sons, Ltd

7 Explain some of the routes into sexual exploitation for young people and the risk factors that can make some more vulnerable than others to exploitation.

8 Describe some of the interventions that can help young people in sexually exploitative relationships to be resilient.

Introduction

Becoming sexually active is a normal and healthy part of growing up. Many important studies have looked at the pleasures and the pains young people go through when developing sexual identities that they feel comfortable with. An essential part of this process lies in taking risks and recovering from various setbacks. This chapter explores our understanding of some of the risks young people face while they become sexually active. It focuses on both the risk factors that can make them vulnerable and the protective factors that can help them avoid or survive harm. Looking at sex and risk in relationships, the chapter acknowledges that while risky, harmful sex can be the result of an attack from a stranger, it can also take place within intimate relationships between peers or people known to each other and considered to be friends. Our analysis of sex and risk must, therefore, include consideration of relationships and risk.

In the second section we look at the risk factors that have been shown to make some young people vulnerable to harm within their sexual relationships. We address the critiques that have challenged our worries about harm and danger. These have noted a 'risk-aware society' that is increasingly preoccupied with identifying and managing risk. Finally, we consider the relationship between risk and resilience, looking at how young people's resilience to harm is affected by the scope for them to take risks. In the third section we look at some of the risks that young people who are becoming sexually active might face. These might include hostile reactions from friends or family, the risk of unwanted pregnancy or of STIs. In the fourth section we look in a little more detail at 'risky relationships', considering the risk factors that can push a young person into a potentially dangerous relationship and the protective factors that can help to protect them from harm. We then go on to consider some case histories illustrating the issues concerning risk and resilience relevant to sexually exploited young people, and finally, in conclusion, we summarize suggestions for policy and practice to support protective factors that can build young people's resilience.

Risk and Resilience

Categories of Risk

Existing research has identified common risk factors that can contribute to making some young people vulnerable to harm as they grow up. These risk factors have been categorized under three areas (see Coleman and Hendry, 1999; Newman, 2002; Rutter, 1985 for further details).

Firstly we have risk factors encountered at an individual level such as low self-esteem, poor physical and/or mental health and problematic attachments to friends, family or carers. These, plus other difficulties facing the individual young person, can all undermine their

capacity to take risks or to manage the impact of risk-taking. In essence, they can undermine the young person's coping skills.

Secondly we have familial risk factors such as parental mental and/or physical health problems; patterns of neglect, of physical, sexual or emotional abuse; criminality within the family, or family histories of being looked after or being in care. These risk factors can mean that resources within the family are stretched and strained, limiting the family's capacity to support the young person.

Thirdly we have environmental risk factors such as poorly resourced housing and local community support provision; inadequate public transport; local safe play and sport facilities; and poor schooling or local employment opportunities (Fergusson *et al.*, 1994).

One, or as is often the case, a combination of these three types of risk factors can result in a young person being more vulnerable to the dangers associated with sexual experimentation during adolescence, or can result in them demonstrating behaviours that are seen as risky to others.

Critiques of the Risk Society

Are risk factors real, or are they socially constructed by anxious adults wanting to protect young people from harm? We need to take a critical look at how information defining categories of risk is derived, and at why we have such a strong focus on the concept of risk. It has been questioned whether we are increasingly becoming a society that is unduly focused on developing strict and rigid structures for 'risk management', in some cases with an ultimate (and yet impossible) aim of eradicating all risk (Adam *et al.*, 2000; Beck, 1992). Is the focus on risk identification and risk management helpful or is it part of a desire by adults, and in this case the young people they feel responsible for, to avoid the strong feelings of emotional pain that are just an inevitable part and parcel of life (Cooper and Lousada, 2005)?

In terms of young people's sexual activity for example, different societies have had different expectations of young people's capacity to manage sexual risk. Some European countries give young adolescents responsibility for their sexual relationships, setting the age of consent at 14 (Germany). Other countries place it at 15 (Denmark and France). We could question whether in the UK, where the age of legal consenting sexual activity for boys and girls is 16 (Sexual Offences Act 2003), we are trying to over-protect young people, perhaps being dismissive of, or punitive towards, those younger teenagers who are sexually active?

Also, we must note that while adolescence is associated with risks such as teen smoking, high suicide rates, binge drinking and high teenage conception rates, there is an alternative story that focuses on how such problems can mask a more positive picture of resilient youth (Sharland, 2005). Less advertised data shows alternative stories of declining conception rates, albeit they are still the highest in Europe, increasing numbers of young people in education and employment (Coleman and Schofield, 2007) and of young people more likely to be victims, rather than perpetrators, of crime (Goldson *et al.*, 2002). Indeed, Rutherford (1986) shows us that risk-taking is part and parcel of the dynamic of growing up, and that media and political responses might over-sensationalize risk-taking behaviour, begging the question why young people are, and have been, through generations, so demonized as 'risky' (Pearson, 1983). Central to this debate is awareness of the important relationship between risk and resilience: risk-taking being argued to be essential to the development of a resilient character (Howard *et al.*, 1999).

Risk and Resilience: A Pair in Partnership

It is helpful therefore to look at resilience in a little more detail. Resilience has been defined by Gilligan (1999) as the capacity to transcend adversity, or by Fonagy *et al.* (2002) as normal development under difficult conditions. Just as there are risk factors that can make some young people more susceptible to danger, so there are protective factors that can help young people to manage danger without undue harm to themselves. As argued by Newman (2002):

> *Risk factors heighten the probability that children will experience poor outcomes. Resilience factors increase the likelihood that children will resist or recover from exposure to adversity. Positive child development is not simply a matter of reducing or eliminating risk factors and promoting resilience. The successful management of risk is a powerful resilience-promoting factor in itself.* (p. 3)

Building resilience to the impact of negative experiences can only occur if the occasional risk is taken. Taking risks and building resilience do, therefore, work in partnership with each other, meaning we need awareness of protective as well as risk factors when considering young people's experimentation with sexual relationships. 'Protective factors' that can help to increase resilience have been located within similar categories as those proposed for risk factors: individual, family and environmental categories. The difference is in the nature of the experiences within these categories. For example, focusing on the individual young person, their poor mental or physical health or low self-esteem might be a risk factor, making them vulnerable to harmful sexual relationships. Alternatively, a history of positive mental or good physical health or of high self-esteem might build the young person's resilience. Similarly, a disrupted family or care history and an under-resourced, fragmented local community might increase the young person's vulnerability to harm, while a cohesive family history and a supportive local community might increase their resilience to identify and cope with danger.

However, we need to be cautious about becoming too deterministic about this. Not all children with low self-esteem or fragmented care histories necessarily become vulnerable adolescents. Neither too are all young people with strong self-esteem, supportive families and communities immune from harm. As argued by Newman, it is never too late to build resilience. He draws on evidence from longitudinal studies which show that where protective factors are put in place, children and young people tend to recover from short-lived childhood adversities better than when they are not in place (Newman, 2002, 2004). Where adversities are continuous and severe and where protective factors are absent, young people are less resilient and less able to recover from trauma or distress. However, even in these circumstances, there are still opportunities to build a young person's resilience. Resilience is dynamic, having the capacity to emerge later in life after earlier periods of coping problems. Research from the USA and UK shows that if the individual young person can be encouraged to be active and independent, and can be supported by a parent or a parent substitute, resilience can be enhanced. In other words, it is not too late to provide protective factors for adolescents whose earlier childhoods might have been disrupted.

It is on this note that we start to focus in more detail on the relationship between risk, resilience, young people and sex. We will look first at the research that explores the relationship between sex and risk. Then we will focus on risk and sexual health before looking at risky violent and sexually exploitative relationships. In conclusion, we will draw on the relationship between risk-taking behaviour, risk factors, protective factors and the development of resilience.

Summary

In this section we have:

- Identified risk and protective factors.
- Looked at the relationship between risk and resilience.
- Introduced caution of a 'risk society' that is focused on protecting young people from risk.

Sex, Risk and Sexual Health

The Management of Risks

Moore and Rosenthal (2006) focus on the relationship between sex and risk by referring to Irwin and Millstein's (1986) 'risk-taking model' in relation to adolescent development. This model places biological maturity (the timing of puberty) at the centre of the young person's development. The model looks specifically at the impact that biological maturity has on the young person's

- psycho-social development (self-perception, self-esteem),
- developmental needs in relation to peers (peer affiliation, intimate relationships),
- cognitive scope (academic achievements, capacity to question and understand social situations),
- perception of the social environment (awareness of relative influence of parents and peers),
- personal values (independence and self-determination).

By looking at the young person's maturity and their understanding of risk for each of these variables, the model can be used to identify the likelihood of emergence of risk-taking behaviour. However, Moore and Rosenthal note that when looking at sexual risk-taking, the model has its limitations as

> an understanding of young people's sexual risk taking must include consideration of the nature of sexuality (both heterosexuality and homosexuality), the social norms that underpin sexual practices, and the understandings of sex that ensue.
>
> (Moore and Rosenthal, 2006, p. 63)

For a risk-taking model to be applicable to sexual risk, we need additional focus on sexuality and the impact that social, economic and political influences have on the way sexuality is constructed and understood. This is returned to later in the chapter, following discussion of work with young people facing high risk and harm in their sexual relationships.

Before we consider 'high-risk' relationships, we need first to look at some of the risks that can face a young person when they start to become sexually active. To give some examples, three different sorts of risks that could be encountered by a young person follow below.

1. To start a sexual relationship, a young person might have to first establish a close friendship with their potential partner. This might start with asking the friend out for a drink, to see a film or go to a party or other social event. If the young person is rejected at this early stage, their confidence and self-esteem could be undermined. The impact that this rejection could have on the young person, and their capacity to manage this, will, of course, vary. It will depend upon the strengths of the protective factors: their existing friendships, the support they receive from family, carers and local community provisions. If there are few protective factors but many risk factors such as tensions with friends, little support from any established peer group, family or local community youth work provision, a rejection at this early stage of trying to establish an intimate relationship could undermine a delicate confidence base, increasing the young person's isolation and potentially damaging their self-esteem. Here, in this very first example of risk, we see how the individual, family and environment can impact on the young person's capacity to manage risk.

Let us look now at another, potentially more damaging risk that could arise from a young person challenging cultural norms.

2. A young person might want to establish an intimate relationship with someone of whom the family or local community might not approve. Recent media attention has focused on certain religious communities where young people might face reprisal for disrespecting family 'honour' if they develop a relationship with someone from a different culture or

religion. However, the notion of 'honour', and of the extreme danger of 'honour killings', is not specific only to one religion or community. Just who a teenager develops a relationship with and why has been seen to carry risks to some families and communities for generations in a range of different cultures and religions (Meetoo and Mirza, 2007). The capacity of the individual to manage the dynamics within their family, and the capacity of the family to manage the conflicts within their community, will vary.

And finally, let us look at a third example of a risk that might be encountered by a young person experimenting with their sexual orientation.

3. Research has shown that many lesbian and gay young people face the risk of rejection from family or friends when they experiment with same-sex sexual relationships or when they 'come out' (Savin-Williams and Diamond, 2001; Troiden, 1989). Discrete processes can operate to isolate lesbians, gay men and bisexuals within their families and push them to the margins within schools, colleges and workplaces (Valentine *et al.*, 2002). Managing the risk of being isolated and discriminated against in this way is a tall order for a young person to face. If protective factors are in force, the damaging impact might be better accommodated. However, if individual risk factors are high and communication and understanding is already limited within the family, school and local community, the young person could be badly damaged by such discrimination.

In the above we have looked at some risks that face young people when they initiate a friendship that could develop into an intimate, sexual relationship. We have also noted some of the ways that these risks can be managed and how certain protective factors can help the young person to cope. Looking at the above we can begin to see how resilience to harm can be built through the management of risks.

We continue now to look at research findings from studies that have focused on what might be seen as specific sexual health risks that young people can face when they are sexually active.

The Risk of STIs and of Unintended Pregnancy

Whether it is approved of or not, it is clear that an increasing number of young people are sexually active in their early to mid-teens, with substantial increases of reported sexual activity over the last few decades (see Figure 4.1). Farrell's (1978) study of 2000 15- to 19-year-olds in Britain found that while 20% of boys and 12% of girls were sexually active in the early 1960s, this had risen by the late 1970s to over 50%. Currie (2004) shows a significant increase in the number of sexually active school-aged young people in the UK and abroad in the early 2000s. With this in mind, it is helpful to explore whether there are genuine risks facing sexually active young people or whether concern for the young people arises, in the main, from moral and value judgements.

As many countries do place the legal age of consent in mid-teenage years (15 or 16 in most European countries), there has been a consensus of belief that young teenagers should be protected from the negative impacts that early sexual activity might have. Some research has shown that sexual activity at an early stage of adolescent development can have detrimental effects on physical and emotional health and well-being. One longitudinal study noted a positive association between problem drinking, marijuana use and delinquent behaviour (school truancy, anti-social behaviour and offending behaviour) and early sexual intercourse

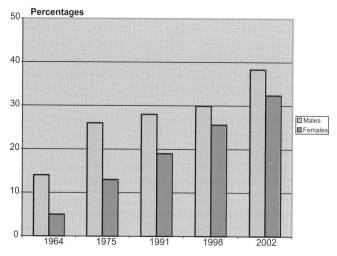

Figure 4.1   Reported first sexual intercourse before the age of 16, by gender, in Great Britain, 1964–2002

Source: J. Coleman and J. Schofield, *Key Data on Adolescence, 2007.* Trust for the Study of Adolescence, Brighton.

(Jessor *et al.*, 2003). Younger teenagers are less likely to use contraceptives, finding it difficult to access good advice on sexual health. The National Survey of Sexual Attitudes and Lifestyles (NATSAL) found that up to 50% of sexually active young people under the age of 16 used no contraception and regretted that it happened so early in their life (Wellings *et al.*, 2001).

In the main, the most detrimental impact has been noted to be related to feelings of regret and the impact that this has on feelings of self-worth and self-esteem. Wight *et al.* (2000) found, from a questionnaire survey of 7395 13- and 14-year-old school pupils, that 18% of boys and 15.4% of girls had experienced sexual intercourse and felt regretful that it had happened. For both, the regret was related to feelings of control within their sexual relationship. The young men felt that they had lacked control within their peer groups, responding to peer pressure to have sex and exerting control over the young women by pressurizing them into sexual intercourse. The young women felt that they lacked control. The lack of perceived control has been shown to be an indicator of low self-esteem and low self-worth, both of which can undermine a young person's healthy sexual development (Aggleton *et al.*, 2000).

Young people who start sexual relationships early in their teens might find themselves isolated without support or information. As noted by Coleman and Schofield (2005, p. 69), many young people do not know of sexual health services in their area where they can access support. Irrespective of the age of the young person, a number of studies have shown teenagers to first become sexually active when under the influence of alcohol or drugs. Wight *et al.* (2000) found from their study of teenagers that 39% of young women and 40% of young men said that they were 'drunk or stoned' the first time that they had sexual intercourse. The sexual activity was not always desired. Coleman found that from a sample of 39 interviewees aged 14 to 17 who had sexual experiences while drunk, 32 regretted the activity. Also, his work showed that drunkenness could result in 'an inability to control or recognise a potentially risky situation' (Coleman and Cater, 2005, p. 27).

Essentially, these works suggest that 'problem behaviours' cluster together (Jessor and Jessor, 1977; Jessor *et al.*, 2003) and that the younger the young person, the less equipped they might be to manage the complexities of multiple problems. If the young person is isolated from support or advice, if they feel regretful, embarrassed or ashamed, early sexual activity can contribute to lower self-esteem, bullying from friends and conflict with family.

However, it is important to note that early intercourse need not, itself, on its own, have negative consequences. As noted above, many of the anxieties about sexual risk can be motivated by moral concerns, often as part of religious beliefs, about sexual activity amongst young people. These need not be overt, but can be hidden under the guise of concerns about sexual, physical and emotional health. At the core of these concerns is a worry that the young person will have unprotected sex and contract harmful STIs or become a parent before they are ready or equipped to manage.

Bearing this worry in mind, it is important to note that figures do show a dramatic increase in the number of young people infected with STIs in the UK. Figure 4.2 shows that there has been a rise of 250% in cases of reported chlamydia infections of 16- to 18-year-old young women and 400% of young men, and an increase of 175% where cases of gonorrhoea amongst young women are concerned.

Although there are only a few known cases of HIV infections amongst young people, the number of known infected young women has risen between 1994 and 2003 from approximately 10 to approximately 90 (Coleman and Schofield, 2005, p. 68), as can be seen in Figure 4.3.

Similarly, data on conception rates and terminations show young people in Britain still to have worryingly high levels of unintended conceptions, despite evidence in recent years of significant decreases in these rates. It is important to note the geographical variations in these figures; some areas having higher conception rates than others. While being mindful of the problems that can face young parents who might not have the income to support their

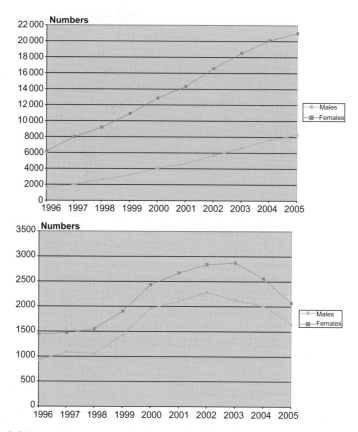

Figure 4.2   (a) New diagnoses of chlamydia infection presented at GUM clinics in the UK, among 16- to 19-year-olds, by gender, 1996–2005. (b) New diagnoses of gonorrhoea infection presented at GUM clinics in the UK, among 16- to 19-year-olds, by gender, 1996–2005

Source: J. Coleman and J. Schofield, *Key Data on Adolescence, 2007.* Trust for the Study of Adolescence, Brighton.

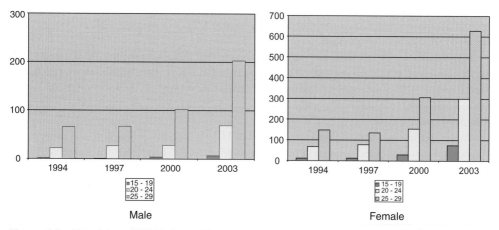

Male   Female

Figure 4.3   Numbers of HIV-infected individuals, by age and gender in the UK, 1994–2003

Source: J. Coleman and J. Schofield, *Key Data on Adolescence, 2007.* Trust for the Study of Adolescence, Brighton.

family or might not have the opportunity to access and engage with training and education, it is important to note that not all teenagers necessarily understand conception and pregnancy to have a negative impact on their lives. Teenage pregnancy in poor, deprived local areas may be welcomed as an advantage, providing the young woman with a sense of purpose when few other opportunities are available (Hoggart, 2006). If protective factors are strong, the family is supportive and the local community well resourced, early pregnancy need not have such a negative impact on young people.

We have noted above some of the risks that face sexually active young people and we have been aware of some of the critiques levelled against perceiving all sexual activity as harmful and dangerous. We have noted that the young person's resilience will impact on their ability to manage these risks, and that the provision of services within the community plays a part in enhancing good sexual health. We move now to focus in more detail on some of the more extreme risks that can be experienced by some young people, on their vulnerability to these risks and on the resilience they develop in order to cope.

Summary

In this section we have:

- Identified some of the risks that could be experienced by a young person when they start a sexual relationship.
- Looked at the sexual health risks for young people, including the risk of conception and early pregnancy.
- Questioned whether all early conceptions or teenage pregnancies are necessarily negative.
- Linked other risk factors such as risky drinking, offending behaviour and violence with vulnerability to early sexual relationships.

Risky Relationships

We are now going to explore some of the risks that can face young people when they are in ongoing, intimate, sexual relationships with their partners. In the last decade there has been awareness that sex education on its own does not adequately prepare young people for healthy sexual relationships. The government now provides guidance for Personal, Social and Health Education (PSHE) lessons on both sex and relationship education. This appreciates that young people might need scope to talk about how to manage their relationships as well as their sexual activity (DfES, 2004), and that some relationships can have harmful outcomes for the young people concerned. We look below at some of the dangers that might exist for young people in their intimate relationships, focusing in the main on the risk of violence and abuse.

Risky Violent Relationships

The risk of domestic violence within intimate relationships has traditionally been seen as one facing adults, rather than teenagers. Apart from some occasional press coverage of the increase of violence between girls, most coverage of young women in discourses of violence sees them as witnesses of violence or as victims of rape or sexual assault (Alder and Worrall, 2004; Skinner *et al.*, 2005). Most research into violence between teenagers in intimate, sexual relationships has taken place in America and has been termed Adolescent Intimate Partner Violence (AIPV).

This work has shown that the risk of violence can occur in a range of different relationships, including some same-sex relationships, and can occur within all social strata, not necessarily only within deprived communities. Halpern *et al.* (2004) showed that one-quarter of the total 117 young people in same-sex romantic relationships reported partner violence victimization, while a study in Scotland reported AIPV from pupils in schools in economically privileged as well as deprived areas (NHS Health Scotland, 2005). In this Scottish survey, students in 10 secondary schools from urban and rural areas took part in a total of 12 focus groups. Between 15% and 20% of both girls and boys reported a range of physical violence and, more surprisingly, 2% of girls and 4% of boys reported trying to force a partner to have sex.

Although there are not, as yet, published findings from empirical research on this topic in the UK, an unpublished survey undertaken by the London Borough of Southwark 'Safer Southwark Partnership' showed that 42% of the respondents experienced some form of abusive behaviour from a partner. The survey covered 135 young people from nine different ethnic groups living in 23 different postcode areas. The young people were between the ages of 12 and 24, including 74% of respondents aged under 18, 41.7% of whom were under 16 years old. Analysis showed that there was a positive correlation between experiencing some form of abusive behaviour and demonstrating behaviour that was abusive (Schutt, 2006, pp. 45–46).

One of the key and important findings from this body of research in America, and the preliminary work done in the UK, is that physical violence is more likely to occur between teenage couples once a sexual relationship has been established. Two surveys show a correlation between the beginning of sexual activity and the beginning of violence in the relationship. A study of 6548 adolescents aged 12 to 21 showed that

> *violent victimisation was more likely to occur in romantic relationships that included sexual intercourse, 37% of the respondents reporting sexual relationships experienced at least one form of verbal or physical violence victimisation, compared to 19% of those reporting relationships with no sexual intercourse ... sexual intercourse was significantly more likely to precede violence rather than the reverse.*

> (Kaestle and Halpern, 2004, p. 386)

The second study showed that 78% of adolescents experiencing violence during the 3 months after giving birth had not experienced violence before delivery (Harrikson *et al.*, 2002).

Although these surveys do not imply that sexual activity between young people necessarily results in physical violence, they do note that managing a sexual relationship or having a child can place additional strain on young people, strain that may result in violence. So, when we consider the relationship between sex and risk, we need to be prepared to move beyond an immediate focus on sexual health, contraception and STIs and move into an analysis of risk factors such as violence and abuse. Within this we need also to focus on the resilience factors that might help support a young person to challenge their progression on to either being a perpetrator or a victim (or both) of domestic and sexual violence within intimate relationships.

Sexual Exploitation, Risk and Resilience

To continue with this theme, we are going now to focus on young people's vulnerability to violent sexual relationships or sexually exploitative relationships. The latter, the process whereby young people are coerced or forced into selling or swapping sex for favours (be they a bed for the night, drugs or drink), has been shown to involve high levels of violence (Melrose and Barrett, 2004). We will look at some case studies of young people who have experienced both domestic violence and sexual exploitation to identify ways that they have been supported to develop resilience to cope with their situation. This will draw on research that identified case studies of 55 young women at risk of or experiencing sexual exploitation. The research was funded by the Joseph Rowntree Foundation and was undertaken in partnership with the NSPCC (Pearce *et al.*, 2002).

The policy context: a vulnerable victim or a risky perpetrator

Before we look at the case studies, it is important to consider how young people can be resilient despite facing high risk and despite being equipped with few protective factors. Although it is recognized that sexual exploitation is a form of sexual abuse, it has been asked whether all sexually exploited young people do actually see themselves as victims. Can a young person under the age of 18 actually exercise some choice in choosing to sell sex (Pearce, 2007; Phoenix, 2002)? Hidden within this question is the issue of the young person's agency: do they see themselves as a victim of sexual exploitation, a vulnerable victim of abuse who is overcome by risk, exercising no choice in the matter; or are they exercising some choice, showing some resilience in coping with poverty and isolation by deciding to earn money through the sale of sex?

Legislation and guidance appears to be confused about this question of victimhood and agency. Although the recent Sexual Offences Act 2003 makes it an offence for someone to entice a young person under the age of 18 into prostitution, placing the young person clearly as a victim of abuse from exploitative adults, the Prostitution Strategy 2006 still allows for young people themselves to be arrested as a perpetrator of offences relating to prostitution. The Prostitution Strategy (HO, 2006) provided an ideal opportunity for a consistent message to be given positioning sexually exploited young people as victims of abuse. Instead, it upholds the caveat in the original guidance from the Department of Health (2000) that allows those who persistently and voluntarily return to selling sex to be arrested for offences relating to prostitution.

The message, therefore, is mixed. The young person who is overcome by the risks they face, and who responds to social service intervention, can be deemed to be a victim of abuse. On the other hand, the young person who persistently and voluntarily returns to selling sex, and who exercises choice in rejecting welfare support, is an active perpetrator of criminal offences (despite research evidence showing that the latter, the rebellious young person selling sex on the street, is often the most isolated and most in need; Pearce, 2006). This distinction between victim and perpetrator is important for us here as it is informed by a polarization between a compliant young person at risk from the harm others can do to them (the child 'at risk') on the one hand, and a challenging young person who creates risks (the child as 'a risk') on the other hand. The policy implications of this distinction are important. The victim 'at risk' receives welfare care while the perpetrator 'at risk' becomes a young offender, despite their underlying needs and their experiences of exploitation being similar. While this needs challenging in policy, the issue of interest for us here is how to support a young person who is making the transition from being 'at risk' of sexual exploitation to being free from risk without necessarily becoming 'a risk' to themselves or others.

Central to this is how we can support young people to build their own resilience against the harm and abuse that can be inflicted upon them by others. To do this we will look first at the research that has identified common risk factors that can pull some vulnerable young people into prostitution and then identify some case studies that show how a young person can be supported to build resilience against abuse without necessarily being a risk to others. Within these case studies, we will return to the relationship between alcohol use, violence and risky sexual relationships as explored above.

Risk Factors: Routes into Sexual Exploitation

Different explanations have been put forward to account for how and why some young people become vulnerable to sexually exploitative relationships. Looking at individual, family and environmental risk factors we can see the way each contributes to routes into sexual exploitation.

Individual influences

The grooming model of sexual exploitation, where an adult encourages a young person to become dependent upon them, focuses attention on the individual vulnerability of the young person to abuse. Young people who are vulnerable to this form of abuse have been identified by research and practice as having low self-esteem, serious drug and alcohol problems, mental health problems, poor school achievement and low perceived control, finding it difficult to assert themselves and form constructive and rewarding interpersonal relationships (Chase and Stratham, 2005; Harper and Scott, 2005). Indeed, as said by a young woman who contributed to the case study research:

> *It's only possible to protect yourself if you think you're worth protecting*
>
> (Rachael, aged 17, in Pearce *et al.*, 2002)

The message here is that if your self-esteem is low, if you are self-harming and feeling bad about yourself, a violent or abusive relationship is a continuation of this self-harm. To stop it, to protect yourself, you need to feel that you should not be hurt. Otherwise, you will, as Rachael says, fail to protect yourself. The study of 55 young women showed that 34 of the 55 regularly self-harmed, 26 had been bullied at school, 18 had attempted suicide and all 55 had problems with binge drinking, being drunk at least once a week.

These individual risk factors make the young people particularly vulnerable to abusive adults who are skilled in flattery and manipulation. Short-lived flattery and raising of morale can encourage someone who feels low about themselves into what they think will be a supportive relationship, only to find that the violence and abuse they are familiar with returns. This 'grooming' model has also been applied to the way that particular young people who are looking for friendship are enticed into abusive sexual relationships by paedophiles over the internet (Palmer and Stacey, 2004).

Family influences

Problems within the family have also been identified as risk factors for sexual exploitation. In the study of 55 young women, 53 were regularly running away from home, 47 had experienced physical abuse within the family, and 25 had known experiences of sexual abuse within the home. Thirty nine of the young women had been taken into care by the local authority (Pearce *et al.*, 2002). It is known that a disproportionately high number of sexually exploited young people have been 'looked after' by the local authority and that being in care can, in itself, be a risk factor for prostitution. Evidence suggests that most adults working in the sex industry began their work when under the age of 25 (McKeganey and Barnard, 1992; Sanders, 2005) and that many had histories of being in local authority care, particularly residential care (Melrose and Barrett, 2004; Pitts, 1997).

Cusick *et al.* (2003) conducted a retrospective study of women and men involved in prostitution. Forty-two per cent of the total 125 participants had experience of being 'looked after'. Of the 18 'most vulnerable' young people involved in prostitution before the age of 18, 14 had been looked after. Of those, 10 had been living in, or running from, local authority care when they first 'prostituted'. Such histories are prevalent across all racial and cultural barriers (Ward and Patel, 2007). Considering this, it could be argued that 'care' does not necessarily safeguard individual young people from harm but can become a risk factor in its own right (Lee, 2002). What is evident from this research is that a history of previous disrupting care and of violence or abuse within the family home can heighten a young person's vulnerability to entering sexually exploitative relationships. The confused feelings that Ellie (case study 2 given below) notes when she talks of simultaneously loving and hating her mother and her boyfriend, who are both violent towards her, demonstrate this point well.

Environmental influences

If these individual and familial risk factors are compounded by unsupportive environmental factors such as poverty, poor local provision and disrupted schooling, the young person is particularly disadvantaged. All but three of the 55 young women who contributed to case studies lived in under-resourced local areas where outreach youth work was limited, if existent at all. The 21 of the 55 young women who did self-define as prostitutes, selling sex from the street, were the most isolated from any service delivery, relying on the occasional visit from outreach sexual health workers for the limited support that can be available from a mobile van. The impact of poverty and deprivation has been identified as a key risk factor for many young people entering sexually exploitative situations. The need for money, accommodation, drugs or rewards may, in the young person's eyes, be obtainable only through the sale or exchange of sex. It is in such circumstances that the question of agency becomes apparent. Faced with such adversity, the young person may feel that they can choose, albeit a constrained choice, to sell sex as a means of getting money when they see few other alternatives available.

Summary

In this section we have:

- Explored the prevalence of interpersonal violence between young people in sexual relationships.
- Noted the existence of domestic violence between young people in intimate relationships with peers and with older partners.
- Defined sexual exploitation, looking at its relationship with domestic violence.
- Described different accounts for some young people's routes into sexually exploitative relationships, identifying risk factors that can make young people vulnerable to exploitation.

Case Studies: Lessons For Practice

Analysis of the case studies of 55 young women (Pearce *et al.*, 2002) showed three categories of risk. These categories have since been used by a number of local authorities within their protocols for safeguarding sexually exploited young people, including the London Safeguarding Children Board procedures for children abused through sexual exploitation.

The three categories below show a shift from low to high risk, ranging from a young person being vulnerable to sexual exploitation through to them self-defining as a prostitute, selling sex for returns.

- *Category 1 (low risk)*. A vulnerable child or young person who is at risk of being targeted and groomed for sexual exploitation.
- *Category 2 (medium risk)*. A child or young person who is targeted for opportunistic abuse through the exchange of sex for drugs, accommodation (overnight stays) and goods, etc. The likelihood of coercion and control is significant.
- *Category 3 (high risk)*. A child or young person whose sexual exploitation is habitual, often self-defined and where coercion/control is implicit.

(Categories taken from Pearce *et al.*, 2002, adapted by http://www.londoncpc.gov.uk/Sexual ExploitationFinalJune06.doc. See website for further details, including risk assessment and models of intervention.)

Category 1 (low risk) included 19 young women identified from the research project. For these young women protective factors such as a consistent relationship with an identified key worker, access to good preventative work within school – such as access to a lunchtime club, after-school facilities or education social work – and contact with other social services could help divert them from harm. These were young women whose individual behaviours of risk-taking sexual relationships placed them at risk of manipulation and exploitation but who were not involved in swapping or selling sex for favours or reward. The individual risk factors facing these 19 young women were significant, but they still had enough contact with family and community to expect that good protective factors could be built upon.

Category 2 (medium risk) included a further 15 young women from the research project. These young women did not self-define as sex workers or prostitutes but did talk about swapping sex for accommodation, for drugs, alcohol or for gifts. These young women were beginning to lose contact with their school and carers. The familial and environmental protective factors that might be able to support them in managing the risks that they were facing were becoming more distant, while individual risk factors such as low self-esteem, problem drug and alcohol use were escalating.

Category 3 (high risk) included young women from the research who self-defined as selling sex. The 21 young women in this category were the most in need, carrying the most problems, including sexual health problems, homelessness, self-abuse and serious drug and alcohol problems. They were regularly running from home and truanting, if not excluded from school. Despite this high level of need, they were the most isolated from any service provision. Few had contact with any members of their family or with past carers and most were unable to make appointments with service providers, saying that they felt too low: "too depressed and the journey takes too long" (Iona, aged 17), too ill: "would like to get off drugs but am too weak" (Sue, aged 16) or too angry and disillusioned: "if services wanted to heal they should have helped in the past" (Fiona, aged 16).

None of these young women had regular access to any service that might be able to help them to cope with the risk factors that they experienced. They all relied on outreach services to provide them with sexual health advice and with drug harm minimization programmes. However, as will be seen later, although the temptation might be to focus on the dangers they experienced and the risk factors that placed them in harm, the way that they managed their everyday lives and sought to survive in their circumstances showed resilience that should not be overlooked. This will be explored in more detail below.

Case Studies

The case studies below are used to explore some of the contradictions that exist for sexually exploited young people who are trying to manage the risks that they face. They are drawn from the research developed in partnership with the NSPCC mentioned above. As this particular research was with young women, the case studies below cover three young women's circumstances. Work with sexually exploited young men has shown that, although the ways that young men are identified and worked with may vary, the personal and familial histories are invariably similar. However, more work is needed to explore the gendered nature of risk and resilience within work with sexually exploited young people. Specific details within the case studies have been compiled from a number of different young women's situations to ensure anonymity. Together, the three case studies give us the opportunity to look at the resilience demonstrated by young people who are trying to survive the adversities they face. The protective factors that can help to build resilience amongst sexually exploited young people are identified in the conclusion below.

CASE STUDY 1

Sima was 16 when she was contacted through the research and placed in category 1 'at risk'. She had dropped out of school in the last year but was keen to return at some point to complete her GCSEs. She had been an A* pupil prior to meeting her boyfriend. Sima lived with her family in overcrowded conditions on a deprived housing estate. Her family were of Bangladeshi origin and Sima was second generation in the UK. She had become increasingly frustrated with the overcrowding at home and saw her relationship with her boyfriend as a means of escape. She was in touch with a local drop-in project. Workers there were concerned that her boyfriend was forcing her into unwanted sexual relationships with other men. However, she denied this and said that she was in love with her boyfriend, and wanted to stay with him when she was on the run from home. She arrived at the local project 'drop-in' one evening with severe bruises after a row with her boyfriend. Although very angry and hurt, she was going to return to him because:

- If she leaves him before the police can do anything her family may suffer.
- She has had a miscarriage with his baby and she wants to tell him so he knows how much she has suffered.
- She thinks that if she stays with him for long enough she can change him – make him treat her differently.

Although Sima did return to her boyfriend, she also continued to use the drop-in sessions, meeting with and talking to project workers and other young women in similar situations. After an 18-month period she left her boyfriend's accommodation and moved back home. Although she continued to see her boyfriend, and felt obsessed with him "he takes all my head space" the amount of contact did slowly decrease. She visited her teachers at school who helped her attend a lunchtime class which was linked into courses provided by a local college.

The case study shows some of the problems that can face child protection teams working with young people who are at risk of sexual exploitation while in a relationship with a violent boyfriend. Sima wanted to continue her relationship with her boyfriend and was determined to stay with him. In these circumstances, child protection guidelines could helpfully be supported by referring to approaches used in working with victims of domestic violence. The latter have, as a starting point, an acceptance that the victim might not leave the abuser. While child protection procedures might be focused on 'removing' and 'rescuing' a child from abuse, domestic violence policies and procedures are more likely to accept that this may not be possible. Whatever interventions are put in place, the victim might find different ways of returning to the abusive relationship. Instead, the practitioner might work with time, accepting that change will be slow and offering support throughout periods of failure as well as through times when success is more evident. This is based on the premise that the young person might, eventually, build enough resilience to make some changes to their circumstances themselves.

This does not mean condoning violence between young people, or ignoring risk, but it does accept that the dynamics involved are extremely complex, involving the young person's feelings about love, hate and personal autonomy in interpersonal, sexual relationships. It also accepts that some protective factors can be accessed and developed even after the young person has experienced trauma and abuse. Individual protective factors such as self-esteem and self-awareness were supported through Sima's contact with the project workers and through the continued support of the school that she had originally rejected.

The following quotes are from discussion with Ellie about her case study following her 17th birthday. They show that she is confused between the feelings that she has for her mother and those she holds for her boyfriend.

Talking of her boyfriend:

> *I know he did all that to me, he was just taking it out on me because I was only 16 and he thought I didn't know lots of things about the world but I did. What he did to me really hurt me, but in a way I don't, but in a way I do forgive him because I love this boy deep down in my heart.*

CASE STUDY 2

Ellie is a white young woman of English origin, aged 17 at the point of contact with the research. She had a history of truanting from school and running away from her home where she lives with her aunt. Her aunt is caring for her because her mother has mental health problems and has been violent towards Ellie. Despite her aunt providing care for her, there are often arguments about how they manage to live together and Ellie runs away to "get some headspace". When she runs she stays with her boyfriend, aged 25, who lives on the local estate. She has had a sexual relationship with her boyfriend for the last two years, although she knows that he has sexual relationships with different girlfriends and has a reputation for being a 'pimp' on the estate. Ellie has spoken of swapping sex with her boyfriend's friends in return for drugs, although she rejected any idea that she sold sex for money. During the two-year period of her relationship with this boyfriend, she was increasingly bullied at school and her attendance had dropped.

Talking of her mother:

> *Sometimes I wish she was dead. That is really horrible to wish someone dead but its how I feel. But she's my Mum. I love her … It's funny you know that it is really confusing when you really hate somebody and you care for them. That is really bad.*

We can see in the above the tangle between love and hate and the confusion that might exist when someone says that they love you but is also abusive. Ellie is, in effect, repeating the feelings that she had in her relationship with her mother in her relationship with her boyfriend. The important point to this case study was that it was at the time that Ellie was being bullied at school and beginning to truant, that she became more dependent upon her boyfriend. While it is recognized that schools need additional resources to be able to support vulnerable young people, an intervention at an earlier stage of the truanting career might have helped Ellie to recognize the risk factors she was facing.

The other important consideration here is the importance of Ellie's contact with a youth project worker. By engaging with the research project, Ellie did start to attend the drop-in sessions of a local outreach support group. In so doing, she began to articulate the feelings she had towards her mother and her boyfriend. She was able to make connections between the ways that she felt about both, reflecting on her own comments as above. Supporting her to be able to build on these connections was an important part of the work with Ellie, one that was hastened because of her own intellectual capacity to understand some of the dynamics within her relationships with others. She was able to remember some of the achievements she had made at school prior to meeting her boyfriend and some of the positive inputs to her development that she had received from her aunt. Here, the individual protective factor of personal achievement, self-worth and self-esteem was important for practitioners to focus on. Indeed, it became more worthwhile building on this during the course of the project work than it was to focus on the negative risks that she experienced in her relationship with her boyfriend.

Having looked at the importance of both individual and community or environmental protective factors when working with young people at risk of harm in risky relationships, we draw on a case study of a young person who was regularly selling sex and whose circumstances and behaviour would place them in the 'high risk' category. The case study is referred to as it illustrates both the young person's vulnerability to risky relationships and the resilience they have to manage some of their circumstances (case study 3).

This case is a clear illustration of the immediate problems facing a child protection service that aims to support a vulnerable young person who is facing a number of risks. Lucy's drug dependency and her initial attachment to her boyfriend meant that she would not stop swapping or selling sex. While she was in this situation, there was little that she would accept as an alternative to living with her boyfriend and she saw no other way of earning equivalent money to fund her own, and her boyfriend's, habit. Despite her extreme health and welfare needs, she was, during the period that she was selling sex on the street, at risk of being criminalized for committing offences relating to prostitution as she was 'persistently and voluntarily' returning to sell sex.

However, sensitive work between outreach workers, social services and police ensured that this did not happen. Instead, the outreach sexual health worker was able to accept Lucy's

CASE STUDY 3

Lucy was 18 when interviewed and was living in refuge accommodation, waiting to be moved into a flat. Much of Lucy's life had been spent adapting to a number of crisis situations. She had spent her early childhood with her parents who were both drug users and alcoholics, but by 13 she had started to truant and spend time with older young people on the local streets. At 14 she was taken into care and placed with foster parents. She ran away repeatedly, having mixed feelings about her new 'family', wanting to settle in but also resenting being placed in care. Just after her 15th birthday she met and fell 'in love' with a local heroin dealer and moved in to live with him, becoming attached to a relationship that involved swapping sex with him and his friends in return for the heroin that she was becoming addicted to.

Lucy's dependence on drugs developed and she started to sell sex on the street to fund her own, and her boyfriend's, habit. She was aggressive and challenging to practitioners who wanted to support her, being 'a risk' to others she came into contact with. However, when she was 16 she started to develop contact with an outreach sexual health worker. She became more confident in the relationship with the worker and after an 18-month period, she moved into the refuge and began to recognize the traumas she had experienced and wanted to start a recovery programme.

decision to stay with her boyfriend while maintaining a non-judgemental outreach support service. The outreach worker maintained contact by visiting the same street at regular intervals, establishing and following a fixed routine that Lucy was able to follow. As opposed to being continually negative about Lucy's situation, the outreach worker noted Lucy's strength and tenacity in going out onto the street and negotiating the sale of sex.

Without inappropriately romanticizing or glamorizing Lucy's circumstances, it was possible for the outreach worker to help Lucy to see the skills that she used in managing her situation. This intervention did not ignore the risks that Lucy was facing through her drug misuse, through selling sex and through the exploitative relationship that she was in. However, these risks were not the central focus to the intervention. Instead, the worker concentrated on Lucy's strengths, noting how she managed the violence she experienced, how she employed negotiating skills with those who purchased sex, how she managed her time and her routines around her day-to-day lifestyle. Such a focus enabled Lucy to feel some confidence in her ability to manage parts of her life, a confidence that later developed into meaning that she wanted to leave her boyfriend. As she noted once she had gained enough confidence to attend a part-time college course:

> In college you see lots of young kids smiling. Why can't I be like that? It's about time that I put my life together. I've learnt my mistakes now with boys and everything. I'm not getting involved with a boy again. I'm going to concentrate on my studies and become someone someday.

Summary from the case studies

Each of these case studies endorses the need for awareness of the risks that young people can face within some sexual relationships. The case studies also show that interventions with young people in risky, violent and sexually exploitative relationships need to focus on protective factors that can offer support and encouragement to the young person, despite the extreme risks they face. This means accepting that it may not be possible to rescue the young person from risk, or alternatively prevent them from repeatedly returning to risky situations.

From the case studies above we have identified how some protective factors could have been accessed for young people at risk of sexual exploitation. Before we conclude, it is helpful to return to the risk model identified by Irwin and Millstein (1986), referred to earlier in the chapter. What we do here is adapt and build on the model, identifying some key protective factors that might support vulnerable, at risk young people as they mature into adulthood. The four groupings below refer to some of the themes noted by Irwin and Millstein but include interventions that are suggested as ways of enhancing the resilience of damaged and difficult young people who are in risky relationships.

Psycho-social Development (Self-perception, Self-esteem)

- Maintain a key worker as available despite the key worker being rejected.
- Demonstrate through the worker that setbacks can be recovered from, for example, if the young person rejects a worker, the service will survive and continue to be available to the young person. If the young person returns to an abusive relationship, the worker will continue to be available.
- Continue to offer support and encouragement, identifying strengths demonstrated by the young person, even if the strengths are within behaviour that needs to be discouraged.
- Offer small, achievable tasks for the young person to undertake, for example, meeting at a street location, same time, repeatedly. Attend a drop-in session offering transport at first.

Developmental Cognitive Scope (Academic Achievements, Capacity to Question and Understand Social Situations)

- Take short leaflets, information sheets out on outreach to young people.
- Develop or use existing distance learning packages designed for vulnerable and excluded young people; show them to the young person at regular intervals.
- Show videos, DVDs of young people who have survived abuse. Listen to recorded information from young people who have experienced damaged relationships.
- Engage in educational outreach activities such as creative writing, expressive drawing, life story work, even if this has to be done on the street or in a van.
- Try to build group work activities, even if between a small number of young people (two or three). For example, eating a snack together, recording a conversation and playing it back to the speakers, discussing a picture or magazine entry.

Personal Values (Independence and Self-determination)

- Showing the young person that they are important to other people. This can be achieved by mapping who is in a relationship with them and noting how important they are to these people.
- Keeping record of the individual achievements that the young person is making, however small they might appear to be.
- Keeping discussion going about what are important personal values to the young person. Being respectful of the values that the young person notes. Praising positive values.
- Demonstrating, through example, how positive relationships with others can occur.

Perceptions of the Social Environment (Awareness of Relative Influence of Parents and Peers)

- Keep ongoing work alive about relationships. This means encouraging the young person to talk about services or practitioners they have been in touch with.
- Keep a picture diary or personal account with the young person of where they go and what they do. Placing importance on their whereabouts, activities and identifying what they cope with, what they are able to manage.
- Map services for the young person, identifying knowledgeable workers who will be available to vulnerable young people within each of the services and supporting the young person to access them by arranging transport, escorting them on visits.
- Find access to supported respite accommodation, short-term training through outreach services.

These activities rely upon resources being committed to support specialist workers who are in touch with young people who are vulnerable and at risk of harm or abuse. The essential issue is that the workers themselves identify ways of building a positive relationship with the young people being supported to give a model of how a good relationship can exist. This cannot happen without support and supervision for the practitioners concerned. For sexual health services to access and engage those young people who are marginalized and at high risk, those undertaking outreach and providing contact will need support themselves. It is through such specialist facilities and approaches to work that the dangers of high risks can be understood and protective factors developed.

Summary

In this section we have:

- Identified three categories of risk for sexually exploited young people.
- Looked at three case studies that illustrate some of the contradictions and difficulties facing practitioners working with sexually exploited young people.
- Looked at different forms of resilience demonstrated by young people who are experiencing exploitation.

- Identified ways that practitioners can support young people who are in sexually exploitative relationships to build their resilience, with the aim of supporting them to choose to leave violent and damaging partners.
- Linked the capacity to gain self-determination and independence with the need for good, supported outreach work, and with accessible education and training resources.

Conclusion

At the start of this chapter we noted that experimentation with sexual activity was a normal and essential part of a young person's transition to adulthood. We noted that for this to take place, the young person will need to take some risks. Although a 'risk-aware' society might want to protect young people from harm, this aim may not be either desirable or achievable. Young people may need to take some risks in order to build resilience to cope with the set-backs that they might experience in their relationships of the future. They may also continue to seek out risk, and risky relationships, despite being advised otherwise. Indeed, by putting themselves 'at risk' they may also become 'a risk' to others.

With this in mind we can see from the remainder of the chapter that interventions that focus on sexual activity, be they preventative or treatment, also need to help the young person discuss and understand their sexual relationships. To focus solely on poor sexual health, early conception and pregnancy as risks to young people is to miss the opportunity to build good preventative work around how to expect, build and maintain positive and healthy relationships.

Also within the chapter we noted risk factors that can make young people vulnerable both to poor sexual health and to entering into risky relationships. However, we were cautious not to assume that all young people experiencing these risk factors became vulnerable. We looked at the protective factors that can help young people build resilience to harm, even if they have been abused or exploited. The building of a more positive self-esteem, a supportive family or care arrangement and better resourcing within the community can each contribute to a young person taking steps towards coping and changing their behaviours and circumstances. As noted in the introduction to this chapter, it is never too late to build protective factors and to enhance resilience. Protective factors can be introduced to a young person in their teens, with a positive impact even if the young person has experienced previous abuse or deprivation. Service provision could place more attention on how to support young people to build their resiliencies, noting that "The successful management of risk is a powerful resilience-promoting factor in itself" (Newman, 2002, p. 3).

Further Reading

Lowe, K. and Pierce, J. (2006) Young people and sexual exploitation. *Child Abuse Review*. Volume 15 Issue 5. John Wiley & Sons, Ltd: Chichester.

Luthar, S.S. (2003) (Ed.) *Resilience and vulnerability: Adaptation in the context of childhood adversities*. Cambridge University Press: Cambridge.

Moore, S. and Rosenthal, D. (2006) *Sexuality in adolescence: Current trends*. Routledge: London.

Pearce, J.J. (with Williams, M. and Galvin, C.) (2002) *It's someone taking a part of you: A study of young women and sexual exploitation*. National Children's Bureau: London.

Discussion Questions

1. It is suggested that resilience is the capacity to recover from harm. Do you agree with this or can someone become a resilient adult without necessarily experiencing any setbacks in their childhood? In other words, do you need steeling experiences in order to develop resilience?

2. Thinking of a 13- or 14-year-old known to you, consider whether you feel that they are mature enough to enter into a sexual relationship with a partner of similar age. What sorts of risk do you think they would need to be able to manage? What sorts of support might they need?

3. If a 16-year-old becomes pregnant, is she necessarily inhibiting her own development and her capacity to explore her potential in the future? Consider the impact of her internal world, i.e. her own individual resources, and the impact of the external world, i.e. her family and community resources, in your answer.

4. Drawing on the section in this chapter, what do you consider to be the differences and similarities between adult and young people's experiences of domestic violence or of sexual exploitation? How do the risk factors differ, or are they the same irrespective of age? If they do differ, what are the specific features of being a young person that makes them particularly vulnerable to violence from intimate partners or from sexual exploitation?

5. Why do you think some young people who have experienced disrupted and violent childhoods and who live in poverty might be vulnerable to entering sexually exploitative relationships while others may not? Consider the impact of community resources and the relationship between social work, domestic violence units and policing policies.

6. How might schools, further education and community work plan to support sexually exploited young people in the three different stages of risk identified above?

Chapter 5

Mental Health and Mental Disorders

Panos Vostanis

Professor of Child and Adolescent Psychiatry, University of Leicester

- Introduction
- Mental health needs of adolescents
- Finding out the extent of mental health problems and disorders in adolescence
- How do adolescents perceive mental health issues?
- Factors that promote adolescent mental health
- Vulnerable young people: factors involved in the development and continuation of mental health problems
- Types of mental health problems and disorders in adolescence
- Mental health promotion and prevention: everybody's responsibility

Learning Objectives

Once you have read this chapter you should be able to:

1 Understand the mental health needs of adolescents.

2 Appreciate the range and types of mental health problems that adolescents may face.

3 Recognize the role of mental health promotion and prevention in increasing resilience.

Adolescence, Risk and Resilience: Against the odds. John Coleman and Ann Hagell (eds.).
Published in 2007 by John Wiley & Sons, Ltd

Introduction

Adolescence encompasses a range of changes and transitions in different aspects of the young person's development. All these aspects (emotional, behavioural, social and communication functioning) are related to the broad concepts of 'psychological development' and 'mental health'. There are factors that facilitate this process and protect young people, and factors that make them vulnerable by hindering smooth transitions and adaptive functioning in one or more areas of their life. The objective of this chapter is to discuss the evidence and implications on adolescents' mental health needs, ways of helping them and improving services across all agencies in potential contact with them and their families. In addition, we will link mental health issues with broad topics discussed in detail in other chapters, such as the role of the family, anti-social behaviour and ways of increasing resilience.

The chapter is structured in three broad areas. The first seeks to explore adolescents' mental health needs, and when these become problematic or pathological, or different from the expected process of adolescent development. The second describes related concerns or behaviours, on the spectrum of severity and complexity that adolescents experience and seek help for. Finally, the role of agencies and services in enhancing adolescent mental health will be discussed across all sectors (education, health, social care, non-statutory).

Mental Health Needs of Adolescents

'Mental health' can be defined as a young person's ability to: develop psychologically, emotionally, intellectually and spiritually; have a sense of personal well-being; sustain satisfying personal relationships; develop a sense of right and wrong; and resolve problems as well as learn from them (Mental Health Foundation, 1999). If one or more of these components are hindered (for reasons discussed later in the chapter), problems of varying severity can gradually develop.

Mental health *problems* in young life are thus conceptualized as emotions or behaviours outside the normal range for age and gender, either linked with an impairment of development/functioning and/or the young person suffering as a result. The term *disorder* indicates the presence of a clinically recognizable set of symptoms or behaviours linked with distress and interference with personal functions for at least two weeks' duration (Health Advisory Service, 1995). Most symptoms are quantitative shifts from normality within a developmental framework, for example, the behaviours appropriate for a 12-year-old would not be demonstrated by an older adolescent of 16 years and their family.

As mental health cannot be viewed independently of the adolescent's functioning along other parameters (relationships, education, personal and life skills), and mental health problems affect some or all of these areas of life, the broader concept of mental health *needs* is often used to indicate the requirements in these aspects for the young person to function as expected for their chronological age. For example, this might include changes that might need to happen within the family, peer group or educational setting.

Behaviours and Concerns in Adolescence: Usual Developmental Changes or Mental Health Problems?

The above definitions suggest that mental health operates on a continuum, and at multiple levels, i.e. a young person may be experiencing difficulties in one area (such as relationships with their peers), whilst functioning well in most areas (in the previous example, relating well to their family and progressing with their educational work). For this reason, no single behaviour can be distinguished as either 'normal' or 'abnormal' or pathological. A number of factors will determine the judgement whether the adolescent is developing mental health problems. These include the duration of the particular behaviour, its severity, the co-existence of other signs of distress or difficulty in coping (mental health problems usually consist of a number of inter-related presentations) and, most importantly, the impact of the behaviour on the young person or other people (family or peers).

This applies to all individuals, from early childhood to adult life. However, there are additional issues that are particularly difficult to differentiate in adolescents. This is because of the substantial changes in all aspects of psycho-social development during adolescence, which can easily be misinterpreted as 'unusual' or 'strange' behaviour, or being outside the expected norm. Also, because these changes will not happen at the same time for different young people. Some young adolescents may have better developed cognitions or communication than young people in their late teens, and consequently perceive and share their distress in more appropriate ways.

Many behaviours falling within the 'problem' spectrum are also part of usual adolescent changes. Is being uncommunicative and withdrawn to be expected, or is it a subtle sign of the onset of mental illness? What is the difference between being shy and tense in social situations, and suffering from an anxiety condition that requires help? Similarly, when does sadness and unhappiness turn into depression? The answer usually lies in the contextual interpretation of behaviours, which should be based on the overall picture and impact on the young person's life, rather than on the narrow description of a single behaviour in isolation from the young person's development and functioning. The most common types of mental health problems will be discussed below. Before doing so, however, it would be useful to provide some evidence from epidemiological research on the frequency of these problems.

Finding out the Extent of Mental Health Problems and Disorders in Adolescence

Interpretation of epidemiological research must take into account several methodological aspects, which explains the variation of findings in the literature. The sample may not represent the general population, as it may be associated with mediating factors, such as socio-economic deprivation, which could account for the high rates of mental health problems. Studies adopt different definitions of symptoms, behaviours, problems or disorders, which are often not comparable. Research with young people faces additional difficulties, in particular the reliance on multi-informant reports. Because of continuous changes in cognitive development, different instruments are used for different age groups. There are several self-report measures (for depression, anxiety, post-traumatic stress or behavioural problems) for adolescents (12–16 years), although even in this age group corroborative information from parents and teachers is important. The concurrent presentation of mental health problems is not unusual in this age group, for example, depression may present together with either anxiety or conduct problems, or both. Adolescent mental health problems often co-occur with learning difficulties and developmental delays.

Studies based only on questionnaires usually give a good account of broad mental health problems, but can over-estimate disorders that would require specialist help. Two-stage designs or large-scale studies using both questionnaires and diagnostic interviews with young people, their parents or carers and their teachers are more accurate in estimating rates of specific mental health disorders. The British Child and Adolescent Mental Health Survey (Meltzer *et al.*, 2000) is a good example of such a design. This detected a rate of 9.5% for all disorders among both children and adolescents, which increased with age (11.2% among 11- to 15-year-olds, compared with 8.2% in children aged 5–10 years). Male adolescents reported higher overall levels of disorders (12.8%) than female adolescents (9.6%). This difference was mainly accounted for by behavioural (conduct) problems, whilst the reverse pattern was established for emotional problems such as depression. These will be discussed in more detail below.

Similar patterns have been established by studies in North America (e.g., McDermott, 1996; Whitaker *et al.*, 1990). Recent evidence suggests a real increase in mental health problems in Western societies, i.e. not merely accounted for by better recognition and likelihood of seeking help (Collishaw *et al.*, 2004). This increase is mainly accounted for by adolescent depression, substance abuse, self-harm and conduct problems. Trends in non-Western and developing societies are more difficult to establish, because of methodological differences (mainly in sampling and measures) and the potential trans-cultural differences in the perception and detection of mental health problems. However, two-stage epidemiological studies, such as by Fleitlich-Bilyk and Goodman (2004) in Brazil, are not that different in their overall prevalence rate, with similar risk factors involved. This may even apply in relation to behavioural problems in societies with different parenting and family norms (Thabet *et al.*, 2000).

How do Adolescents Perceive Mental Health Issues?

Considering the lack of clarity among services and professionals on what constitutes mental health and the remit of each service in relation to adolescent mental health (from promotion to specialist services), it comes as little surprise that this confusion filters down to the young people themselves. For example, Armstrong *et al.* (2000) found that adult terms such as 'mental health' were unclear to young people. In another study with young people in contact with the judicial system (Anderson *et al.*, 2004), a number of themes emerged from their perceptions of mental health problems, with associated negative connotations. The themes were associated with severe mental illness ('mad', 'gone', 'no right mind'); impact of emotional trauma ('affected by past', 'can't cope'); learning difficulties ('disabled', 'thick'); and aggressive behaviour or offending ('can't control', 'causing injuries'). This misunderstanding of various concepts and attached stigma often prevents them from seeking help. Such stigmas have a tendency to shape future beliefs and negative attitudes towards services. Young people's problems may be trivialized, with the belief that they are not important enough compared with adults. Adults' tendency to disparage problems from the young person's perspective can further exacerbate such beliefs.

Such negative perceptions are often associated with services experiences. Smith and Leon (2001) talked to older adolescents and young adults (aged between 16–25 years), and found substantial service user dissatisfaction. Young people often found professionals detached from their developmental needs, i.e. either relating to them as children or as adults, resulting in their disengagement and falling through the service net. Such problems are exacerbated for vulnerable young people such as those who leave public care, or who become homeless (Taylor *et al.*, 2004). Adolescents attending specialist mental health services asked for privacy away from parents, not being treated as children and being given more information (Taylor and Dogra, 2002). Less is known on the perceptions of ethnic minority young people, but emerging evidence suggests that their views are affected both by their family and by their peer environment (Dogra *et al.*, 2005).

Factors that Promote Adolescent Mental Health

The role of different factors that protect young people and increase their resilience, as well as those that make them vulnerable, were discussed in detail at the beginning of this book (Chapter 1). Some of these factors are also considered briefly here, in the particular context of mental health and related problems. Young people's psycho-social development involves different aspects and stages, which interact with their environment and are processed by the adolescent as s/he uses the experiences and influence of others (predominantly family and peers) to understand their self and wider systems, experiment and learn, as they strive towards autonomy and independence in young adult life. In that respect, their positive mental health is promoted by a number of internal and external factors. These operate even in the face of adversity, a positive message for interventions that will be discussed in the last section of this chapter.

Indeed, even young people who have experienced trauma and a negative early upbringing, such as those raised in substitute care (discussed in Chapter 3), have inbuilt protective qualities

and can benefit from opportunities provided by their carers and other important individuals in their life. Such factors have been shown to protect them from stressors and adversities (Rutter, 1985). These include children's and carers' coping strategies (self-efficacy, ability to self-reflect, self-reliance, maintaining a positive outlook and problem-solving), positive experiences of secure relationships, social and educational attainment, qualities which engender a positive response from others and friendships. Several of these factors are inter-related, for example, educational attainment is predominantly important in terms of positive relationships and impact on the young person's self-esteem rather than narrowly on their academic achievements. An overarching key factor is the existence of a secure and nurturing environment (particularly their immediate family), which will enable other protective mechanisms to operate successfully.

Vulnerable Young People: Factors Involved in the Development and Continuation of Mental Health Problems

Biological Factors (Temperament, Genetic and Neurodevelopmental)

The term 'personality' is not used for adolescents, as this is not fully formed until late-teens or early adult life. However, even young children have individual patterns of functioning (often defined as *temperament*), which are held to be genetically determined and therefore reasonably stable over time, and which may be altered by experience and environmental influences. Temperament is an interactional concept where the adolescent is an active participant in their own development, shaping the reactions of others. Difficult temperament is a risk factor for subsequent behavioural problems if it interacts with an adverse environment, but is not a reliable factor of psycho-social functioning if considered in isolation of environmental circumstances.

There is a genetic contribution to most mental health disorders, although this is not due to single gene effects. Autism probably has a strong genetic component, transmitted by several genes, but there may be non-specific heritability of elements such as language delay. Other disorders with a significant genetic component include bipolar affective disorder, schizophrenia and severe learning disabilities (e.g., Fragile X) and, to a lesser extent, anorexia nervosa, ADHD and depression. Mediation of mental health disorders may lie in early environmental factors in utero not determined genetically. Such factors have been implicated in the aetiology of disorders like autism, ADHD and schizophrenia, although their development is possibly related to multiple factors including genetic predisposition (Gillberg, 1995). Prenatal environmental factors influencing the development of learning disabilities, although uncommon, include infections (e.g., HIV), as well as toxins such as alcohol in foetal alcohol syndrome and also serious systemic maternal disease. Perinatal factors are seen usually as markers of learning disabilities that reflect pre-existing causes.

Acute Stressors

These imply sudden or rapid onset, marked by intense fearfulness. Adolescents can demonstrate post-traumatic stress reactions following major life-threatening stressors, with the prognosis depending on the severity of trauma, its meaning and the support networks following the trauma. Psychopathology is mediated by a number of factors such as adolescents' cognitive maturity and parents' responses to trauma.

Chronic Adversities

Chronic familial adversities significantly associated with adolescent mental health problems include severe marital discord, socio-economic adversities such as overcrowding and larger family size, paternal criminality, parental psychiatric disorder or alcohol abuse, experience of violence, parental rejection and lack of warmth. These risk factors have a cumulative effect, and may predict psycho-social outcomes in adult life.

- *Parental mental illness.* The nature and severity of that illness is of less importance than how it affects the young person through diminished parenting capacity. Contributing mechanisms are lack of family and social support networks, disrupted family life because of recurrent episodes or hospital admissions (although this only applies to a minority of severe cases) and reduced opportunities for the adolescent's development. Protective factors include a mentally healthy partner, restoration of family harmony and secure attachment with one parent.
- *Parental loss and separation.* Children and adolescents who experience parental loss, through death or permanent separation, are more vulnerable to develop mental health problems. None of these factors per se result in psychopathology, but this is usually the outcome of a number of interacting events. Early loss may lead to inadequate care and lack of emotional stability. Parental death or institutionalization may predispose to poor-quality relationships and further family disruption, particularly in the presence of violence. Divorce is now one of the most common life events impacting upon children and adolescents. It is a complex and often ongoing process with cumulative stressors. Remarriage and subsequent divorce may subject to chronic adversity, by exposure to hostile disputes; hence impact on adolescents depends on the quality of the divorce rather than divorce per se. Protective factors embrace a secure relationship with either or both parents, sibling or extended family support, friendships and a positive school environment.
- *Parenting skills and strategies.* Certain parenting characteristics impact negatively on adolescents' self-esteem, locus of control and self-reliance. Hostility and rejection, punitive parenting and marital discord can all impact on young people as acute or chronic stressors. This may be the disruption of essential parenting functions such as stability, consistency and emotional warmth; facilitation of development, fostering of self-esteem and the provision of rules and structure; most importantly, the experience of secure attachments upon which to build successful relationships in later life.
- *Abuse.* All three types of abuse (emotional, physical and sexual) in childhood and adolescence constitute a risk factor for the development of mental health problems. However, despite the high risk involved, most young people who suffered such traumatizing experiences will not present with mental health problems. The outcome of physical and emotional maltreatment is likely to be influenced by the nature and severity of the abuse or neglect, and by the subsequent relationships and circumstances in the young person's life. Consequences of abuse include impaired psychological development, impaired physical

development (which improves when a child or adolescent is placed in a more nurturing milieu), attachment difficulties and disorders such as depression. There is also increased risk, particularly among male victims of abuse, of becoming perpetrators in later life.

• *Physical illness and disability.* Chronic childhood physical illness affects about 10% of adolescents, with 1–2% being seriously affected, and constitutes a strong risk factor for mental health problems. This risk increases substantially if the central nervous system is affected. Multiple hospitalizations, especially with resulting separations from parents, may also impact on young people's psycho-social development. Also, school absences and loss of social opportunities. The resulting frustration, social restrictions and learned helplessness may lead to an external locus of control, demoralization and low mood. Parents' understanding of the illness, their supports and coping strategies are essential in maintaining family and emotional stability during this period. These effects can be bi-directional. Emotional stressors can exacerbate physical symptoms such as asthma. Related to this is somatization or the manifestation of psychological difficulties through somatic symptoms such as abdominal pain, chronic fatigue syndrome (physical weakness and exhaustion, tension headaches, sleep disturbance, worries) or conversion disorders (partial or complete loss of bodily sensations or movements), and associated physical or emotional complaints in the parents.

Types of Mental Health Problems and Disorders in Adolescence

All young people will express isolated behaviours and symptoms of distress at different stages of their life, which, however, do not constitute mental health problems or disorders. As discussed above, a substantial proportion of adolescents (at least 10% at any one time) will present with a number of such behaviours or signs that will have a sufficiently severe impact to merit help outside their immediate environment of friends and family. The most common presentations of mental health problems and disorders in adolescence are therefore discussed in more detail, including the nature of the problems, how they develop, what might contribute to them, and types of help and intervention which can be applied across a number of agencies that the adolescent and their family could come into contact with. As anti-social behaviour is discussed in a separate chapter, this has not been included here.

Anxiety

The frequency of all anxiety disorders is approximately 5.6% in adolescence, with higher prevalence among girls (Meltzer *et al.*, 2000). Causes include acute or chronic life events (bereavement, accidents or other traumas), personal predisposition (vulnerability) or a combination of these factors. Symptoms of *generalized anxiety* are irritability, inability to relax, muscular tension, poor sleep, nightmares, physical complaints (nausea, abdominal pain, sickness, headaches, sweating, heartbeats) and panic attacks (sudden onset, extreme fear, faintness). *Phobic disorders* are characterized by persistent and irrational fear of specific objects, activities or situations, which lead to their avoidance. The most common form in adolescence is social phobia, including speaking or eating in front of others. *Obsessive–compulsive disorders* resemble adult-like states, and include intrusive and persistent obsessive thoughts (for example, thoughts of counting, urge to wash hands or touch wood a certain number of times) and compulsive actions related to these thoughts. The young person is aware that these phenomena are unreasonable and tries to resist them, but often gives in.

The treatment of anxiety disorders includes behavioural therapy, i.e. gradual and increased exposure to the object or situation that brings anxiety, relaxation techniques and psychotherapy (brief or longer term) in order to gain understanding into the causes of anxiety. Milder anxiety problems have a good outcome, while chronic and severe cases are at risk of persisting or recurring in adult life. Depending on severity, these principles (particularly of behavioural therapy) can be applied by non-specialist professionals, for example, within education or youth services.

School refusal is not a mental health condition, but is often associated with anxiety and depression. It is defined as an irrational fear of school attendance, and should be distinguished from *truancy*, i.e. the disguised absence from school that is linked to behavioural problems but without an accompanying fear of the school situation. School refusal often starts at the time of school change or after absence for other reasons (e.g., minor illness), and usually has gradual onset and a history of previous absences. Adolescents may present with physical symptoms of tension/anxiety linked to attendance, which tend to remit at weekends and holidays, and have peer relationship difficulties. School refusal is not generally associated with learning difficulties. One or both parents may be 'worriers' and overtly close to the young person, and there may be stressful factors at school, such as bullying or exam-related anxiety. Although minor forms of school refusal are common and difficult to measure, this has been found to occur in about 1–2% of the school population. It is important to exclude an underlying physical illness, treat concurrent anxiety or depression, and aim for a gradual but quick return to school. Liaison with teachers and education welfare officers, and parental involvement, are essential. With this approach, the majority of mild problems and many severe cases of acute onset will be resolved.

Depression

The presence of depression in adolescence has only been recognized in the last decade, although practitioners often use classification systems (ICD-10 and DSM-IV) that adopt adult criteria. Depression occurs in 1% of young adolescents (girls and boys), which may rise to 4% in later adolescence (higher in girls). Teenagers may present with depressed mood (persistent for at least two weeks), poor or excessive sleep, change in appetite (usually decrease), weight changes (usually loss), self-harm thoughts, poor concentration, loss of interest for previously enjoyable activities, fatigue and negative cognitions (feeling useless, inadequate, ugly, guilty, hopeless). Young people with depression often have other mental health problems such as anxiety, behavioural problems or eating disorders. Established causes are life events (trauma/loss), personal predisposition (genetic) and physical illness. Treatment includes management of underlying family, school or social problems, cognitive-behavioural therapy (aimed at changing maladaptive and negative ways of thinking), brief psychotherapy, antidepressant medication and social skills training (improving self-esteem and interpersonal relationships) (AACAP, 1998). The depressive episode usually remits, but there is high risk of relapse (one-third of young people over two to three years). In a small proportion of young people, depressive symptoms may become chronic and there is a risk of depression persisting in adult life.

Recognition of depressive presentation is important for professionals in regular contact with young people, as changes can be subtle and go unrecognized until they become severe enough to be noticed, and hence more difficult to treat. The principles of cognitive therapy (changing negative cognitive patterns to more adaptive thinking) and social skills training (gaining confidence in relating to their peers and dealing with social stressors) can be applied by school counsellors, youth workers and other professionals. It is, however, important to monitor the young person in case they develop more serious and entrenched symptoms or self-harm behaviours that will require involvement of specialist services.

Deliberate Self-harm

Vague suicidal thoughts can occur in up to one-third of teenagers, with an annual prevalence of deliberate self-harm (hospital-treated) of about 0.2% in the general population. It increases with age, is more common in females (3:1) and low socio-economic groups, and is often precipitated by arguments with family, friends or partner. The method is usually either by overdose of analgesics, antidepressants or other medication, or by inflicting lacerations (Hawton *et al.*, 2003). There are often associated mental health problems such as depression, behavioural problems and alcohol/drug abuse. There is a high risk of eventual suicide (in up to 10% of the young people who self-harm).

Suicide in young life is rare, although it is possibly an underestimate, due to often being defined as accidental death, i.e. about 10 adolescents/young adults per 100 000 general population (or 14% of all deaths). There is an increasing trend in 15- to 19-year-old males. In contrast with deliberate self-harm, suicide is more frequent in males; often there has been a history of previous attempts (in 25–50% of young people), and it has no association with social class. Methods tend to be more violent in males, while overdoses are more frequent in females. An important finding for professionals working with adolescents is that about 50% of young people who committed suicide had talked about their intent during the previous week, and there had usually been underlying depression, or concurrent substance abuse or behavioural problems.

Post-traumatic Stress Disorders

Exposure to trauma is a vulnerability factor for a range of mental problems (Vostanis, 2004). In particular, it is strongly associated with a presentation of emotional symptoms, defined as post-traumatic stress disorder (PTSD). High rates of PTSD have been established in studies with children and young people exposed to natural disasters such as earthquakes, human-induced accidents, war conflict, community and domestic violence, and life-threatening physical illness (Yule, 1999). Post-traumatic stress reactions are characterized by intrusive images or recurrent thoughts about the event, reliving their experience (flashbacks), associated sleep disturbance, physical symptoms, avoidance of stimuli associated with the trauma, emotional detachment or numbing, irritability and poor concentration. As professionals from different agencies increasingly come in contact with a wide range of traumatized young people, it is important to consider the possibility of persisting post-traumatic symptoms, whilst at the same time not attributing all problems to the potential impact of trauma.

Post-traumatic stress symptoms respond well to brief psychotherapeutic interventions (cognitive or psychodynamic, individually or in groups) as long as the underlying stressors have been removed. There is less conclusive evidence on the effectiveness of psychological debriefing, i.e. verbally re-experiencing the trauma in order to work through its consequences. Families often need to be involved in the intervention, as their own emotional responses may maintain the young person's distress. Post-traumatic stress disorders are often undetected, as these are internalized by the adolescent, or overlap with problems such as depression or oppositional behaviours. If untreated, symptoms can persist for a long time, or recur at a later stage.

Attention Deficit Hyperactivity Disorders

This condition has attracted publicity in the last few years, and is an example of how changes in the diagnostic and classification systems affect clinical practice. ADHD has an onset before the age of five years, and is characterized by continuous (pervasive) motor hyperactivity, restlessness, poor attention and concentration, distractibility and impulsivity. In recent years, there has been greater diagnostic convergence among clinicians in different countries. However, there are still problems in both under-diagnosing (by considering it a behavioural problem) or over-diagnosing ADHD (by applying very loose criteria). There is less knowledge or agreement on the nature of ADHD in adolescents, but recent findings indicate a prevalence of 2.3% in boys aged 11–15 years and 0.5% in girls of the same age (or ratio 4:1) (Meltzer *et al.*, 2000). In adolescence, the condition may predominantly present with attention and concentration difficulties (attention deficit disorder – ADD), without the physical restlessness and overactivity seen in younger children.

Between 30% and 50% of children and adolescents with ADHD also have behavioural problems (this combination is more difficult to treat). No single cause has been found, but there is some evidence that biological/neurodevelopmental factors are involved. Treatment includes behaviour modification (to improve concentration and adverse behaviour), school intervention (these adolescents benefit from structured teaching in a small size class, if possible) and medication (usually centrally acting stimulants). A combination of approaches is often required. Medication may have a positive effect on attention, concentration and activity, but not directly on behavioural problems. There is limited research on long-term outcome. Hyperactivity, restlessness, attention deficit and impulsivity improve with age, but other problems such as poor school performance, impaired social skills and relationships, low self-esteem and behavioural problems may persist.

Eating Disorders

Problems related to eating, weight and body image are particularly prominent and possibly on the rise among teenagers in Western societies. These appear to relate to a combination of underlying difficulties in emotional and social maturity, family conflict and societal pressures on losing weight, through the media and peer pressure. The vast majority of young people who may wish or try to lose weight are not a cause for concern, as this is usually a transient phase that does not impact on the young person's life. A minority of them will, however, develop more serious presentations that can become entrenched and difficult to resolve. For this reason, it is important that carers, teachers and young people themselves are aware of the differences between a wish to remain slim and a health-threatening condition, and seek help at an early stage. If preoccupation with eating and weight reaches the pathological part of the spectrum, this can be expressed through two broad types of disorders, although a mixture of the two can also occur.

Anorexia nervosa is characterized by a low body weight, 15% below the expected for age and height. This loss is self-induced, by food avoidance, self-induced vomiting, purging, excessive exercise and use of diuretics or appetite suppressants. The adolescent has a distorted image of how their body appears and so employs such tactics as a method of slimming down a perceived fatness. Older adolescents will cease to have their menstrual period, and pre-pubertal girls have primary amenorrhoea as well as delayed physical development. Young men may describe a loss of interest in sexual activity whilst pre-pubertal boys will retain juvenile genital development. Children as young as eight have presented with anorexia, although the majority are between 14 and 19 years. The average prevalence rate is 3%, with a female to male ratio of 11:1. A number of approaches can be helpful, as part of a plan to help the young person. Sharing the 'control' of their weight is important by setting realistic targets, preferably in conjunction with their family. This can be informal in mild cases, and more structured and targeted if there is ongoing weight loss. Family therapy can help improve communication, reframe family relationships and resolve conflict, whilst cognitive-behavioural therapy may help the adolescent change their negative beliefs and perceptions of their body image (Treasure and Schmidt, 2003). If there is rapid weight loss and/or no response to the above interventions, inpatient treatment may be necessary, as severe anorexia can have a number of physical complications, and in its extreme forms can be life-threatening.

Bulimia nervosa rarely presents in children under the age of 11, with recent surveys suggesting that 1% of 11- to 20-year-olds meet the diagnostic criteria, and a female to male ratio of 33:1. Presentation includes fear of being overweight, binge eating and attempting to counteract this by self-induced vomiting, purgatives or appetite suppressants. The adolescent may also be involved with substance abuse as a method of appetite control. Evidence supports the effectiveness of cognitive-behavioural therapy, which focuses on the binge–purge cycle to help the adolescent map out strategies and develop healthier eating patterns (Gowers and Bryant-Waugh, 2004). Physical management consists of education and monitoring of weight.

Early-Onset Psychosis

Mental illness usually refers to psychotic disorders (schizophrenia, bipolar affective or drug-induced) and severe depression. All these conditions are more likely to occur during adult life, at least as a combination of symptoms and behaviours that will lead to such a diagnosis. These disorders are uncommon in adolescence. However, young people can present with psychotic-like symptoms (described below) that may indicate the gradual onset of a psychotic disorder or may have a different explanation (often anxiety-, trauma- or drug-induced). For those young people who have been found to develop a psychotic disorder, the national average annual incidence rate is around 15 per 100 000. Not every incident of psychosis will progress to a diagnosis of schizophrenia; sometimes this is restricted to a single episode linked to substance abuse or trauma. It can also be associated with severe depression or mania.

Early (or 'prodromal') features of psychosis may be very difficult to distinguish from usual adolescent behaviours, or non-psychotic mental health problems. These include anxiety, suspicion, sleep disturbance, perceptual difficulties and isolation. A careful assessment is required to determine whether the young person's developmental, social and family history might suggest an alternative formulation to psychosis. For the few young people who will go on to develop an illness such as schizophrenia (often about two years from onset, based on clients' and carers' retrospective recollection), typical (florid) psychotic symptoms include beliefs outside the social and cultural norms (delusions); distortion of sensory perceptions (hallucinations – usually auditory); deterioration in the thought process (thought disorder); and gradual decline in social functioning. In bipolar affective disorder (manic depression), teenagers' moods can swing between severe depression and mania (irritability, restlessness and elated mood).

In many cases, the concerns may not indicate an underlying illness, but rather changes in social relationships, loss of confidence or social anxiety. This should be established following assessment and/or close monitoring of the young person, corroborating observations with reports from carers, teachers and even his peer group. In other cases, young people may experience severe anxiety, often following trauma such as abuse or a death in the family, which can be misinterpreted as psychotic symptoms. The adolescent may describe very plausible (and real for them) sensory phenomena, often defined as 'pseudohallucinations'. A typical example following the death of a loved one is seeing their image or hearing their voice, usually at bedtime. A distinctive feature is that the adolescent recognizes the symptoms as unusual, despite not being able to resist them or to deal with the resulting distress. In contrast, a psychotic young person will accept such experiences as normal.

Unfortunately, the frequent gap between early recognition and initiation of treatment means that symptoms become so severe that 80% of first episode individuals are hospitalized, 50–60% of them under the Mental Health Act. This can be a terrifying experience for the young person, who is already likely to be coping with such positive symptoms as delusions, hallucinations and thought disorder. This process can be shameful and stigmatizing for the adolescent, and may disengage them in the future from services. Therefore, treatment at this stage is aimed at reducing the impact, as well as the symptoms of psychosis, and can include antipsychotic medication; psychoeducation on the nature of problems and coping strategies for the young person and their family; cognitive-behavioural therapy on dealing with the symptoms; and family therapy in helping the carers, siblings and the young person cope as a unit with the impact of the illness. Training and education are essential for the young person to return to ordinary social activities as soon as possible. There is some evidence that the first three years following the initial onset is a critical period that reduces the impact of the illness (Birchwood *et al.*, 1998).

Mental Health Promotion and Prevention: Everybody's Responsibility

The definition of a mentally healthy adolescent, and the understanding of the multiple factors that enhance their mental health or place them at risk of developing problems, should guide suggestions on developing and improving services. As mental health covers a broad spectrum and range of aspects of functioning in young life, all agencies and professionals have a role to play. This is a key concept of several policies in the UK (Department for Education and Skills, 2003; Department of Health, 2004). The key is to define the remit of each agency in enhancing young people's mental health, as well as the interface between agencies to provide accessible and engaging services, with continuity rather than fragmentation of care. These roles are discussed below in the context of adolescents' mental health needs and characteristics (i.e., in contrast with children and adults).

The role of educational, leisure and youth services is central in promoting and enhancing young people's mental health. This arises from evidence on the protective impact of support networks, friendships, sense of achievement, self-esteem and opportunities for training and employment. Interventions on any of these components can break an adverse cycle in a young person's life, whilst operation of multiple protective factors can have a 'snowballing' effect and help the adolescent strive smoothly towards independence. This will largely also depend on the security of the young person's family environment; otherwise, agencies need to engage and involve parents. Such involvement could range from education on the importance of 'letting go' and encouraging the adolescent to function within their peer group and wider society; empowerment of parents in initiating such activities; 'mediation' between the young person and their parents in negotiating the young person's autonomy within the family boundaries; and different levels of family work in reframing family roles and relationships, resolving conflict and improving communication.

Despite the evidence on the protective function of these aspects of a young person's life, there is actually limited evidence on the effectiveness of preventive or mental health promotion programmes or service models (Carr, 2000). With services and interventions predominantly focusing on the severe end of the mental health spectrum (educational services targeting school exclusion, social care agencies primarily targeting child protection and statutory duties and specialist mental health services geared towards treatment of disorders), such initiatives have inevitably been low in the priorities of resource allocation. However, in recent years there has been a trend of policies, organizational structures and funding streams adopting an inter-agency and more preventive philosophy.

The integration of mental health and other community services, which are more youth-friendly and acceptable to young people, provides an opportunity for education on what constitutes positive mental health, what helps and ways of accessing other kinds of help if needed. This, together with joint work between teachers, youth workers and specialist mental health professionals, can change the perceptions and stigma of mental health problems and related services. School counsellors, mentors, connexions officers and school nurses can offer advice and brief interventions, within a stable and secure environment, where young people can feel listened to away from the family. This obviously raises potential ethical dilemmas on protecting confidentiality from peers and parents, whilst ensuring the young person's safety and collaboration with all carers (e.g., in the case of self-harm). Other professionals, such as social workers for adolescents in public care and youth offending teams officers for young people in contact with the courts, can apply the same principles of enhancing their emotional well-being, albeit under more difficult circumstances, or where there is conflict between the statutory and the therapeutic role. Although it can be more difficult for a young person to be convinced of the importance of social activities and education if these are enforced by the courts and the supervising worker, these are nevertheless important components of an integrated care plan (Callaghan *et al.*, 2003).

This objective of promoting mental health is now considered integral to a comprehensive child and adolescent mental health service (CAMHS) (Department of Health, 2004), but is unlikely to attract much investment in the near future, because of the substantial gaps across specialist services. There are, however, innovative services that integrate educational, health and social care (occasionally the non-statutory sector), although the majority target younger children and families (Window *et al.*, 2004), with relatively few projects for teenagers, and hardly any for those in transition between adolescence and adulthood. Similarly, there is

generally limited help for parents of teenagers, who have different issues and require different strategies from parents of primary school age children. Most interesting examples come from the voluntary sector, although such projects are often constrained by short-term and uncertain funding, consequently shifting the service objectives to meet current policy priorities.

Improving Specialist Mental Health Services for Adolescents

Specialist mental health services for children and adolescents (CAMHS) are faced with a number of priorities for the next decade. Most apply to both children and adolescents, whilst some are specific to the older age group. The general issues include the need to define the role of the specialist service in relation to the assessment and treatment of mental health disorders described earlier in this chapter; establishing clear links with inter-agency services within a comprehensive service model (i.e., continuity of care, rather than fragmented service contacts – these are particularly evident in relation to behavioural problems; Vostanis *et al.*, 2003); increase of skilled workforce; and evidence-base for effectiveness of interventions and services.

Despite the acknowledgement that children and adolescents require different approaches, the level of resources allocated to CAMHS is unlikely to allow the development of separate adolescent services in the foreseeable future. Some services have, however, expanded their adolescent inpatient and day facilities, with specialist staff working predominantly or exclusively with teenagers and their families. There has also been some attention on the upper end of the age spectrum (16–19 years) and the transition to adult mental health services, albeit the picture remains disappointing (Richards and Vostanis, 2004).

Recent policies in countries such as Australia and the UK have recognized that young people in late adolescence and early adulthood have specific mental health needs, which are often related to their transitions in different aspects of their life. When these transitions are disrupted, young people will require co-ordinated support from different agencies. In reality, service provision is fragmented and there are different philosophies and priorities for agencies working with adolescents as opposed to adults, with resulting service gaps and young people disengaging from services during the transitional period of high-level need. Encouraging early findings on interventions and service models arise from different research fields, albeit not necessarily directly from the mental health literature (Vostanis, 2005). Health services have been faced with these issues in relation to chronic physical conditions for many years, and have developed standards of care, transfer protocols and cross-over arrangements between adolescents' and adult services. Within mental health, there has been expansion of early psychosis services, with promising evidence on the importance of early detection and treatment. Such an approach is likely to also suit young people with non-psychotic mental health problems and disorders.

Engagement and Ethical Issues

There are additional difficulties in engaging adolescents with mental health services above those faced by either children or adults. These usually involve a balance of appropriate information, preparation at the time of referral, involvement of the young person in decision-making whilst acknowledging their developmental needs and parental responsibilities. A referring professional should make every attempt to gain consent from the parents and the adolescent before making a referral, and ensure that the young person understands the reasons, even if they are not in full agreement with them. Otherwise, they are likely to disengage sooner or later, and retain a negative experience from their brief contact, thus depriving them of further help. It would be preferable for the adolescent to be given a choice of not re-attending, but to develop a trusting relationship with the therapist, thus keeping the door open to seek help again in the future. The vast majority of adolescents will be Gillick-competent to understand the reasons for referral and what treatment might involve. However, their learning and developmental capacity will differ, even within the same chronological age, therefore these factors will need to be considered and assessed in parallel with the mental health issues.

Ethical dilemmas can arise when adolescents do not wish their parents to be aware of their attendance. Their reasons can be discussed and understood, hopefully leading to an agreed invitation to the parents to meet with the therapist. In many cases, the adolescent's wishes to seek help for themselves should be respected. The therapist should, however, avoid either colluding with maladaptive behaviours ("I will harm myself if you tell my parents") or be identified with other adults who may take a punitive or rejecting position towards the young person. If adults need to be informed or contacted for safety reasons such as child protection, self-harm or being on medication, all efforts should be made to gain the young person's consent. If there is no alternative, it is again preferable to be honest and let the young person know, rather than act without their knowledge. The same applies to liaising with teachers and other professionals involved with the young person, that also requires consent from the adolescent and their parents. Sometimes, a direct approach may be required, explaining why professionals need to share information and/or meet, to adopt a consistent plan to help the young person.

Throughout such difficult scenarios, the key is often to remain sensitive to the young person's experiences, anxieties and wishes, whilst remaining conscious of parenting and care issues. This applies to all contacts with young people, from assessment to completion of treatment. Engagement can be enhanced by first meeting with the young person in the presence of an adult s/he trusts, in an environment of their choice. Some young people may find a mental health setting frightening, and thus prefer a familiar community venue such as a youth service, while others may perceive the mental health service as neutral and confidential. An adolescent-friendly environment is important, as many CAMHS are geared towards younger children, and adult mental health services can deter young people. Adolescents can contribute to audit and service evaluation, adding valuable user perspective (Taylor and Dogra, 2002). However, their involvement should be tailored to their developmental needs, rather than alienating them further from services.

Finally, it is important to comment on the applicability and evidence of effectiveness of therapeutic interventions for adolescents. There is now supporting knowledge on the benefits of a range of modalities for adolescent mental health problems and disorders (cognitive-behavioural, psychodynamic and family therapy; more recently, solution-focused and interpersonal therapy – Carr, 2000). Individual therapies can also be provided in groups, with emerging examples of school-based and other preventive programmes. There is, however, a need for further development of applied interventions for adolescents with complex difficulties (e.g., in public care) that require a more flexible approach, as well as evaluation in real (in contrast with research) settings.

Further Reading

Goodman, R. and Scott, S. (1997) *Child psychiatry.* Blackwell Science: Oxford.

Meltzer, H., Gatward, R., Goodman, R. and Ford, T. (2000) *The mental health of children and adolescents in Great Britain.* HMSO: London.

Department of Health (2004) *National service framework for children, young people and maternity services: The mental health and psychological well-being of children and young people.* HMSO: London.

Discussion Questions

1. How does adolescent mental health impact on other areas of adolescent life as discussed in other chapters in this volume?
2. Are there particular risk factors that are implicated in psychiatric disorders?
3. In what way does the concept of adolescent mental health represent a continuum?
4. How do we all have a role to play in enhancing adolescent mental health?
5. How does the concept of resilience apply to those with mental disorders? What particular strategies can be used to promote resilience with this population?

Chapter 6

Young Disabled People

Kirsten Stalker

Reader, Applied Education Research Centre, University of Strathclyde

---

Learning Objectives

Once you have read this chapter you should be able to:

1 Think about a range of risk factors facing young disabled people.

2 Understand young disabled people's strengths and aspirations and their right to take 'normal' risks as part of growing up.

3 Be aware of the relevance of social models of disability to disabled adolescents.

4 Think about the views and experiences of young disabled people.

5 Have some knowledge of research about young disabled people and mental health.

Adolescence, Risk and Resilience: *Against the odds.* John Coleman and Ann Hagell (eds.).
Published in 2007 by John Wiley & Sons, Ltd

6 Be aware of the potential risks attached to young disabled people's transition from adolescence to adulthood.

7 Discuss the evidence relating to abuse of young disabled people.

Introduction

This book is informed by four different – but potentially overlapping – conceptualizations of *risk*. These are: first, risk factors which may contribute to poor outcomes for adolescents; second, risk behaviour which adolescents may engage in; third, risks relating to child protection; and last, the risks which adolescents may be seen as posing to others or to society at large. These notions of risk all have some relevance to young disabled people, who are the focus of this chapter: like non-disabled adolescents, they also drink and take drugs, while those with mental health problems or behavioural challenges may be demonized. However, the evidence suggests that risk factors and being 'at risk' have particular resonance for disabled youngsters, many of whom face a range of barriers as they go about their day-to-day lives. In addition, the incidence of child abuse is higher among disabled than non-disabled youngsters. At the same time, it must be stressed that it would be wrong to automatically equate *disability* with risk: adolescents are not generally 'at risk' just because they have a physical, sensory or cognitive *impairment*. In addition, disabled adolescents can be both resourceful and resilient, for example, by developing a variety of strategies for dealing with the challenges they face.

The chapter begins by outlining theoretical models of risk and of disability. The emphasis will be on social models of disability, which take the focus away from individual impairment and place it firmly on social and attitudinal barriers to inclusion. Next, research evidence from four recent studies about disabled children is presented. For many years social research in this area focused on parents' experiences of looking after disabled children or professionals' views about them. Research seeking the young people's accounts of their everyday lives is still uncommon, although increasingly researchers are seeking their opinions about service provision. Three of the studies discussed in this chapter focus on the views and experiences of young disabled people. These will be presented chronologically: the first spans children aged 7–11, the second deals with adolescents aged 11–16, while the third moves on to explore the experiences of young adults aged 16–24. The fourth piece is somewhat different: it is a review of recent research rather than an empirical study in its own right. It deals with the important topic of child protection. Research suggests that carers and practitioners are not always well informed about child protection issues in relation to disability. Finally, the summary section highlights the key points made in this chapter.

Theoretical Frameworks

Models of Disability

For many years, policy and practice relating to disabled people was dominated by the medical model of disability. This approach equates disability with illness, ascribes a 'sick role' to the individual and focuses on physical 'dysfunction'. People are categorized in terms of their diagnosis or impairment, while professionals direct their energies towards rehabilitation, recovery or cure. Within this perspective, the experience of being or becoming disabled is viewed as a tragedy, likely to trigger a grief reaction similar to bereavement. The best way forward for the individual is to 'come to terms' with the tragedy and adapt to society as best s/he can.

Finkelstein (1993) identified an administrative model of disability. Here, disabled people are subject to endless professional and bureaucratic intervention, supposedly in order to meet their psychological, emotional or practical needs. In reality, however, Finkelstein argues, the aim is to create and perpetuate the power, stratus and financial rewards which accompany professional standing. This in turn serves to maintain disabled people in a state of dependency.

In reaction against these models, which take little or no account of the views or *collective* experience of disabled people, UPIAS (Union of the Physically Impaired against Segregation) laid the foundations for the social model of disability 30 years ago. It drew an important distinction between impairment and disability, as shown in Box 6.1.

Box 6.1   UPIAS definitions of impairment and disability (1976: 3–4)

Impairment is defined as:

Lacking part or all of a limb, or having a defective limb, organism or mechanism of the body.

Disability is defined as:

The disadvantage or restriction of activity caused by a contemporary social organisation which takes little or no account of people who have physical impairments and thus excludes them from the mainstream of social activities.

The social model argues that we should focus on dismantling the material, economic and social barriers which disable and exclude people who have impairments (Oliver, 1990; Swain *et al.*, 2004). It provides the theoretical basis for the disability movement, which has had significant impact on changing policy and attitudes relating to disabled people.

At the same time, the social model has been criticized, by people within the disability movement, for putting too much emphasis on external barriers and neglecting the role of impairment – the day-to-day implications of being unable to see or hear, for example, and the interaction between particular impairments and the social environment. Thomas (1999) developed the "social relational model of disability" to take account of these missing dimensions. She stresses that disability is rooted in unequal social relationships, seeing it as a form of *social oppression*, like racism or sexism. Importantly, however, Thomas incorporates personal and inter-personal experience within her model, which has three different but related dimensions, as outlined below (Box 6.2).

In summary, and at its most simple, the social model of disability locates the 'problem' within society rather than the individual. Recent thinking has given greater prominence to the implications of living with impairment on a daily basis and also to the corrosive effects on the individual of 'psycho-emotional disablism'.

Box 6.2   The social relational model of disability (Thomas, 1999)

Impairment effects: restrictions of activity resulting from living with a specific impairment. This could include the fatigue or discomfort associated with some conditions, or the inability to do certain things; for example, a person with visual impairment being unable to recognize facial expressions.

Barriers to doing: physical, economic and material barriers, such as inaccessible buildings or transport, which restrict or prevent people from undertaking certain activities; for example, an agency failing to provide a lift in its premises to enable wheelchair users to access upper floors.

Barriers to being: hurtful, hostile or inappropriate comments or behaviour which have a negative effect on people's sense of self, affecting what they feel they can be or become; for example, calling a person with learning disabilities derogatory names. Thomas calls this process "psycho-emotional disablism". Exclusionary institutional policies and practices can have the same effect; for example, failing to provide a lift not only excludes a wheelchair user from accessing certain spaces but may also be construed as meaning that they are not worth the effort and expense of installing a lift.

Understanding Risk

The late twentieth century saw the emergence of the 'risk society' and a preoccupation with identifying and managing a whole host of perceived risks (Beck, 1992; Douglas, 1982; Giddens, 1990), ranging from terrorism to 'anti-social behaviour'. This has been accompanied by a widespread loss of faith in 'experts', professionals and their agencies, who are seen as largely ineffective in reducing risk and sometimes responsible for exacerbating it. This climate of opinion has had a significant impact on the way that work with children and young people is seen and interpreted, with ever-increasing fears of the risks children and young people are said to face and to pose, coupled with calls for more effective 'risk management'.

Risk Factors Affecting Disabled Adolescents

Disabled adolescents may face a range of risk factors. At the macro level, there is ample evidence of attitudinal barriers, which can take the form of bullying and harassment by other children (Watson *et al.*, 2000), as well as ignorance and prejudice on the part of adults (Connors and Stalker, 2003). In addition, these young people's lives are constrained by physical and material barriers such as lack of accessible transport, accessible buildings, failure to provide information in accessible formats, lack of inclusive leisure opportunities and so on (e.g., Baker and Donnelly, 2001; Hughes *et al.*, 2005). In particular, adolescents have been let down by shortcomings in policy and practice, for example, in the transition to adulthood. Research has shown they may be excluded from, or not meaningfully involved in, planning for their futures (SHS Trust, 2002).

This is particularly true for those with communication impairments (Cameron and Murphy, 2001) and from black and minority ethnic communities (Hussain *et al.*, 2001). Young disabled people and their families often have difficulty finding out information about post-school options, with many youngsters being directed towards day centres and segregated courses in colleges of further education (Heslop *et al.*, 2001). Not enough consideration may be given to the kind of opportunities routinely presented to non-disabled young people, such as higher education, employment and a move away from the parental home towards more independent living (Dean, 2003). There is ample evidence of disabled adolescents being at risk of failing to make a successful transition to adulthood (see Morris, 2002 for a review).

At micro level, another set of risk factors face the families of disabled children. It has been documented for many years that families with disabled children are at risk of unemployment, low income and poverty, while at the same time facing the additional costs associated with impairment such as dietary requirements, housing adaptations, aids, equipment and paid sitters or carers (see Cunningham-Burley and Coates, 2005 for a review). Russell (1996) notes that families with disabled children face a wider range of risk factors than others, for example, they are more likely to be single parent families, and the health of both parents and siblings may be adversely affected by the pressures of caring. In addition, the quality of support services is very variable, described by the Audit Commission (2004) as "a lottery of provision". At the same time, research has pointed to the different ways in which parents develop positive coping strategies (Beresford, 1994) and to the rewards and benefits which disabled children can bring to family life (Audit Commission, 2004).

Disabled Adolescents at Risk

Despite a widespread assumption that disabled children are seldom subject to abuse, the limited research evidence available indicates that the prevalence of abuse is higher among disabled than non-disabled youngsters. The scale of the problem has become evident since the 1980s through a number of large-scale studies carried out in the United States, as illustrated in Box 6.3.

Box 6.3   Reported incidence of abuse in disabled children

Method: analysis of computer records for over 40 000 children in an American city.

Findings: compared with non-disabled children, disabled children were

- 3.8 times more likely to be neglected,
- 3.8 times more likely to be physically abused,
- 3.1 times more likely to be sexually abused,
- 3.9 times more likely to be emotionally abused.

Overall, 31% of the disabled children had been abused, compared with 9% of those who were not disabled.

Sullivan and Knutson (2000), cited in Miller (2003, pp. 19–20)

It is of concern that local authorities in the UK cannot usually provide statistics about numbers of disabled children on child protection registers. However, small-scale studies by Kennedy (1989) and Westcott (1993), both cited by Miller (2003), point to high levels of abuse in Britain. Child protection is discussed in more detail later in this chapter.

A Positive Approach to Disabled Adolescents and Risk

One way of looking at risk management is to see it as a continuum, moving from 'risk avoidance/elimination' at one end towards 'risk-taking' at the other, with 'legitimate authority' occupying the middle ground (Gurney, 2000). Risk avoidance is associated with a controlling approach and a drive to find scapegoats when things go wrong. The pressure on practitioners working with children to be constantly looking over their shoulders has been increased by sensationalized press reports of child abuse scandals, high-profile public inquiries and the rise of litigation.

When working with disabled adolescents there are strong arguments in favour of risk-taking – so long as it is well planned, supported and within reasonable limits. This approach is based on a view of young disabled people as active citizens with rights and responsibilities, whose expertise about their own lives should be valued: professionals are not the only experts (Murray, 2000). Risk-taking is part of normal everyday life, one way of empowering young people and promoting personal development. Practitioners working with disabled adolescents have both a duty of care and protection *and* the duty, enshrined in the United Nations Convention on the Rights of the Child (1989) and current UK childcare legislation (The Children Act 1989; The Children (Scotland) Act 1995; The Northern Ireland Children's Order 1995), to consult children about their views and wishes and take these into account in decisions affecting them. Achieving this delicate balance can be a complex process when disabled children want to take risks, or may be considered at risk: children lack adults' experience and arguably, depending on age and ability, judgement in terms of weighing up different courses of action and deciding on the relative risks associated with each. Many disabled adolescents lead more protected lives than their non-disabled peers and may be seen as less able to make such judgements, yet simultaneously more open to exploitation and abuse. These factors may be magnified when the child has learning disabilities.

On the other hand, it can be argued that young people's independence should not be unduly restricted by other people's anxieties. Being over-protective may well compromise another individual's quality of life (Lawson, 1996) and, in the case of disabled youngsters, prevent them from successfully negotiating the transition to adulthood and reaching their full potential. It is striking that service users' views are largely missing from the risk literature (Langan, 1999), and that few if any researchers have sought disabled children/young people's experiences first-hand, most relying on parents' and professionals' accounts. Adolescents' perceptions of risk may of course vary from those of their parents and the practitioners working with them. While most children accept some degree of adult protection, they resent rules and practices seen as restricting their autonomy (Kelley *et al.*, 1998): disabled youngsters are no exception (Connors and Stalker, 2003). Recent years have seen a growing interest in the concept of *resilience*, defined by Jackson (2000, p. 296) as "an interaction between risk and protective factors within a person's background, which can interrupt and reverse what might otherwise be damaging processes". Resilience can stem from individual characteristics, family circumstances and ethos, or environmental factors. Practitioners working with children can enhance resilience by building on existing strengths and reducing perceived risk factors (Jackson, 2000).

In summary, disabled adolescents may face a range of risk factors, primarily in the form of social and attitudinal barriers and, compared with their non-disabled peers, are at increased risk of abuse. Recent international and UK legislation and policy initiatives require practitioners to recognize that disabled adolescents have the same rights as any other young people. Risk management can be seen as moving up and down a continuum, with controlling practices at one end and more empowering approaches towards the other. The latter should include the right to take reasonable, well-informed and supported risks as part of the process of growing up and becoming independent. The rest of this chapter will discuss some findings from four recent publications about disabled young people, within the context of the ideas about risk and disability outlined above. Research participants' real names have been changed.

The Views and Experiences of Disabled Children and Young People: A Positive Outlook

Connors and Stalker (2003) carried out a two-year study, funded by the Scottish Executive, exploring disabled children's daily lives, from their own perspective. The authors visited 26 children aged between 7 and 15, including ten 11- to 15-year-olds, seeing each young person on three or four occasions. The children, who lived in central and southern Scotland, had a range of physical, sensory and cognitive impairments: some attended 'special' segregated schools; others went to 'integrated units' or mainstream schools. The young people took part in semi-structured interviews involving various activities and exercises to engage their interest and facilitate communication. Interviews were also conducted with parents and siblings.

Overall, most young people gave positive accounts of their lives, describing close loving relationships with their parents, fairly typical 'ups and downs' with their siblings and regular contact with extended family members. The adolescents in the sample had very similar preoccupations and interests to other children their age: the boys were keen on outdoor and sporting activities such as football, wrestling and snooker while the girls tended to favour a mixture of sports and home-based pastimes including swimming, drawing and music. With three exceptions, all the young people could identify at least one thing they were good at, while six could not think of anything they found difficult. Most could name close friends and, talking about their experiences at school, presented themselves as helpful pupils, good classmates and active participants in various aspects of school life. One boy said: "It's brilliant. Being at school is better than being at home. I enjoy most things at school" (p. 52). Many of the youngsters were well supported by their parents, some of whom were powerful advocates for their sons and daughters and worked hard to give them the message that they were 'just as good' as their non-disabled siblings and peers. The young people were generally positive about the contact they had with professionals, such as teachers and doctors, and appeared quite happy with the short-term breaks they had in a variety of settings.

In terms of Thomas's social relational model of disability, few of the children described difficulties associated with impairment effects. None conveyed a sense of loss or resentment about having an impairment. However, two youngsters with mobility problems said they wished they could walk and another wanted better vision. Some were active in managing their impairments and had adopted a practical, pragmatic attitude. The mother of a girl with a hearing impairment spoke about a conversation she had overheard between her daughters, including the deaf child. They were each choosing three wishes. Her mother told us:

> *And Julie was last and I was dreading what Julie would say. I thought she might say she wished she wasn't deaf but she didn't mention it... and later on when it was just Julie and I, I said to her; "Do you wish that you weren't deaf?" and she said "No". And I said "Why is that?" and she said, "Because I wouldn't know or have all the special friends that I've got." And I thought that was a lovely thing to say.*

(Connors and Stalker, 2003, p. 105)

Other benefits of having impairments identified by the children included being able to go to the front of the queue at Disney World, getting free tickets to wrestling matches and receiving a football signed by members of a famous football team. However, a few children did report less welcome aspects of having an impairment. Some talked about the effects on their health. A 14-year-old boy had repeated chest infections leading to regular hospital admissions; a girl talked about the pain associated with her impairment.

At times the children also identified what Thomas calls "barriers to doing". Physical restrictions they had come up against included lack of accessible transport to events, lack of access to leisure facilities and clubs, and aspects of the built environment. Adolescents and teenagers were more affected than younger children. While there was a range of organized activities for the latter, there were fewer attractive and/or accessible social and recreational opportunities on offer to help disabled teenagers progress from what Cavet (1998) called the 'organised' leisure of childhood to the 'casual' leisure of adolescence. This has been described as the peak time of leisure need (Hendry *et al.*, 1993) yet many disabled adolescents are excluded. One 14-year-old boy reported that his local Shopmobility scheme only had adult wheelchairs while another teenager, complaining about the inaccessibility of a local youth club, commented:

> *I think it would be better if they [disabled teenagers] could join in with everyone else because they should be treated the same as everyone else and do the same things.*

(Connors and Stalker, 2003, p. 49)

As these examples imply, sometimes the young people were made to feel different from others, in an uncomfortable way. The incidents which upset them most, and which were reported more often than barriers to doing, were what Thomas calls "barriers to being". Almost half the youngsters reported incidents of being bullied, including name-calling, being excluded from peer conversations and activities, money extraction and occasionally physical violence. Bullying took place at school and in the local neighbourhood.

However, the young people were not necessarily passive victims of bullying. Some had taken steps to deal with it, apparently successfully. Strategies ranged from reporting the bullies to parents or teachers, facing up to them with parental support in the background or, in a couple of cases apparently, giving as good as they got. Several children said the bullying was now a thing of the past. For a small number, however, it was a relentless and very distressing experience.

Some young people reported barriers arising from institutional policies or parenting strategies. First, it seemed from the children's reports, often supported by their parents' separate accounts, that a number of mainstream schools had not thought through their

inclusion policies. Having welcomed disabled children into the classrooms, the tendency was then to ignore their difference, rather than provide the support necessary to accommodate each child's individual needs. For example, during a fire drill at one school, a 14-year-old boy who used a wheelchair had been the only person left in the building. Lifts were out of bounds during fire practice but no contingency plan had been made to evacuate him. Not only did this incident make him feel like the odd one out, he was worried about what would happen if there was a real fire. Another report concerned a wheelchair user taken into the younger children's playground by her Special Needs assistant at break time, the latter apparently thinking she was 'safer' there. Not surprisingly, the girl wanted to be with her friends in the other playground. Complaints from her parents had not been effective in changing this practice.

Secondly, while some parents encouraged their children to lead as 'ordinary' a life as possible, others adopted a more cautious and protective approach. This could cause conflict with adolescents who were at the stage of wanting greater independence and freedom from parental stricture. For example, two young people with mobility difficulties were not allowed to cross busy roads, which meant they could not visit friends. One girl was challenging her mother's efforts to keep her as a 'little girl', a phrase her mother also used. The daughter said:

> *She's got to understand that she can't rule my life any more. Because when I get older she's just going to tell me what to do but I just want to make up my own mind because she's always deciding for me, like what's best for me and sometimes I get angry. She just doesn't realise that I'm grown up now but soon I'm going to be 14 and I won't be a wee girl any more.*
>
> (Connors and Stalker, 2003, p. 41)

There is nothing in the girl's words to indicate that she has an impairment: she was probably voicing the views of many non-disabled 13-year-olds. However, it is possible that the mother was more protective of her daughter because of the perceived vulnerability arising from her impairment.

In summary, overall, the young people presented themselves as having relatively happy and ordinary lives, with many similarities to non-disabled children's experiences. Most had a pragmatic attitude to their impairment. Some had come across barriers to doing, notably inaccessible buildings or transport. What bothered the young people most, however, was what Thomas calls psycho-emotional disablism, whether originating from individuals or institutions. Through these different manifestations of disablism, the youngsters were at risk of being excluded from certain activities and relationships, of feeling hurt and/or patronized and in some cases, over-protected. Nevertheless, at this relatively young age, difference was not a major theme and the risks do not appear to differ greatly from those faced by other young children and adolescents.

Life as a Disabled Young Person

This two-year study (Watson *et al.*, 2000), conducted by a team of researchers from the Universities of Leeds and Edinburgh, was part of a research programme called *Children 5–16: Growing into the twenty-first century*, funded by the Economic and Social Research Council. The research aimed to explore disabled adolescents' experiences and perceptions of impairment, and their relationships with family, peers and professionals, taking account of structural and cultural factors shaping the children's lives. The young people in this study were aged between 11 and 16, had a range of impairments and lived north and south of the border. The researchers used ethnographic methods, beginning with participant observation involving 300 children in 14 schools, followed by in-depth work with 165 youngsters who took part in one-to-one, paired or group interviews. The study was informed by the social model of disability.

Watson *et al.* report four key findings. First, they found that the young people were subject to a high degree of adult surveillance. Some wanted greater privacy: one child said "It may be hard to believe but even I have things that I want to keep private" (p. 13). Some said that their relationships with non-disabled children could be adversely affected by the constant presence of their adult assistants. As a result, for many children, the nature and scope of their social relationships, both within and outside school, were restricted. They tended to spend a lot of their leisure time with parents in adult places and have few social contacts outside the family. In addition, it was often difficult for them to access the kind of spaces where adolescents like to hang out, such as fast food outlets or shopping malls. At the same time, some of the young people found ways to resist or subvert adult surveillance and to assert their independence. They spoke to the researchers about feeling more capable and independent than adults realized. Box 6.4 contains an extract from Davis *et al.* (2000), a paper presenting findings from the same study, and reports the following interaction at school between the researcher John, a pupil called Bobby and an assistant called Sharon. The latter seriously underestimates Bobby's abilities:

Box 6.4   A conversation between a teaching assistant, a researcher and a pupil

Sharon: Well John did you see the [football] game last night?

John: Aye, a wis there . . .

Sharon: Bobby, did you watch the game last night?

Bobby: Aye

Sharon: [*looking at John as if to say "I don't believe him watch this I'll catch him out"*] Who won then?

Bobby: [*puts his hands in the air and gets frustrated*] uh uh uh [*like he's trying to spit something out but he just can't*]

Sharon: See he doesn't know [*said in a triumphal tone, then whispers, even though Bobby can still hear her*] A don't think he really knows what's going on. A really don't think he understands.

John [*Bobby is really pissed off with this and shakes his hands and head. I'm sure he watched the game because he spoke to me in signs earlier. Also I think he's finding it difficult to answer her question because the game was a draw and he can't say that word . . .*] Look a know that he doesn't usually watch the football but A'm sure he saw this game. Aye, Bobby, now you tell me with signs, how many did Rangers score?

Bobby: [*puts up one finger*]

John: . . . and how many did we [Celtic] get?

Bobby: [*puts up one finger*]

John: So the score was one one?

Bobby: Aye [*said with triumph and gestures at Sharon with his hand as if to say so there*].

John: And which team were lucky?

Bobby: [*really laughing at the assistant because she's a Rangers supporter, he uses a word John has rarely heard him speak*] Isss [us].

Sharon: . . . That's really good Bobby a nivir realised that.

The second main finding was that the children were at risk of being seen only through the lens of impairment. For example, when children were 'naughty' in class, teachers attributed this to impairment. One boy displaying what the authors call "age appropriate bad behaviour" was labelled as having Attention Deficit Hyperactivity Disorder. When disabled pupils in mainstream schools were late for class or failed to complete their homework, such transgressions were ignored. They were not tolerated among non-disabled children, however, who resented what they saw as the unfair privileges accorded to their disabled peers: thus difference was reinforced in a negative way. Other ways in which individual children may have differed from their peers, as well as the similarities they shared, were often overlooked by adults. Within most children's services, impairment took precedence over dimensions of gender and ethnicity. The perceived boundaries between what was considered 'normal' and what was seen as 'different' were constantly reinforced at school in the way physical and social space was used, and through the policy of inclusive and segregated education. Even the children attending mainstream schools were often separated from their non-disabled peers:

> They were labelled and put together in the class, told which table they should sit at for lunch and they were supervised as a group. Often this reinforced their sense of difference. One care worker said "They find it very difficult to make up their own minds. We have to tell them what to do, help them decide."
>
> (Watson *et al.*, 2000, p. 14)

Thirdly, the disabled youngsters encountered various difficulties in relationships with their peers, including bullying. They described physical, emotional and verbal bullying, including name calling, being kicked and hit and excluded from peer groupings. In the course of participant observation, the authors witnessed these behaviours, and noticed the impact this had on young people's social relationships and sense of self. Watson *et al.* suggest this was also true for youngsters who may not have been bullied themselves but knew that other disabled children were being picked on because of their perceived difference. However, the authors point out that some young people were well integrated within their peer groups, enjoyed many friendships and had positive social relationships.

In several cases, moving from a mainstream primary school to a segregated secondary school led to loss of important friendships. Where relationships with non-disabled children did develop in mainstream settings, these could be dominated by assumptions of need and care, with the latter acting as guides or helpers rather than playmates and equals.

Fourthly, Watson *et al.* explored how the children developed a sense of identity, stressing that identity and ideas about difference are not fixed entities 'out there' but are socially constructed, the result of an interaction of a range of factors including impairment, structure and culture. Unlike those in Connors and Stalker's study, these – on average, slightly older – adolescents apparently did see themselves as different although, as in the other research, this only became an issue for them in certain contexts. For example, one girl described how wheelchair basketball equalized social relationships and, as she put it, "in some situations I'm not, we're not, always disabled" (p. 19). At times the 'disability category' was used to claim special treatment: "Can we go early, Miss, 'cos we're disabled?" (p. 19).

In summary, Watson *et al.*'s findings suggest that disabled adolescents are at risk of experiencing excessive adult surveillance, being viewed only in terms of impairment, facing barriers and inequalities in their relationships with non-disabled peers and being labelled with a socially constructed notion of disability. The young people negotiated, challenged and at times reinforced these different processes. Watson *et al.* highlight periods of transition, particularly from primary to secondary school and from secondary school to adulthood, as times presenting particular opportunities and threats.

What's Happening? How Young People with Learning Disabilities and Their Parents/Carers Understand Anxiety and Depression

It is well established that people with learning disabilities are at greater risk of developing mental health difficulties than the population at large: recent research has shown that this may be particularly true of young people. It is estimated that at any one time about 40% of young people with learning disabilities are experiencing significant mental health problems compared with 10% of their non-disabled peers (Emerson, 2003). The study discussed below explored the views and experiences of young people with learning disabilities who were experiencing anxiety and depression. It is important for practitioners to be aware of this group's vulnerability to mental health difficulties, particularly in the light of evidence that such problems often go unrecognized and thus untreated (Foundation for People with Learning Disabilities, 2002). However, it should also be stressed that, just as disability cannot automatically be equated with risk, it would be wrong to imply that all young disabled people experience anxiety and depression: many do not – or at least to no greater extent than any other young people negotiating the transition to adulthood.

This two-year study, conducted by Wilson *et al.* (2005), was part of a research programme funded by the Foundation for People with Learning Disabilities. It set out to explore understandings of anxiety and depression among young people with learning disabilities who were experiencing these conditions, and its impact on their lives. Seventeen participants aged 16–26 were recruited through a variety of settings, such as schools, colleges and community learning disability teams, in two health board areas in central Scotland. Using an ethnographic approach, the researchers made regular visits to each of the young people over a 6- to 12-month period, spending time with them in school, college or at home. An innovative aspect of the study was the use of disposable cameras and video diaries. The young people were given cameras to take photographs of whatever aspects of their day-to-day lives they wished to record, and some were also lent camcorders. These methods had a number of advantages: they helped facilitate conversation in later meetings as the researcher and the young person looked at the photographs and/or film together, enabled insight into aspects of the young person's life that might not otherwise have emerged while also giving the young people some control over data collection. Semi-structured interviews were also carried out with parents and various professionals working with each young person.

The research identified a number of causes for the young people's emotional difficulties. First, some had complex lives, were living in difficult social or family circumstances and/or had experienced a striking number of traumatic life events, including the loss of loved ones through bereavement or parental separation. Family tensions and conflicts were a source of considerable distress and concern to several participants, some of whom reported that their parents imposed what they considered unfair restrictions on what they were allowed to do. Some young people were acting as carers for parents who had their own difficulties.

The young people also reported ups and downs with their friends. Several seemed to have regular 'fallings out' with their classmates or fellow students and some also reported experiences of being bullied or harassed when they were out and about. A few appeared preoccupied with what others thought about them, perhaps reflecting low self-esteem on their part. For example, a community psychiatric nurse working with one teenager said the girl compared herself unfavourably to her siblings and even her young nephews/nieces who apparently could count better than her. This was echoed by the girl's mother who reported her daughter saying "I wish I wisnae born; I'm different from everybody else".

Several young people talked about their desire to have a boyfriend or girlfriend, and some were depressed about not having such a relationship. Sexuality was a major concern for one participant who reported having a 'terror' of gay men.

Many of the youngsters had little to occupy them during the day and expressed frustration about the absence of meaningful activity and purpose in their lives. One or two spent much of the day sleeping; watching TV and videos was another common way to pass the time. Several spent most of their free time at home with their parents, which could give rise to tensions and, in some cases, rows. Some participants lacked confidence in relation to aspects of everyday life such as travelling by themselves on buses or trains, which significantly restricted their range of activities and level of independence. In addition, some of the young people had medical conditions such as epilepsy or bowel problems, which caused them anxiety and sometimes embarrassment, again limiting their ability and confidence to lead fuller lives. Box 6.5 contains a pen picture of one teenager in the study.

Box 6.5   Case study of Sam

Sam is 16 years old and lives in a deprived inner city environment. He attends a special school. Following his mother's death a couple of years ago, and not knowing his father, Sam went to live with his cousin and her small child. Sam had difficulty coming to terms with his bereavement and the subsequent changes in his life. The relationship with his cousin suffered as a result and she had begun to wonder if she could carry on looking after him. Sam started to harm himself, putting himself at risk of serious injury, if not death. He described how he cut himself:

I kept doing it and I thought I would never do it too deep but then one night I was really, I don't know, I was pure pissed off, don't know how and I don't know what made me feel like that, I just felt pure that I didn't want to be in this world any more. . . . and I just sat up in my room on my bed and then I was doing it nice and slow and then I just went pure deep and it went right through my hand and I was lying in my bed pure screaming and then I stopped screaming and I was just like that, shutting my eyes and I was all blood on my quilt and all that and then my uncle came up the stair and he ran to the phone, he phoned [the carer].

On other occasions, Sam's feelings of despair could turn to aggression and thus he could pose a risk to other people. Sometimes he went out at night, 'growling' at passers by, as if trying to pick a fight. He was also involved in violent incidents at school, where he was convinced that nobody liked him. Fortunately, however, the head teacher was supportive, working with Sam to show him that both pupils and teachers cared about him. She contacted the social services department and Sam was allocated a social worker. It took Sam a few months to trust him but gradually together they explored the emotions and events underlying Sam's difficulties. The social worker referred Sam to bereavement counselling and psychological services where he was diagnosed with low mood/depression and 'impulsivity'.

The social worker helped improve the relationship between Sam and his cousin. Over time, Sam settled down a little better at school and came to accept the structure and discipline of that environment.

In summary, the young people in this study were recruited on the basis that they had either been diagnosed with anxiety or depression, or else professionals working with them were concerned about their emotional well-being. Therefore it is not a representative sample of the population of young people with learning disabilities. Nor, however, is it wholly atypical, given the high incidence of mental health difficulties among this group. The anxiety and/or depression experienced by these young people were caused by a range of factors and circumstances, some of which occur randomly and would be expected to cause distress to any young person, such as bereavement or family conflict. Other issues could be seen as relating to impairment and/or social barriers or, more likely perhaps, an interaction between the two, leaving the young people at risk of running into a range of barriers as they tried to negotiate the transition to adulthood. Thus they experienced difficulties in developing trouble-free friendships, forming romantic and/or sexual relationships, finding or sustaining meaningful occupation, achieving independent travel and, in some cases, dealing with physical health problems. Like the two studies discussed above, ideas of similarity, difference and *identity* are important underlying themes but with this older age group, appear to have taken on greater resonance. The findings indicate a need for a much wider range of support, both practical and emotional, to help young people overcome these obstacles and achieve their full potential.

'It Doesn't Happen to Disabled Children': Child Protection and Disabled Children and Young People

This document is different from the three publications discussed above in that it does not report the results of one study. Rather, it is a review of research (Miller, 2003) which forms one chapter in a report produced by the National Working Group on Child Protection and Disability (2003) set up by the NSPCC. The report explores a number of key issues and concerns about disabled children and child protection, drawing on research findings and practice experience, and makes a series of recommendations for future policy in the field.

There has been limited research in the UK about risk factors facing disabled children in relation to child protection, but Miller discerns three main categories of risk from the literature. First, attitudes and assumptions surrounding disabled children create both a vulnerability to abuse and a risk that disabled children will not be listened to if they try to report abuse. This is compounded by a failure among carers and professionals to recognize the indications of abuse in disabled children.

Second, inadequacies in service provision can exacerbate risk. Families with disabled children may be poorly supported and become physically and socially isolated – known to be a risk factor for abuse. Organizational and skill gaps between professionals working in the child protection system and those working with families with disabled children can create barriers to effective protection. Many disabled children lack effective assistance with communication and even where they do have communication systems, these may not include appropriate words or pictures to convey an abusive experience. Disabled children are often overlooked in consultation exercises with young people so they lack opportunities to express their views and feelings. Many do not receive adequate sex education.

Third, factors relating to impairment may also play a part. Disabled children may require intimate care from a number of caregivers, increasing their vulnerability to abusive practices. They may have less capacity than other children to resist or avoid abuse and in some cases they may have limited understanding of what is being done to them. The latter circumstance does not in any way lessen the offence or the potential harm caused. Disabled children living away from home are particularly vulnerable to abuse (Utting, 1997 cited in Miller, 2003).

On the positive side, Miller reports some lessons from research about how best to protect disabled children from abuse. At the level of society, a major shift in attitudes is needed so that disabled children are seen and valued as equal citizens with the same rights as any others. The safeguarding of disabled children must be made a priority, with individuals in all settings recognizing their responsibility to act when appropriate. At community level, a choice of safe

---

Box 6.6   Experiences of abuse among young disabled people

"It ruined my life. I still find it difficult to talk about"
            24-year-old disabled adult, sexually abused by a care worker in school

"She couldn't tell us she had been hit but I couldn't see what else could have caused the bruises. But nothing happened...as far as I know, whoever did it still works there"
            Mother of a 13-year-old girl with learning disabilities

"I worry that we accept levels of neglect and really poor quality of care that we wouldn't if it was an able-bodied child"
            Social worker

Report of the National Working Group on Child Protection and Disability (2003, p. 9)

and accessible community and leisure services is needed, along with effective networks and support systems and policies and practices within schools and services which safeguard, respect and empower disabled children. This will include guidelines on intimate care, behaviour management and the recruitment, screening, training and supervision of staff. At carer level, there is a need for better co-ordinated and multi-agency support for carers, consultation with disabled children about aspects of their care, and awareness-raising among carers about disabled children's vulnerability to abuse and the indicators of it. As far as children themselves are concerned, policy makers and practitioners must consult them, offer choice and ensure individual children do not become isolated. Disabled children should be given sex education and made aware of safety issues.

In summary, children with impairments are at significantly higher risk of all forms of abuse than their non-disabled counterparts. This can be attributed to a number of factors which can in turn be related to Thomas's social relational model of disability encompassing impairments (such as reduced capacity to understand or resist), barriers to doing (inadequate provision) and barriers to being (attitudes towards and assumptions about disabled children). It is not helpful for practitioners to adopt an overly controlling approach. Rather, research highlights various ways in which disabled children can be better protected. However, we still do not know enough about child protection in relation to disability.

Summary

- It should not be assumed that adolescents are automatically 'at risk' because they have a physical, sensory or cognitive impairment.
- Nor, however, can it be assumed that these children are immune from abuse. The incidence of abuse is over three times greater among disabled children than their non-disabled peers.
- At any one time, approximately 40% of young people with learning disabilities are experiencing mental health difficulties.
- Disabled adolescents face a range of barriers in their everyday lives, ranging from material and physical barriers to social and attitudinal ones. This opens them to risks of social exclusion and denial of their human rights.
- Research suggests that the transition from primary to secondary school may present particular risks for some disabled adolescents, including loss of friendships and moving into segregated educational settings.
- Many disabled children develop effective strategies for dealing with the barriers they face.
- Disabled adolescents should have the right to take reasonable, well-informed and supported risks as part of the 'normal' process of growing up and becoming independent. Like other youngsters, they should be allowed to learn from their mistakes.

Further Reading

Grant, G., Goward, P., Richardson, M. and Ramcharan, P. (2005) (Eds) *Learning disability: A life cycle approach to valuing people*. Part 3: *Independence: Adolescence and the younger adult*. Open University Press: Maidenhead.

Priestley, M. (2003) *Disability: A life course approach*, Chapters 3 and 4. Polity Press: Oxford.

Sellars, C. (2002) *Risk assessment in people with learning disabilities*. Blackwell Publishing: Oxford.

Shakespeare, T. (2006) *Disability rights and wrongs*. Routledge: London.

Discussion Questions

1. What are the main risks facing disabled adolescents today and how can young people be supported to deal with them?
2. How far are the risks facing disabled adolescents a result of impairment and/or material and social barriers?
3. How can we think about disability within a resilience framework? What can be done to promote resilience among such young people?

Chapter 7

Anti-social Behaviour

Ann Hagell

Programme Director Adolescent Mental Health, Nuffield Foundation;
Editor, Journal of Adolescence

- ■ Introduction
- ■ Describing anti-social behaviour
- ■ Causes and pathways to anti-social behaviour
- ■ Time trends at the population level
- ■ Conclusions – what do we need to do?

LEARNING OBJECTIVES

Once you have read this chapter you should be able to:

1 Understand the causes of anti-social behaviour and the way that negative cycles develop.

2 Appreciate the overlap between being anti-social and being vulnerable.

3 Appreciate the differences between causes of individual behaviour, and causes of time trends at the population levels.

4 Have a sense of the real extent of the problem and the importance of media and public discussions in our perceptions of what is going on.

5 Appreciate individual differences and what can be done to foster resilience.

Adolescence, Risk and Resilience: Against the odds. John Coleman and Ann Hagell (eds.).
Published in 2007 by John Wiley & Sons, Ltd

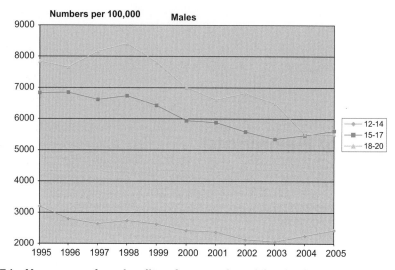

Figure 7.1   Young men found guilty of, or cautioned for, indictable offences per 100 000 population, by age group, in England and Wales, 1995–2005
Source: Chart 6.2 (MALES ONLY) from *Key Data on Adolescence, 2007* (Coleman and Schofield, 2007).

Introduction

There has rarely been a period in recent history when so much attention, debate, resources and law-making activity have been focused on anti-social behaviour by young people. We seem rather obsessed with the topic. Newspapers are full of it, solutions are suggested by everyone and the causes (and thus appropriate targets for intervention) are discussed everywhere you turn. We run the risk of thinking that we are overwhelmed with anti-social behaviour in the younger age group, but in fact youth crime among young males has been falling for a number of years (see Figure 7.1). The problem is that anti-social behaviour acts as a sort of lightning rod for our concerns about our lives, the society we live in, the position of children within it, and our philosophies on rights and responsibilities.

It is quite difficult to find a way through the mass of material and opinion that is available on the topic and to get an accurate sense of what is actually happening. At the start it is worth just trying to ensure we keep some kind of perspective in mind. Most young people in the 10–20 years age group are essentially not anti-social in the way they interact. Most are networked into their local communities through their schools, their neighbours, their leisure time activities and their part-time jobs. The main task of adolescence is to firm up a sense of identity. Taking some risks and testing boundaries is part of that. However, despite the importance of their peers at this time, most are attached to their parents (even if they do argue), fond of their siblings (ditto) and, although they may occasionally let loose and take risks, they are not fundamentally criminal. We do them a disservice, as an age group, to think otherwise.

On the other hand, virtually everyone gets involved in something that would be classified as anti-social at some point, often when they are teenagers or young adults. To this extent it is also useful to be reminded that anti-social behaviour is both (a) very varied and (b) on a continuum. Most of us are capable of doing things that offend other people. In fact, one-third of adult men will have acquired a criminal record by the time they are in their thirties. This sounds shocking, but with criminal records given for a very wide range of behaviours it is not so unlikely. Figures from the Home Office's 2003 Crime and Justice Survey (a nationally representative self-report offending survey including around 4300 young people aged 11–25 years) reported one-third of young men and one-fifth of young women committing acts of anti-social behaviour in the previous 12 months. This went up to about 40% of the 14- to 16-year-olds (Hayward and Sharp, 2005).

These two sets of statements (most young people are not persistently anti-social, and most people get involved in some anti-social behaviour at some time) are not as contradictory as they seem. The figures cited above cover nuisance anti-social behaviour, and violent anti-social behaviour forms a very small part, yet we often think anti-social behaviour means violence. In addition, it is important to remember that anti-social behaviour is often something that people get involved in for a short length of time, but that then passes. Most people grow out of it. Persistent young offenders are much rarer, and account for only about 3–6% of the general population of this age group (Rutter *et al.*, 1998).

Describing Anti-social Behaviour

In England and Wales, the Home Office's definition of anti-social behaviour is "any behaviour that impacts on other people in a negative way" (Home Office, 2006). The first thing to note here is that this is a socially determined construct. If no one is offended or upset, then the act is not defined as anti-social. The sorts of behaviour involved as described in the Home Office's current website are rowdy, nuisance behaviours, dealing and buying drugs on the street, anti-social drinking (and, slightly oddly, misuse of fireworks). In research terms the focus is often *crime* by young people, rather than all anti-social behaviour, and it is important to note that most juvenile crime is theft. This is largely shoplifting, but there is also a certain amount of car crime such as

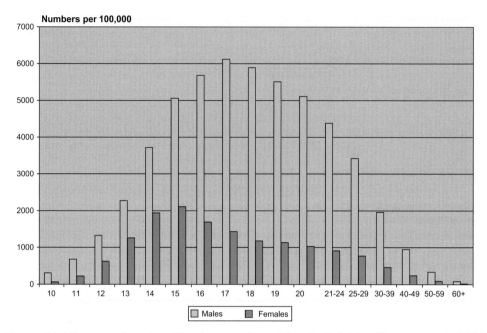

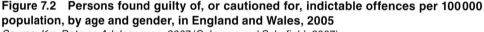

Figure 7.2   Persons found guilty of, or cautioned for, indictable offences per 100 000 population, by age and gender, in England and Wales, 2005
Source: *Key Data on Adolescence, 2007* (Coleman and Schofield, 2007).

taking and driving away ('TWOC' as it is known), offences involving drugs and alcohol, vandalism and burglary, and then there are officially defined violent crimes such as robbery, fighting and using weapons. In official UK statistics, approximately 17% of juvenile crime leading to a police or court disposal (a reprimand, final warning or conviction) is violent offending against the person, and a significant proportion of these offences are relatively minor (NACRO, 2006).

Young men are more anti-social than young women, at least by these definitions, but for some offences such as shoplifting the ratios are almost equal. The peak age of offending (see Figure 7.2) is usually in the late teens, and shows higher rates of offending for young men than young women (Rutter *et al.*, 1998).

With respect to our discussion about notions of risk, as outlined in Chapter 1 of this volume, anti-social behaviour provides a good illustration of the many different ways in which it can be conceptualized. First, there is a wealth of research on the *risk factors* that predict anti-social behaviour, and we will look at these in the next section. Second, anti-social behaviour is often what is thought of when '*risky behaviour*' is considered. Third, being anti-social clearly puts young people *at risk*, through, for example, dangerous driving, binge drinking and fighting. Finally, the way in which the term is most often encountered in the media is in relation to our fourth category, that of young people who *pose a risk to society*.

Causes and Pathways to Anti-social Behaviour

A considerable amount of research work over the last three decades has gone into determining the pathways to anti-social behaviour and the characteristics of the best interventions.

A certain amount, it is fair to say, is now known about these pathways. However, we do need to be careful not to muddle up what is *associated* with anti-social behaviour with what *causes* it. There is far too much cross-sectional work in this area, where assumptions are made about the directions of influence. In fact, we do know from longitudinal research that people select themselves into their environments, and are not just passive pawns in their own development. The processes are dynamic and iterative. All of the following feature in the story:

Individual Factors

- *Attention deficit and hyperactivity disorder (ADHD).* The spectrum of problems that come under the heading of ADHD have been shown to have clear links with later anti-social behaviour, and of all the individual factors, this group of problems are the strongest predictors of later difficulties. The link, however, is not just to anti-social behaviour, but tends to be with generally poor social functioning rather than with crime per se. ADHD consists of two main elements: hyperactivity (children who cannot sit still, fidget constantly, find it hard to get through a lesson and have higher than normal levels of activity) and attention problems (difficulties in concentrating on any task, inability to focus or to complete things). ADHD is generally considered to have strong neurobiological elements, and can run in families, suggesting genetic components.
- *Temperamental factors* are also predictors of later anti-social behaviour, and there is some overlap with ADHD in this respect. Impulsivity, for example, a heightened need for sensation-seeking, lack of control and aggressivity are all temperamental factors that seem to enhance the likelihood of problems developing, as people may not be able to (or want to) control their behaviour to the same extent as calmer children.
- *Cognitive impairment* is sometimes related to later anti-social behaviour, although as with all the risk factors, not all children with cognitive impairment will have behaviour problems. The links seem particularly through the child's verbal and planning skills, which relate to an ability to understand the consequences of actions.
- *A distorted style of social information-processing* has also been implicated, and this includes a tendency to wrongly attribute negative intentions to other people's behaviour, to misinterpret social interactions and to focus on aggressive behaviours by others.

There are likely to be at least some *biological substrates* for some of these factors, which operate in a probabilistic fashion as part of the multifactorial causation. Genes (probably lots of different ones) act to set up a liability to develop anti-social behaviour in childhood through dimensions such as impulsivity and hyperactivity, *given the presence* of other environmental risk factors as well. That last bit is very significant. There is little of the original 'nature–nurture' argument left in the science of human development any more; what is clear now is that dispositions interact with environments and both work together (Rutter *et al.*, 1997a).

Psycho-social Features

- *Parenting* is the central and critical risk factor here. Research has shown that coercive/hostile parenting, abuse and neglect, and ineffectual parenting are all associated with an increased risk of challenging behaviour in the children (e.g., Patterson, 1982). The more negative the features of parenting, the worse the outcome for the child. Parenting possibly has an impact through the maladaptive development of social relationships, or through the learning of inappropriate and coercive behaviour patterns. The mechanisms are not quite clear.

• *Delinquent peer groups* is another key risk factor. Disruptive young people seek out like-minded friends and peers, and then those groups of friends continue to reinforce disruptive behaviour. Delinquent peers may not be the root cause of the problem in the first place, but they may make it more likely that initial liability is translated into actual behaviours.

What is parental monitoring? The problems of sorting out cause and effect

Håkan Stattin and Margaret Kerr from Örebro University in Sweden have shown that parental monitoring in adolescence may not be quite what it was originally conceptualized to be. Monitoring older children's whereabouts, and what they are doing, is often held to be a crucially important element of effective parenting for reduction of anti-social behaviour. But what does this sort of 'monitoring' really mean?

They suggest that parental monitoring in later years may in fact be a *result* of aspects of the relationship between parent and adolescent, rather than a predictor of it. They claim that, contrary to earlier writers, controlling, supervising and monitoring do not on their own lead to better outcomes. Instead, what is underlying the relationship between the variables is the accuracy of parents' knowledge about their children. They say that "monitoring is not what the term implies, a parental activity. It is more a child's activity". In other words, it relates to what the child decides to tell the parent. By unpacking monitoring, and revealing parental knowledge, they have questioned the constructs we are using to define parenting.

Rather than teaching people to 'monitor', Håkan and Margaret say "Parents should try to optimise conditions for the child to disclose information about his or her everyday experiences". This often gets a laugh in an audience of people including parents of adolescents, who struggle to extract much useful information from their moody teenagers! However, there is a serious point to make about the importance of communication and trust, as well as supervision.

If the positive associations between monitoring and outcomes actually just reflect how much the children tell the parents, the first thing one obviously thinks about is where does parental knowledge come from? What is it based on? We need more research on this.

Stattin and Kerr (2000)

Environmental Factors

• *School effects* can contribute to anti-social behaviour, both through the quality of the school as a social institution, and through the influences of other pupils through bullying and delinquent peer groups. It is very important to acknowledge how large a part of young people's lives school forms.

- *Area differences* may also be important. Their precise role is still open to debate, but some data are emerging that the area sets a context for parenting, and that certain sorts of parenting might be difficult in certain sorts of neighbourhoods if it goes against the general trend. Area features such as community disorganization and neglect, and lots of community instability in terms of people moving in and out, can also contribute.
- *Media*, again, is a topic that is still subject to considerable (and heated) debate, at least with respect to its effect on individual behaviour. However, at the collective level the media clearly has some role to play, and this is partly their role in our shared representation about young people and their tendency to be anti-social. There is currently a great deal of interest in our vision of childhood and youth, and in the damage that can be done by constantly negative portrayals. Rob MacDonald touches on these topics in his chapter on social exclusion (Chapter 8).
- *Availability of guns, weapons and drugs.* It is likely that the social change witnessed in drug use and misuse over the last 50 years has some part to play in current trends in anti-social behaviour. There has been a sustained and long-term increase in drug use by young people since the Second World War, and at least for some types of behaviour crime and drugs are related. Use of drugs may lead to stealing to sustain an addiction, or may lead to involvement with organized crime and violence, for example. However, the peak for drug use is later than that for anti-social behaviour, and the ways in which the two activities influence each other are not yet entirely clear. In addition, availability and preparedness to use weapons are also likely to be important. Where gun laws are more relaxed, more young people die from gunshot wounds.

Causes sometimes operate in their own right (such as inconsistent parenting) or sometimes they may be indirect. In the case of poverty, for example, research has suggested that it operates by making it more difficult for parents to parent effectively rather than lack of money being a direct cause (Conger *et al.*, 1994). *Most of these are not either/or* – the way we parent our children will affect their choices of peers at adolescence, for example. It is also important to bear in mind the bigger social context in which all these variables are situated; as we commented in Chapter 1, the status of young people, the media's collective sense of young people as problematic, the readiness of the public to interpret behaviour as threatening and uncomfortable, all these things play a part in understanding and managing risk.

Resilience

It is clear that some children are *more resilient* than others, even if they experience the same patterning of risk factors. The research literature is beginning to point to a number of protective factors that may help promote resilience in the face of adversity. The evidence here is not very extensive, but might include: higher intellectual ability, a redeeming and warm relationship with one person in the family, positive school experiences and having fewer delinquent peers. As we noted in Chapter 1, resilience is not just the absence of risk factors, it is the ability to cope even in the face of a range of difficulties.

Another important concept in resilience models is the *turning point* – such as moving out of a neighbourhood, which might interrupt the flow from risk factors to delinquency. In Chapter 1 we described the importance of interrupting chain reactions of negative events, and this is particularly relevant to anti-social behaviour where things tend to build on each other in a downward spiral. In this regard, Michael Rutter, one of the leading researchers in this field, has argued that it is not just the 'individual factors' that count, but the 'processes', the ways in which things develop – that is, the 'knock-on' effects. He has thus concluded that in order to try to increase resilience, we need to increase positive chain reactions by opening up new and better opportunities.

In a report on the protective factors identified in the American National Longitudinal Study on Adolescent Health, Benard et al. (2001) show how a range of parental, school and individual characteristics all help. As with earlier studies, caring relationships, high expectations and opportunities to take part and contribute all have a positive influence in the face of adversity. The authors particularly emphasize the importance of strong relationships in all domains of life, and conclude that "Prevention and education reform efforts must focus on environmental change – on creating healthy, inviting climates and systems – versus 'fixing youth'" (p. 5). Goldstein and Brooks (2005), who have written extensively on resilience, also note the importance of helping young people to develop and improve a skill set that includes stress-management skills and problem-solving skills, empathy and communication, in order to enhance their ability to face daily stressors.

Finally, this leads us to an important point about the *lack of specificity*. The risk factors described in the previous sections are interesting, but they are also the same as those for lots of other outcomes. Children with a full deck of risk factors are likely to have all sorts of other overlapping needs, relating to drugs and mental health, for example. The research is clear, for example, that young offenders have elevated rates of depression, anxiety and self-harm (Hagell, 2003). Understanding and being prepared to tackle multiple needs is a key aspect of addressing anti-social behaviour in children. In addition, there is little specificity in our understanding of what makes young people resilient; it is not clear that there will be anything special about the factors that help in anti-social behaviour, when compared with factors that help in other situations of risk.

What we do know is that we cannot predict very accurately who is going to become anti-social, and we know that children with a pile-up of problems will have a range of difficulties and will need extra support. Early intervention has to be relatively benign, and to focus on bolstering resilience; we must not run the risk of stigmatizing young people by labelling them anti-social. If we do, this just becomes a self-fulfilling prophecy.

Time Trends at the Population Level

Has anti-social behaviour by young people increased, decreased or remained constant? This is a complicated question, and it depends in part on what time period we are looking at; it also depends on what constructs or aspects of anti-social behaviour we are interested in. Taking the longer perspective, anti-social behaviour *has* increased this century, and this is (a) an international trend and (b) accompanied by rises in a whole range of psycho-social problems experienced by young people (Rutter and Smith, 1995; Rutter et al., 1998). On the other hand, official crime statistics suggest that youth crime has fallen since the early 1990s (NACRO, 2006).

The first question is, are these real trends or are they artefacts of the data? Whole books have been written on this topic. There are two main sources of information, either accounts from individuals themselves or statistics from central records such as those collected by the police. Although there are differences, they match reasonably well. Self-report studies tend to show higher rates of offending, partly because they include crimes for which people are not caught. On the other hand, there tends to be more variation in official data, where changes to the law and processing recommendations can have dramatic effects on the numbers in the system. Overall, we are reasonably confident that the last 50 years of the twentieth century showed a considerable rise in anti-social behaviour by young people in the Western world, and that these rises were levelling off by the end of the century, if not earlier. This was not confined to anti-social behaviour but applied as well to other types of psycho-social problems (Collishaw *et al.*, 2004). More recently, the trends have been stable or downwards.

If we look at all the data from official as well as other types of studies, some particular things to note in the trends are:

- *Young women account for a greater proportion of youth crime than they used to.* The ratio of young men to young women in official crime statistics was around 11:1 in 1957, 7:1 in 1967, 4:1 in 1977 and nearly down to 3:1 in 1997. Differences remain most dramatic for the more serious crimes (13:1 for burglary). There is a possibility that biological sex or psychological gender add a risk all of their own, but this cannot explain the speed of this downward trend. Factors associated with offending in girls seem to be the same as in boys – we have no concrete research evidence to the contrary yet. So sex differences must be to do with differences in the occurrence and frequency of those underlying risk factors. Is parenting of young women becoming more like parenting of young men, perhaps? Are the peer groups that young people spend time with becoming more homogenous? We do not yet know the answers to these questions, but they raise interesting issues to do with social change and socialization patterns.
- *Violence is a growing problem (but it is important to keep this in context).* There were rises in violent anti-social behaviour in most European countries and the USA in the 1980s and 1990s. This included a rise in violence by young women but baseline for these statistics is very small indeed, so a large rise does not indicate a great increase in actual events, and in addition, violence by young women tends to be more expressive and less instrumental than that by young men. With respect to violence, the use of guns and other weapons represents a significant part of the problem, and this is on the increase.

Secondly, we need to know both why the population trends go up, and then why they come down again. The explanations for population trends can vary from explanations for individual behaviour. Take height, for example, which is approximately 80% inherited (and thus mostly genetic). Most parents will have come across a standard calculation for the prediction of their child's adult height from their own heights minus adjustments for parental gender. This is generally pretty accurate. However, in the first half of the twentieth century, the average height of boys in the country as a whole went up around 15 cm. This was due to diet (and thus the environment). The point is that while at the individual level genetics can be an excellent predictor of some variables, at the population level big changes can be seen that are essentially environmentally driven (Rutter *et al.*, 1998).

The explanations for the rises in anti-social behaviour during the twentieth century have to be about social change. There are a range of possible candidates, although at present there

is very little research evidence to guide the development of theory. The options (as suggested, for example, in Nuffield Foundation, 2004) might include:

- Issues relating to *education and educational experiences.* In the UK there is a sense in which the transition to secondary school may be becoming more demanding for certain groups of adolescents. In addition, with more emphasis on academic testing, and less in the way of alternatives for the non-academic members of the 14–19 age group, it may be that this period has become more stressful for some than it may have been in previous decades.
- Beyond education, are the changes in adolescent behaviour and well-being something to do with *non-school time*? Is the balance right in terms of structured and unstructured outside school activities? Has something changed about peer group interactions and non-family socialization?
- Does *employment* play a role, in a world where both (a) a significant proportion of children work during their school years, yet (b) far fewer than before have any kind of full-time work at the end of compulsory education? What sort of economic role do young people have compared with a quarter century ago, and how does this affect how they see themselves and their contribution?
- What is the role of issues relating to the *family context*? It seems that changes in family structure only make a modest contribution, but the possibility remains that there are other aspects of family context that make a difference. Are we parenting differently?
- Other issues relating to the *changing social situation*, particularly for young men, including increasing numbers remaining single or divorcing, high unemployment rates, increasing risk of imprisonment, increasing availability of drugs and alcohol.

These are interesting questions needing further research. But the underlying point here is that we need to consider whether something fundamental has changed in our society and we need to know how it has impacted on adolescents and their behaviour. It seems likely that changes in how they behave and relate to the rest of society should not be considered 'their fault', but should be thought of as a reaction to the context that we all provide for them. Can that context be improved?

What can we do to Help?

What does all this say about interventions? Interventions have to play to the positive, to enhance resilience, to reinforce good behaviour and to accept the limitations of what can be achieved. They have to tackle the family and peer influences, and to engage very hard-to-engage clients with assertive outreach. They have to be set within a context that appreciates the contributions young people can make to society as a whole, and that values their role. Policy also has to acknowledge that many will simply grow out of it, and that interaction with the criminal justice system can, in some cases, further damage young people. Because of this, every court in the UK has a statutory requirement to consider the welfare of any young person brought before it.

Programmes to stop offending

We know from a number of extensive reviews of the relevant research that there are some key elements of programmes that successfully intervene to reduce anti-social behaviour. These are:

- They should target specific behaviours (rather than offering counselling) and include social skills training and problem-solving.
- They should be clearly matched to the particular needs of the young person.
- They should be well structured and planned.
- They should be effectively supervised and monitored.
- They should be based on programmes that have been proven to work, and they should then remain true to the original programme model. These programmes tend to be based on a clear theoretical model that explains how they are anticipated to work.

But intervening is about more than this. Because of the extensive welfare needs of most young offenders, at the serious end of anti-social behaviour, intervening is also about supplementing and complementing the strengths of families and communities to provide stability and support for young people over long periods of time, and probably at considerable expense. There is no point in running in with an excellent six-month intervention if the child is without parents in its life, and is living from hand to mouth. Changing behaviour in children and young people is partly about specific interventions, but it is also about changing the context of young people's lives. We are not terribly good at state parenting; at providing an alternative if families cannot cope. Our records for children in care are woefully inadequate. Yet many young offenders who end up in custody, for example, will have spent some time in care first.

Education also plays a role in the general context. Most persistent young offenders are pretty much detached from the education system by about the age of 12 years. We are also not very good at educational provision for those who will be in the underachieving 50% of the population; those who do not get one to five GCSE passes at levels A–C (the national standard set within England and Wales by the Department for Education and Skills). We need to rethink how we provide incentives for underachievers and how we help them to value themselves if they are not contributing to government statistics for better-performing schools. Some will never get there, but they still need to live with us and feel they have a viable and valuable role to play in our society.

Intervention principles fully supported by research

There are a number of principles underpinning successful intervention that we can safely conclude are supported by existing research evidence, and are thus worth investing in:

- *Research says, respond quickly.* It is important, for learning, that outcomes are clearly contingent on behaviour. This works at a number of levels, both at home with families and in the parenting context, and also in schools and within the youth justice system. In this respect, for example, initiatives within the youth justice system, such as halving time from arrest to sentence, are generally a good idea. It also suggests, again within the youth justice system, an investment in detection. When only 3% of crimes result in disposals, then these disposals are unlikely to be having much impact on patterns of behaviour in the broader community.
- *Research says, it is the role of the community that matters.* Children need to live in communities, and even if they are removed because their behaviour is too troublesome to be dealt with locally, they will inevitably return to those communities relatively swiftly. We cannot thus ignore the importance of investing in community initiatives and support. Although it will be a necessary component of service delivery for some young people, locking them up will generally not solve the problem, as custody has not been proven to be an effective intervention. In the long term, support in the local community is the only real option.
- *Research says, take vulnerability into account.* The message about the overlap between anti-social behaviour and vulnerability is well supported by the research evidence. Most aggressive and violent young people, or persistent young offenders, are also victims – often of violence and abuse. As we have seen, the problems that lead to anti-social behaviour also predict a range of other poor outcomes. When helping young people in these situations, it is crucial to *expect* there to be drugs and alcohol problems. *Expect* them to have been abused and neglected, for their schema for close relationships to have been knocked about. Base your work with these young people on the assumption that they are difficult, needy, and will not respond.
- *Research says, things start to go wrong early and then escalate* in a cycle of negative reinforcement. The principles underlying large-scale preventative initiatives such as On Track and Sure Start are sound. However, a recent evaluation of a home-visiting intervention called Home-Start found that improvements measured among women visited by Home-Start were not significantly greater than among mothers with similar problems who were not visited (McAuley *et al.*, 2004). The evaluation of Sure Start suggested that for some very needy groups the outcomes were worse (Rutter, 2006b). Actually, putting this research

principle into practice requires a considerable degree of sophistication about targeting, in the sense of being very specific about what the programme is intended to achieve and how, with whom. It is important that findings about programmes that do work are not simply taken on trust and generalized to new populations without proper testing. It is often more complicated to get the intended effect that anticipated (see below).

Mentoring

The early work on the Big Brothers & Sisters programme in the USA was encouraging, yielding some positive intervention results. Meta-analyses showed benefits. In 2003 government funding of £850000 was announced to support mentoring schemes in England.

However, in a recently published article (Roberts *et al.*, 2004), researchers from an international team from the UK and USA revisited the evidence. They found that some intellectual 'jumps' had been made, and when they looked just at objective measuring tools, rather than self-reported improvements, then there was no evidence for an effect. This was particularly the case for non-directive mentoring programmes delivered by volunteers.

The authors worked with practitioners to identify what could be done to make mentoring work – this seemed to include being more directive, and including cognitive behaviour therapeutic elements. A blanket notion of mentoring as a positive input did not seem to be helpful; it was important to tighten up the elements that actually held the key to positive impacts.

Roberts *et al.* (2004)

- *Research says, intervene multimodally.* There are now a number of well-documented examples of what are known as 'multimodal' interventions, where attempts are made to help on a number of fronts at the same time. These include the introduction of Community Courts, based on models developed in the USA, where single buildings hold both courts and also treatment options such as drugs clinics, so that problems can be dealt with immediately and in the same location. Other examples include multi-systemic therapy (Henggeler *et al.*, 2002) and treatment foster care (Chamberlain, 2003). Evaluations of treatment foster care have shown that at 12 months, young people spent 60% fewer days incarcerated, had fewer arrests, ran away three times less often and used fewer hard drugs. Caregivers are paid around $30k per year, but overall there are financial net benefits. They deliver encouragement, and follow a behaviour management programme with clear rewards and sanctions. There are weekly family therapy sessions once the young people go home. The main message here is that it is not possible to solve these deeply entrenched problems just by targeting one risk factor. It is the pile-up of risk factors that matters. Similarly, other interventions that have been properly evaluated in the USA and Australia combine a parenting programme with a classroom management programme for teachers, and a training programme for the children themselves to improve cognitive skills (Seattle Social Development Project,

CASE STUDY: TOM

At the time that we met Tom he was in a Secure Training Centre, following a fairly spectacular and extensive history of offending. According to his files he was first convicted at age 12, and his offences included theft, taking cars, receiving stolen goods, burglary, shoplifting and failing to surrender to custody. Before he arrived in custody he had been of 'no fixed abode'.

He had a difficult and disrupted childhood. Around the time he turned 10 his mother and stepfather were reporting increasing problems in coping with his behaviour. As a result he had a number of placements outside the family and a failed reconciliation. He had been in children's homes and other secure placements before arriving in custody.

When he arrived the staff described him as being "one of the worst trainees". His communication skills were poor, and he was thought to have learning problems. He couldn't meet anyone's eye. He was tall and well built, so that he could seem threatening, and had a history of propensity to violence in previous settings.

Yet despite the poor auspices, good relationships were formed inside the centre. In custody he had anger management sessions, which he thought had helped the way he thought about problem solving – "I'd think before I smashed that window", he told us, "Before I'd just do it without thinking. And I can sit in a meeting now as well… before, I couldn't". He was given some skills, some ways of coping. This was a start. He also flourished in the stability of the environment, presumably because it was such a contrast to what he had known in his recent past.

On release, when we met with him again, he had continued to face a range of obstacles such as confusion in the family about where he was to live, resulting in continued instability in living arrangements, and difficulties getting a college placement, despite promises from services. In the meantime he had found a part-time job in a bakery, acquired through his father, and had been going to the gym. He strongly claimed to us that he had not offended and did not intend to (although he admitted to cycling whilst drunk, carrying a weapon, fighting and buying drugs, but he did not consider these proper offending), and he had reduced his drug use from cocaine to cannabis.

Tom was a complicated and difficult person, but he had a reservoir of charm that may have been a protective factor that allowed him to make the most of the opportunity for a change in direction. He had a good relationship with his youth justice worker; it was an unusual relationship of trust and endurance in his life. It was not clear whether he had enough resources to cope if things got more difficult, but with continued regular and intensive support it seemed possible that he could pull through. This was likely to be the real challenge to youth justice; it was the long haul, not the short intervention that would influence the final outcome.

Source: This case study is based on a young man taking part in a research evaluation of Medway Secure Training Centre (Hagell *et al*., 2000).

Hawkins *et al.*, 1999). This combined approach led to less violence, less drinking, more school commitment, etc. at age 18. However, it is important to note that, for example, with treatment foster care, the support needs for foster parents and staff working with them are very high, and consequently very expensive.

- Research says, even programmes with the strongest research credentials are at risk of failure at the delivery stage unless they are *faithfully replicated and implemented.*
- Research says, we have to be *in it for the long haul* if we are looking at a deeply entrenched problem. Work has to be reinforced over time, and in different settings.
- Research says, *there isn't one cause*, and then one effect. It is all reciprocal and dynamic, and there will be no simple solutions.

What we should not do

We can also be fairly clear from the research evidence that there are some things that do not work well. These include:

- Relying on punishment to change behaviour.
- Locking people up.
- Using short-sharp-shocks. Research on boot camps has shown that some elements of the supported life in the 'camps' may be useful but the punitive components are generally not.
- Allowing relaxation of gun laws or making it easier for people to acquire and use weapons.

Conclusions – What do we Need to do?

There are a number of ways in which we need to develop our approach to supporting and intervening in families where young people are difficult to manage. The underlying message of this book is that, in the face of a number of challenges, many young people can be encouraged to become more resilient and be supported to change direction, even when faced by a series of negative events and contexts that are making their lives (and those of the people around them) rather difficult. Anti-social behaviour is similar in this way to other issues tackled by other chapters. What makes it a particularly sensitive area is the overlap between anti-social behaviour and youth offending, and thus the overlap between child care needs and the need to protect other people. Media representations, policy initiatives, the need to be seen to be tackling issues that frighten people, all make it particularly difficult to see through the rhetoric to the clear messages arising from research about what we can do to help.

There are a number of important points to make in conclusion. First, we need to *get more sophisticated* about the role of different causal models in the development of problem behaviour. It is clear from research, for example, that different factors set off behaviour as triggers, compared with those creating long-term risk. Some factors act as proximal mediators for more distal risks – for example, parenting relationships provide the link between poverty and problems with children's behaviour. The challenge now is finding ways to translate this sophistication within causal models into the prevention and intervention programmes.

That said, we also need to be aware of the fact that popular interventions that have been well designed and robustly evaluated still largely *remain black boxes* – the young people go in one side and come out the other and we are not sure what is happening in between. A climate has been created in which it is widely held that these interventions are effective, and so they are rolled out nationally. They seem intuitively sensible; they speak to our common sense. However, we need to be careful until we really understand what is going on.

Second, it is crucially important that we take on board the need to appreciate the *limits of what can be achieved*. Overall reductions in problem behaviour are only likely to be of relatively small magnitude – for most of this chapter we have been discussing deeply entrenched behaviour for which people have been training for 13–14 years. A six-month intervention is unlikely to make the total difference. Research on health care has shown that interaction with the health system explains only around 10–12% of variation in the health of an individual. The estimate for reduction of offending is the same. The causal model for developing persistent offending (in particular) is very complicated. It is too much to expect that the criminal justice system can cure it on its own. We should appreciate and value small changes as they can still be important in the context of the quality of life of the young people involved.

Third, we need to ensure that we continue to *learn from history*. While we have a 200-year history of a secure juvenile estate in the UK, for example, we have a clear preference for reinventing the wheel with each new cycle of youth justice development, and it is hard to compare provision at one time with a new set of slightly different institutions at another time. Some psychologists are concerned that we are losing the expertise that we had build up in the 1970s and 1980s in, for example, the secure treatment centres and places like Glenthorne (Epps, 2006), and we need to ensure we build on what we know rather than simply inventing new initiatives in response to public pressure to be seen to be doing something.

Finally, and most importantly, we need to encourage more work on *resilience* and to design programmes that not only 'fix' problems but also help to inoculate and support young people against stressors and pressures, and address the general context in which they live. We have seen that anti-social behaviour can be thought of in all the various forms of 'risk' that we outlined in Chapter 1 of this volume; there are clear risk factors in evidence, anti-social behaviour involves a range of risky behaviours that also put young people at further risk, and anti-social behaviour is considered a great risk to society. In addition, evidence suggests that the range of features that enhance resilience in other areas also work for anti-social behaviour. The importance of close relationships, of enhancing positive views of the self, of making it clear that we can value the contribution young people make to society, of finding ways of helping young people who are excluded by their behaviour, of enhancing community assets, are all a crucial part of the story.

Of course, we need to take on board that none of this comes cheap. But the savings can be great, and the investments have to be made. The message of this chapter is that anti-social behaviour is complicated, and that intervening is relatively challenging. However, there is much to be hopeful about, and much that can be done. While the general media and many policy initiatives continue to stress the importance of punishment and 'getting tough', there is still a considerable body of support, from both research and policy, for prevention and intervention, not punishment. There is much that can be done to improve the effectiveness of preventative and rehabilitative programmes, and it is crucial that this work is done, as this is where successes are most likely in the long term. Prevention will not, of course, solve all the problems. However, research cited in this chapter illustrates the need to continue to build bridges between criminal justice and child care. Lessons for good practice have not traditionally been shared across this boundary, particularly at the more extreme end, but this is where effort needs to be placed in order to improve outcomes for young people.

Further Reading

Beinart, S., Anderson, B., Lee, S. and Utting, D. (2002) *Youth at risk? A national survey of risk factors, protective factors and problem behaviour among young people in England, Scotland and Wales.* Communities that Care: London. Downloadable summary on the JRF website at www.jrf.org.uk/knowledge/findings/socialpolicy/432.asp

Hagell, A. (2003) *Understanding and challenging youth offending.* Research in Practice Quality Protects Briefing No. 8. Department of Health, Research in Practice and Making Research Count: London. Downloadable at www.rip.org.uk

Hill, J. and Maughan, B. (2001) (Eds) *Conduct disorders in childhood and adolescence.* Cambridge University Press: Cambridge.

NACRO (2006) *Youth Crime Briefing: Some facts about children and young people who offend – 2004.* NACRO: London. Downloadable from www.nacro.org.uk

Sutton, C., Utting, D. and Farrington, D. (2004) *Support from the start: Working with young children and their families to reduce the risks of crime and anti-social behaviour.* Department for Education and Skills Research Brief No. 524. DfES: London. Downloadable at www.dfes.gov.uk/research/

Wilson, D., Sharp, C. and Patterson, A. (2006) *Young people and crime: Findings from the 2005 Offending, Crime and Justice Survey.* Home Office Statistical Bulletin 17/06. Home Office: London. Downloadable from http://www.homeoffice.gov.uk/rds/pdfs06/hosb1706.pdf

Websites

Home Office Crime Statistics

www.crimereduction.gov.uk/sta_index.htm

Home Office Research and Statistics Directorate

www.homeoffice.gov.uk/rds

National Family and Parenting Institute

www.familyandparenting.org

National Youth Agency

www.nya.org.uk

Trust for the Study of Adolescence

www.tsa.uk.com

On Track

http://www.homeoffice.gov.uk/rds/preventing1.html

Youth Justice Board

www.yjb.gov.uk

Discussion Questions

1. To what extent do you think public attitudes to punishment and locking up children can be challenged? Why is there such a need for punishment to be seen to be done when the research evidence suggests it is not very effective?
2. Where do you think we should be investing money within the system for helping young people with anti-social behaviour problems?
3. To what extent do anti-social behaviour problems reflect individual difficulties, and to what extent are they the product of the environment in which the child is living?
4. What is the role of social change in promoting and defining anti-social behaviour? Are young people as much of a 'general risk' to the public as the media makes out?

Chapter 8

Social Exclusion, Risk and Young Adulthood

Robert MacDonald

Professor, School of Social Sciences and Law, University of Teesside

---

LEARNING OBJECTIVES

Once you have read this chapter you should be able to:

1 Review critically some recent key approaches to understanding socially excluded and 'at risk' young adults.
2 Understand some recent sociological research on youth transitions in poor neighbourhoods.

Adolescence, Risk and Resilience: *Against the odds.* John Coleman and Ann Hagell (eds.).
Published in 2007 by John Wiley & Sons, Ltd

3 Be aware of the difficulties in applying, straightforwardly, influential and popular notions of 'risk' to the school-to-work, criminal and drug-using careers of young people growing up in poor neighbourhoods.

Introduction

This chapter is written from a sceptical viewpoint. Whilst concepts of risk and resilience are valuable in understanding the diverse experiences and outcomes of adolescents and young adults, the *application* of risk assessments and predictions to *individual* young people as their lives unfold is less straightforward than implied in some current theory and practice. Unpredictable 'critical moments' and localized, place- and person-specific contingent factors can turn youth transitions in unpredictable directions.

Central to the discussion is recent research carried out with young adults from some of the poorest neighbourhoods in England. This study had at its heart an interrogation of popular, influential theories and concepts – of 'social exclusion', of an emergent youth 'underclass', of a 'lost generation' disconnected from the social, economic and moral mainstream – set against a close-up examination of the life stories of young people who, on the face of it, might best fit these labels. Although notions of 'risk', 'risk-taking' and 'resilience' were not key ones in the original project design, the research does allow for critical reflection on these ideas. The majority of young people in the study shared most of the 'risk factors' normally associated with social exclusion and negative outcomes in early adulthood. Yet a key finding is that youth transitions in places beset by the problems of social exclusion in extreme form are diverse, differentiated and difficult to comprehend without a more qualitative, biographical and long-term perspective.

Social Exclusion, Young Adults and Risk: Some Key Concerns

Numerous labels are applied to young people perceived to be marginal to, or even falling outside of, what might be regarded as 'normal', 'mainstream' transitions to adulthood. Obviously, normative judgements are at work here. Despite critical objections (e.g., Coles, 2000; Skelton, 2002), academics, policy makers and practitioners readily use, often interchangeably, shorthand terms that lump together quite diverse youth experiences, groups and social issues, and carry with them the whiff of pejorative labelling (e.g., the 'disaffected', 'disengaged', 'excluded', 'underclass', 'hard-to-reach' or 'hard-to-help') (MacDonald, 1997). What is deemed to unite young people so labelled is their difference, implied but rarely stated explicitly, from a preferred set of circumstances in which individuals are engaged in more 'conventional', 'normal', 'included', 'successful' transitions to adulthood (e.g., those traditionally associated with more affluent, middle-class young people).

Whilst it is certainly not the objective of this chapter to dispute the real problems and hardships that some young people face, one aim *is* to question some of the assumptions underlying the way that youth transitions are theorized and labelled in current research, policy and practice. As Coleman and Hagell make clear in the introduction to this volume, 'risk' is a term that is used wisely in contemporary social science but often in quite different ways. Put simply, this chapter is concerned with the way that 'risk factors' are used to explain the different sorts of experiences that

young people have as they grow up. The risk factor approach has been used in attempts to understand a wide range of youth problems; those individuals possessing a greater number of risk factors
are said to be at greater risk of experiencing various social problems. Coles (2000) provides a useful
critical summary of risk approaches to teenage pregnancy, unemployment, mental health problems
and social exclusion in general. Scott and Chaudhary (2003) provide a short, accessible review of
research on risk and resilience factors in contexts of disadvantage. This chapter selects two key
areas of risk for young people: the risk of economic exclusion and the risk of criminal involvement.
It describes dominant academic and policy perspectives in respect of them and then draws upon
the research mentioned above to raise some critical questions about these perspectives.

The Risk of Economic Exclusion: 'Status Zer0 Youth'

Much of this academic and policy concern has to do with an understandable fear that those
left out of progressive school-to-work careers (i.e., ones that hold the promise of securing
reasonably rewarding, lasting, satisfying employment in adult life) may become forever
marginal to economic life and languish in 'poor work', poverty or 'welfare dependency' in the
long term. *The* central thrust of government policy in respect of young people in Britain over
recent decades, and given extra momentum by Labour governments since 1997, has been to
incorporate young cohorts into education, training and employment.

This has been the single issue which has most exercised, and which most clearly represents,
contemporary British policy making about 'excluded youth'. It also provides one of the few
examples of youth research having a relatively direct impact on government policy. The story can
be traced from Istance *et al.*'s (1994) small-scale, local study in South Wales that found 20% of
school-leavers were not in education, employment or training (termed by the researchers 'Status
Zer0' youth, because those in education, employment or training were classified as Status 1, 2 and
3), through the political lobbying and further studies of researchers involved in that project (e.g.,
Williamson, 1997), to the newly empowered Blair government's establishment of the Social
Exclusion Unit in 1998 and its early report on the same problem (Bridging the Gap, 1999).

Other studies followed. In a critical discussion of the task the forthcoming Connexions
Service might face, Britton *et al.* (2002) suggested that at any one time 214000 young people
nationally are likely to be 'not in education, employment or training' (or NEET, to use the acro-
nym now favoured in policy circles). Raffe's study in Scotland (2003) suggested a figure of over
30% of the age cohort. The Connexions Service was launched, from 2000, as a multimillion
pound, national strategy with a central aim of ensuring that all young people, not just the
advantaged and affluent, were included in suitable post-16 employment, education or training.

The condition of 'status zer0' or NEET has been tied together with, and is one key example
of, a range of circumstances and behaviours said to cause, predict or exemplify 'social
exclusion' for young people (the exact relationships are sometimes left unclear in policy docu-
ments): see Box 8.1.

Some young people are more at risk of becoming 'status zer0' than others. Socially
disadvantaged youth – for example, black and minority ethnic young people, those with
disabilities or special needs, care leavers, young lone mothers, working-class school-leavers –
are more likely than others to end up in this situation. Being 'status zer0' is also said to predict
later disadvantage. Not being in education, employment and training at age 16 is reported to be
the most powerful predictor of unemployment in young adulthood (Bynner and Parsons, 2002;

Box 8.1   What is 'social exclusion'?

A vague and slippery term (see Hills *et al.*, 2002; Levitas, 1998; MacDonald and Marsh, 2005), 'social exclusion' can perhaps best be understood as a condition in which individuals become excluded from participation in the normal social, economic and cultural life of their communities and society at large. Thus, socially excluded young people are regarded as not just economically excluded (as with the case of 'status zer0' young people) but also as detached from social support, important social networks, community and political participation and expected social and moral behaviour.

MacDonald and Marsh (2005) argue, however, that it is often difficult to match this sort of definition against the lived experiences of young people growing up in poor neighbourhoods. Although economic *marginality* is a common experience, complete and permanent exclusion from the labour market is rare. Furthermore, locally embedded social networks – and the social support sometimes available in adverse circumstances – can generate strong subjective feelings of social *inclusion*. They conclude that popular images and theories of 'disconnected youth' fail to connect with the realities of life in poor neighbourhoods.

Social Exclusion Unit, 1999). Similarly, school truancy (another predictor of 'status zer0') has been linked to wider social fears about the risks of young people falling into a life of unemployment and crime. According to the government, 50000 pupils truant every day (cited in Hayden, 2003). Reducing these figures has been identified by the Social Exclusion Unit as 'a crucial part of the government's wider strategy to tackle and prevent social exclusion' (1997, p. 3). Indeed, its very first report concerned school truancy, with its first page warning that:

> *Truancy and exclusions have reached crisis point. The thousands of children who are not in school on most schooldays have become a significant cause of crime. Many of today's non-attenders are in danger of becoming tomorrow's criminals and unemployed.*

On the one hand, then, 'status zer0' youth are portrayed as disadvantaged by the restructuring of traditional, class-based pathways to adulthood and excluded from the social and economic advantages that accrue from post-16 learning and skills development (i.e., a vulnerable group in need of care). At the same time, these 'idle hands' pose the threat of trouble: a danger that demands intervention and control. Even sensitive sociological accounts, close to the empirical realities of 'status zer0', reflect this long-standing twin concern of 'youth in/as trouble' (Hebdige, 1988):

> *There is a risk of scare-mongering about the wider social consequences (in terms of, for example, homelessness, drug misuse and criminality) resulting from such long-term marginality to mainstream structures of economic opportunity, but that does not mean they will not materialise...//... Status Zer0 young people, if renewed effort is not made to integrate them into training and labour market structures, may be the first generation for whom the underclass is a social reality rather than a political and ideological device.*

> Williamson (1997, p. 81)

The Risk of Offending: 'Criminal Careers'

One of the clearest, best known and most influential examples of the risk approach to under-standing young people's lives can be found in the criminal career perspective. Within crimi-nology there is a well-established and enormous research literature in the USA and UK that is concerned with the study of criminal careers. Whilst there are many important protagonists, perhaps the key exponent of this approach, certainly in the UK, has been David Farrington. He defines a criminal career as:

> ...the longitudinal sequence of offences committed by an individual offender...a criminal career has a beginning (onset), and end (desistance) and a career length in between (duration). Only a certain proportion of the population (prevalence) has a criminal career and commits offences. (1994, p. 509)

As with youth sociology, 'career' is meant in the sense of a 'course or progress through life'. It does *not* mean that an individual involved with a criminal career will rely on crime as a means of earning a living (although this may be true in some cases). The criminal career approach is essentially concerned with human development over time, but 'criminal behaviour does not generally appear without warning...offending is part of a larger syndrome of anti-social behaviour that arises in childhood and tends to persist into adulthood' (Farrington, 1994). The theoretical promise and policy influence of this type of criminal career research is that offenders and offending behaviour can be predicted, known and, with appropriate intervention, controlled. Farrington concludes that a small group of chronic offenders is responsible for a large proportion of crime and that 'these chronics might have been identified with reasonable accuracy at age 10' (1994, p. 566). Central to the approach, then, is the use of quantitative studies (usually of young men) to identify, measure and model the early life influences on (potential) offenders. Individual psychopathology, from an early age, *predicts* later forms of anti-social behaviour and crime:

> ...hyperactivity at age 2 may lead to cruelty to animals at 6, shoplifting at 10, burglary at 15, robbery at 20, and eventually spouse assault, child abuse and neglect, alcohol abuse, and employment and accommodation problems later on in life. Typically, a career of childhood anti-social behaviour leads to a criminal career, which often coincides with a career of teenage anti-social behaviour and leads to a career of adult anti-social behaviour.
>
> (Farrington, 1994, p. 512)

The identification of major risk factors to the onset of a criminal career becomes paramount (see Box 8.2).

Box 8.2   Risk factors for youth offending
(adapted from Farrington, 1996, pp. 2–3)

Prenatal and perinatal	(e.g., teenage motherhood, itself associ-ated with absent fathers, low income and poor child-rearing methods)

Personality	(e.g., impulsiveness, hyperactivity)
Intelligence and attainment	(e.g., low intelligence, poor school performance)
Parental supervision and discipline	(e.g., harsh, erratic parental discipline, physical abuse)
Parental conflict and separation	(e.g., separation or divorce of parents, parental conflict)
Socio-economic status	(e.g., socio-economic deprivation, low parental income, poor housing)
Delinquent friends	(e.g., offenders gravitate to other offenders or peer group membership leads to offending)
School influences	(e.g., schools affect delinquency rates or troublesome children tend to go to schools with high delinquency rates)
Community influences	(e.g., disorganized, inner-city areas, over-crowded households, physical deterioration, high residential mobility, socialhousing)

This positivist, rationalist, 'actuarial' approach to understanding crime (see Young, 1999) has found favour in important policy and practice interventions that seek to identify and control risk behaviours, particularly amongst the young population. A good example can be found in the *Communities that Care* programme for reducing anti-social behaviour (e.g., Beinart *et al.*, 2002). Devised in the United States, this policy intervention has been imported to the UK with major funding from the Joseph Rowntree Foundation (JRF). Indeed, the research and policy review that JRF commissioned made an explicit call for the implementation of this 'large-scale community-based programme against crime… [in order to]… tackle risk factors that are problematic within particular communities' (Farrington, 1996, p. 5).[1]

---

[1]Crow *et al.*'s recent evaluation (2004) highlights some of the difficulties that have been faced in implementing this model, and Coles (2000, p. 194) raises some more fundamental methodological and theoretical questions:

> …*[it] employs a remarkably 'deductive', 'positivistic' and 'normative' approach to problem identification and problem solving. It suggests that social science is supremely confident that it knows the causes of problem behaviours and poor outcomes during youth transitions. This might be a very questionable assumption. A second major worry is that it seems to identify…the problems as clustered around young people, their families, friends and communities rather than the opportunity structures available or inadequacies in service delivery.*

The same stress on detecting risk factors amongst the young and intervening to ward against the predicted, later outcomes (i.e., fuller criminality, more entrenched exclusion) is central to the British government's strategy for reducing youth crime (see Home Office, 2004, p. 41). It is evident in their £20 million programme of *Youth Inclusion Projects* (YIPs), launched in 70 high crime areas from 2000.[2] Based on the finding that 40% of crime occurs in 10% of locations, that 1500–2000 neighbourhoods are blighted by crime and that two-thirds of serious young offenders' are brought up in these neighbourhoods, this £20 million programme draws upon the expertise of local, multi-agency teams to assess the risk of criminal involvement posed by young residents of these areas. Once those 50 teenagers deemed to be most 'at risk' of criminal involvement are identified, they are invited to participate in programmes of support (with substantial targets set for reduction in offending amongst this group and in their community). Although offending is key amongst the risk factors used to identify participants, it is quite possible, given the emphasis on predictive risk factors, that some people are selected for participation who, to date, have no record of offending. The *risk* of an individual offending is sufficient.

Some Critical Questions

It is not the purpose of this discussion to cast doubt on the importance, influence and rigour of studies on risk and criminal career carried out by Farrington and others. Reviewing this work does help to identify, though, some of the methodological and theoretical problems inherent in much current risk-oriented youth research and intervention, not just in relation to problems of youth crime. Whilst there is not the room here for a thorough appraisal (see MacDonald, 2006; Webster *et al.*, 2006), some key points can be mentioned.

The first is that relatively little attention is given in risk factor approaches to the changing historical and social contexts in which youth transitions and criminal careers develop. For instance, the Cambridge Study of Delinquent Development, upon which Farrington's arguments are based, focuses on young people who were growing up during the 1960s and 1970s (see Farrington, 1995). Its findings and theoretical conclusions may be out of date. For instance, Smith and McVie (2003) suggest that the substantial growth of single parent and re-constituted families in the intervening decades *may* have reduced the significance of parental separation as a risk factor in the causation of youth offending.

Secondly, and more generally, criminal career perspectives tend to prioritize individual-level explanations (rooted in concepts of pathological, anti-social personality types) and tend to underplay the importance of changing local and neighbourhood contexts in the creation of criminal careers. According to the research presented later in the chapter, it would be impossible to understand the contemporary nature of criminal careers amongst disadvantaged youth in Teesside without reference to two, crucial historical–spatial processes (Webster *et al.*, 2004, 2006). The first is the rapid and widespread de-industrialization of this locale and the concomitant rise of economic marginality and poverty amongst its working-class young people. The second is the historically

---

[2]See www.crimereduction.gov.uk/gpyc05.htm [accessed 21 October 2004].

unprecedented influx of cheap heroin into Teesside's working-class housing estates in the mid-1990s. The testimonies of drugs workers, police officers, local residents and young people gathered in this research all point to the devastating and recent effects of 'poverty drugs' (MacDonald and Marsh, 2002) in enmeshing some young people in the most intractable and damaging forms of criminal career (damaging for the young people themselves, their families and their communities).

The relative absence of a more sociological perspective on the influence of neighbourhood, community and social agencies (such as the criminal justice system) on *youth* transitions and crime in Farrington's work was one of the theoretical spurs to Smith and McVie's Edinburgh-based study (2003; see also Armstrong, 2003). 'Youth' is stressed here because of Smith and McVie's argument that more needs to be known about how criminal careers shape up (or do not) after childhood (the life-phase usually given most emphasis). An important influence in teenage years is the influence and role of leisure lifestyles and social networks (Armstrong, 2003; MacDonald and Shildrick, 2007; Wikström, 2004). The Teesside research comes to similar conclusions. Criminal – and more conventional – destinies are not set in stone in childhood; teenage events and experiences proved to be critical turning points for some youth transitions.

A further, key theoretical ambition of the Edinburgh study – and a third question for criminal career perspectives – is how to explain the fact that some people with a heavy burden of criminogenic risk factors do *not* evolve criminal careers. As Smith and McVie point out (2003, p. 170), although:

> *individual differences in future offending can be predicted fairly well from character, behaviour, and temperament shown at an early age... the substantial limitation of these predictions is that there are many 'false positives'... [for example] among children who are difficult to control there are many who turn out not to have criminal careers as adolescents or adults.*

Farrington (1996, p. 3) notes that "comparatively little attention has been paid to factors that may protect young people, especially those from high-risk backgrounds, against offending". He goes on to identify those protective factors that are known: "a resilient temperament; a warm, affectionate relationship with at least one parent; parents who provide effective supervision, pro-social beliefs and consistent discipline; and parents who maintain a strong interest in their children's education".

Related to this, and fourthly, it is difficult to disentangle the relative efficacy of different risk factors from the long list that have been identified as playing a role; even more so at the level of the individual case:

> *the basic idea of risk-focused prevention is very simple: identify the key risk factors for offending and implement prevention programmes to tackle them. This idea avoids the difficult question of which risk factors have causal effects... if all modifiable risk factors are targeted, the intervention programme will be effective because at least some of the risk factors will be causes*
> Farrington and Painter (2004, p. 57)

A current ESRC research network on "pathways in and out of crime" has also highlighted the theoretical and methodological "difficulty in attributing causality to single and universal 'risk' factors. For example, life-histories show that the same 'factor' (e.g. parental separation, exclusion from school, etc.) can have different consequences for different people at different

times" (ESRC, 2004, p. 3). The Teesside study reports the same finding and goes further: the same risk factor or risk event can have quite different consequences *for the same individual*, at different points in his or her life-course. Like the Teesside study, the ESRC research network is particularly keen to introduce a more biographical, qualitative understanding of criminal careers from the subjective point of view of the young people involved (Armstrong, 2003). Young people's own lived experience of 'risk' and their perspectives on the processes involved in the onset of – and desistance from – criminal careers is notably absent from most quantitatively oriented studies.

Overall, then, there is a growing recognition of the need for more *sociological* understanding of the role of the individual *and* of social structural and historical influences, mediated through the social conditions of the neighbourhoods in which young people live, in the creation of youth transitions that incorporate criminal careers. Within this, a qualitative, biographical method can throw into question some of the generalizing conclusions of the quantitative, risk factor-based analysis of criminal careers that has been so influential in academic theory and government policy.

The following discussion draws upon some recent research of this sort in order to further explore young people's experience of 'risk' and 'social exclusion'. Echoing the foci of the discussion so far, particular attention is paid to the risk of economic exclusion and the risk of criminal involvement.

Researching Youth Transitions and Social Exclusion on Teesside

The study was carried out in the late 1990s.[3] It was interested in how 15- to 25-year-olds from the neighbourhoods of 'East Kelby' in Teesside, North-east England evolved transitions to adulthood in contexts of severe socio-economic deprivation. These young people had grown up in some of the poorest neighbourhoods in "one of the most de-industrialised locales in the UK" (Beynon et al., 1994; Byrne, 1999, p. 93). The five wards that comprise these neighbourhoods all featured in the top 5% most deprived nationally (DETR, 2000) and two of them ('Orchard Bank' and 'Primrose Vale') were in the worst five – of 8414 – in England. The research incorporated periods of participant observation and interviews with people who worked with young people or the problems of poor neighbourhoods (e.g., youth workers, Benefits Agency staff, 'New Deal' personal advisors). At its core, though, the study relied on lengthy, detailed, tape-recorded, biographical interviews (Chamberlayne et al., 2002) with 88 young people (45 females and 43 males) from the predominantly white, (ex)manual working-class population resident in these neighbourhoods.

This interview sample was selected purposefully so as to reflect a wide range of youth experiences. It included youth trainees, single parents, young offenders, clients of drug advice centres, the employed and unemployed, college and university students and 'New Deal' participants. They were recruited via agency contacts and through 'snowballing', whereby an interviewee would suggest others to be approached. The interviews, which took place in, for instance, people's homes or workplaces, were normally tape-recorded and usually lasted for up to two hours. Second interviews were completed with around 60% of the sample within a year of the first. Notwithstanding the problems often reported in gaining research participation from 'hard to reach' young people (Merton, 1998), this biographical, qualitative research offers an insight into contradictory, lived experiences of 'social exclusion' and 'inclusion' (Hills et al., 2002; Levitas, 1998).

The research used the sociological concept of 'career' (Becker, 1963; Berger and Berger, 1972) to explore the way that individual decision making, informed by young people's cultures and sub-cultures, interacts with socially structured opportunities to create individual, and shared, paths of transition. Coles (1995) argues that youth transitions have three main dimensions: the move from full-time education into the labour market ('the school-to-work career'); the attainment of (relative) independence from family of origin ('the family career'); and the move away from the parental home ('the housing career'). It became clear that 'criminal careers', 'drug-using careers' and 'leisure careers' can also become important in shaping youth transitions (Johnston et al., 2000; these terms are explained in MacDonald and Marsh, 2005). These six 'careers' became the focus of interviews with young people.

There is not room here to set out the study's findings (see MacDonald and Marsh, 2001, 2002, 2005) beyond noting that individuals described differentiated transitions in terms of family, housing, leisure, criminal and drug careers but were united by a common experience

[3]The author is indebted to the ESRC, who funded the study, to Jane Marsh, who undertook much of the fieldwork and initial analysis, to Colin Webster and Tracy Shildrick for their comments on this chapter and to all the participants in the project. All real names of informants and their immediate neighbourhoods have been changed. In interview extracts,...indicates a natural pause and...//...indicates that extraneous information has been edited out. Material in square brackets is added as explanation. Emphasis is as in the original, unless otherwise stated.

of economic marginality. The majority displayed highly conventional attitudes to employment but their school-to-work careers struggled to progress beyond low-paid, low-skill, insecure 'poor work' (Brown and Scase, 1991; Byrne, 1999).

The Relationships Between School Disengagement, Truancy and School-to-work Careers in East Kelby

It has been noted that many youth studies and policy analyses argue for a strong, causal relationship between individual truancy, poor school performance, post-16 experience of 'status zer0' and ensuing unemployment and criminal involvement. These are said to be tied together as part of a causal chain that creates social exclusion for young people. What did the Teesside study find?

Experiences of truancy in the sample were widespread. A minority had no or only very infrequent unauthorized absence from school (19 from 88 interviewees). 29 interviewees reported being occasional truants (i.e., they missed school quite often but not extensively). 40 people were classed as 'frequent truants' (i.e., they had persistent and extensive unauthorized absence that sometimes amounted to weeks, or even months, at a time). The explanations given for affective disengagement from school in general, and for truancy in particular, were familiar ones (Brown, 1987; Carlen et al., 1992; MacDonald and Marsh, 2005; Osler et al., 2002; Ridge, 2002).

A minority sought physical escape from bullying and a minority felt unable to cope with, or felt untested by, the academic demands of school. More commonly, truancy was a reflection of a widespread, informal resistance to academic learning and the authority of schools (that were regarded as offering little to them) (Willis, 1977). Typically, school disengagement ran alongside emotional and physical engagement with the attractions of street-based, sub-cultural activities and identities (see Liam and Adam, Box 8.3). For a significant minority, school disengagement was bolstered by a critical de-bunking of the orthodoxy that individual academic effort translated into success in the post-16 world of work (see Broderick, Box 8.3).

Box 8.3   Experiences and views of school disengagement

All they were learning me when I left school was adds and takeaways and that was in secondary school. The Maths teachers used to take us weight training – didn't do Maths. So I just thought "Sack it" [give it up].

Lisa (24, non-employed mother)

If you didn't show the slightest bit of talent you never got pushed, do you know? If you couldn't be bothered, they didn't bother with you. They get all them people who're clever or the slightest bit clever, push them, so they get all them who pass which makes them look good but the others, they're just not bothered about.

Sarah (23, university student and mother)

I was easy led, very easy led. I'd do anything anyone told me to do. I'd just do it…because I didn't mind going to school. Like, I didn't hate the lessons. If I was there, when I did go to a lesson, I'd do it and I'd enjoy it. It's just I couldn't be bothered or someone'd say, "Away, let's nick off [play truant]. Let's go here today" and I was, "Away then!"

Liam (27, unemployed)

[School] was alright when I first started. I just started mixing with the wrong people, experiencing drugs about 13/14…//…I mean, I was stood outside the Head-master's office all the time… Smoking, fighting, nicking out of lessons, everything. I just didn't take no notice of the rules or nowt…I just wanted to be like the others, you know what I mean? Just like a little gang that used to knock about together: if they done it, you done it.

Adam (20, inmate of Young Offender Institute)

They'd [Broderick's parents] argue about it. Our Neville [his stepfather] come home and he'd say "Hasn't he been to fucking school again?"…He'd just go "He'll never get a job when he leaves school 'cos he's never there". Why? So if you go to school for a full five years, you're definitely getting a job when you leave? All that – full of shit – no!

Broderick (18, unemployed)

In *general* terms school disaffection and absence are, of course, likely to limit individual educational achievement (and the chances of trading in school qualifications for entry to 'better' post-16 options) and to increase the chances of later social exclusion. In this context of overall low educational achievement and a local labour market that still offers work (albeit casualized, insecure, low-paid work) to the unqualified but willing, however, an individual history of persistent truancy may play less of a role in predicting later outcomes. MacDonald and Marsh (2005) show how being tied into informal social networks ('who you know' not 'what you know') actually proved more efficacious than possessing educational qualifications in searching for work in a severely depressed local labour market that still had plenty of low-level jobs on offer.

Certainly these young people were poorly qualified. Only six (from 88) had achieved five GCSEs at grades A–C, at the age of 16 (a common but contested measure of the 'success' of pupils and schools). Given that over half of the 88 had *not* been 'frequent truants' (with 19 reporting no truancy) there is obviously no simple relationship here between educational absence and school attainment. And whilst this level of qualification is staggeringly low by national standards, it compares with what was typically achieved by schools in this place at this time (with one school recording only 4% of its 16-year-olds reaching this level).

This research also casts doubt on the efficacy – *in this context* – of a conventional school history and academic qualifications in guaranteeing more 'successful' transitions into the labour market. Because this was not a statistically representative sample of school-leaving cohorts, it was not possible to assess directly the effect of the extent of truancy and of GCSE pass rates on later outcomes. One method of investigating these questions, though, is to consider the post-school careers of those with the highest levels of school qualifications (i.e., those six interviewees who passed five GCSEs at grades A–C), against those of the majority who had no (n. 34) or lower levels of qualification (n. 48). To what extent *does* the orthodox educational deal work for young people in East Kelby?

Overall, there was remarkable similarity between the longer-term post-school careers of these six and the rest. *All* informants – regardless of their degree of engagement with school or qualifications attained – reported erratic, complex and economically marginal transitions, consisting of training and education courses of mixed quality, spells of unemployment and episodic engagement with usually low-paid, low-skilled and temporary jobs. Virtually all interviewees had been 'not in employment, education or training' at some point. MacDonald and Marsh (2005) criticize the current policy fixation with this concept and category. The school-to-work careers followed by these interviewees were so volatile and unpredictable that employment one day could easily be followed by a return to 'status zer0' the next. Because of the 'poor work' they encountered, for these young people 'inclusion' in employment did not signal an end to 'social exclusion' (Byrne, 1999).

In scanning the later labour market destinations of the sample as a whole it would be impossible to identify those six people who had achieved the most 'success' at school or who had been the most frequent truants: the transitions and outcomes of the entire sample were similarly marked by economic marginality. Virtually all interviewees, regardless of their propensity towards school truancy, experienced recurrent unemployment.[4] In short, for this sample standard risk predictions did not work. Greater experience of truancy did not predict a greater propensity to subsequent unemployment and nor did higher levels of qualification predict easier transitions to secure jobs.

These findings point to the importance of "the structure of opportunities" (Roberts, 1995) in understanding these sort of transitions. This includes not only what is available to young people as they leave school but also what is provided for them in school. A consistent theme was that interviewees felt they had been a low priority in schools that – because of the effect of schools' league tables – were targeting more attention, effort and resources to those pupils deemed capable of achieving grades A–C at GCSE (see Simpson and Cieslik, 2003; see Sarah, Box 8.3). The schools that these young people attended had been judged as 'failing' in Ofsted reports (and two have now been demolished to make way for a new City Academy). Being a 'failing' pupil in a 'failing school' led many to feel that formal education was of little relevance to them, certainly when compared with the hedonistic pleasures and peer approval to be gained from truant days 'on the street'.

For these reasons, school disengagement (and associated truancy and low educational attainment) is interpreted as, in part, an *effect* of social exclusion, rather than an irreversible step towards – or *cause* of – later social exclusion, criminality and unemployment (as implied by the Social Exclusion Unit, 1997). Similarly, the later labour market fortunes of this group are not so much an outcome of the risk and protective factors that might have been ticked off against individual young people, but a consequence – in the main – of the limited employment opportunities that awaited school-leavers and young adults in this locale.

As Ball *et al.* (2000, p. 8) describe: "many of those outside of education and training post-16, the 'others' to the 'learning society', carry with them learner identities often severely

---

[4]In Webster *et al.*'s follow-up study (2004) three individuals had relatively 'successful' school-to-work careers in the longer-term. These people had even *lower* levels of qualifications than the under-qualified majority.

damaged by their experiences in compulsory education. More learning is the last thing they are interested in". The Teesside study, too, uncovered many instances of the lasting, negative impact of schooling upon young people's attitude to education (MacDonald and Marsh, 2005). But interviews also revealed many instances of people who, over the youth phase, moved in and out of education. Learner identities were not concrete. Virtual abandonment of formal schooling at the ages of 12 or 13 did *not* predict educational disengagement at 15 and 16. Some of those with the grimmest memories of school life were now, several years later, studying at college. Equally, early instrumental orientations to school could be supervened by later, full-blown alienation.

Summary

Two important implications for theories of risk and social exclusion are highlighted in summary. Firstly, in contexts of shared and deep social disadvantage, weighing up the standard 'risk factors' accruing to *individuals* helps us little in predicting the later fortunes of these individuals. *Shared*, structural inequalities rooted in class and place can become more important and over-ride the significance of individual behaviour and attributes. Secondly, neither 'positive' nor 'negative' experiences in late childhood and early to mid-teenage years *determined* later outcomes and experiences, as implied in much risk theory. Both these conclusions are borne out by an analysis of criminal and drug-using careers in East Kelby.

The Relationships Between School Disengagement and Criminal and Drug-using Careers in East Kelby

Very many of the sample reported offending in their early teenage years (predominantly infrequent, petty shoplifting). For the majority, their transgressions ceased there. Two key movements can be identified in the consolidation of the most serious, longer-term criminal careers.

The first of these was the hardening up of school disaffection into full-blown disengagement, exhibited in frequent, persistent truancy (Pavis and Cunningham-Burley, 1999). Simultaneous engagement with "street corner society" (MacDonald and Shildrick, 2007) further established oppositional identities and was the cornerstone for the evolution of most careers of crime that extended beyond early to mid-teenage:

> *just me and this other lad used to nick off all the time…//…Just go and hang about the town…that was me starting days of crime and that, yeah…shoplifting and pinching bikes, that's what it was.*
>
> Danny (21, Young Offenders Institute inmate)

Dull truant time was enlivened by the camaraderie of shoplifting jaunts, other petty thieving and speeding around the estates in stolen vehicles: crime as leisure for bored, out-of-school teenagers.

For some, this marked the early phases of criminal apprenticeships. They began to learn the routines of more acquisitively oriented offending (e.g., how and what to thieve from cars) and were drawn into local criminal markets (e.g., the best shops and pubs for fencing stolen property, the market rate for 'knock-off gear', etc.). For many, though, these sorts of infringements – coupled with under-age drinking and recreational drug use – marked the extent, and end-point, of criminal careers.

The large numbers involved in (petty) offending in early teenage years gradually lessened as the years passed. The second, most significant 'moment' – that helped to drag out a smaller number of individuals' criminal careers into later periods and to transmute them into something more destructive – is when heroin enters the scene. Local police and drug workers reported how very cheap, smokeable heroin flooded into the estates of Teesside in the mid-1990s, prior to which the area had had a negligible heroin-using population. MacDonald and Marsh (2002) describe how many of Teesside's young people seem unprepared to resist the temptations of this 'poverty drug' and made speedy transitions from occasional, recreational use of drugs such as cannabis and speed to often daily, dependent use of heroin (and later in the 1990s, crack cocaine).

For this minority of interviewees, dependent use of heroin was the driving force behind exclusionary transitions which distanced them from their families, their previous lifestyles (and sometimes friendship groups), from the labour market, and which entangled them in chaotic, damaging careers of drug-driven crime. Heroin use became central to an understanding of their unfolding biographies. For individuals like Richard (see Box 8.4), increasingly desperate acquisitive criminality was fuelled by the need for daily drug money. By the age of 20, this close combination of drug and crime careers had progressively closed down options for a more 'mainstream' lifestyle. He had failed to complete several government training programmes, had been employed only once (and briefly), had been unemployed recurrently, had become estranged from his family, had been homeless and slept rough, had a lengthy and

Box 8.4 One criminal and drug-using career
The emergence of one criminal and drug-using career: Richard, 20

Age	School to Work	Family/Housing	Leisure/Networks	Crime	Drugs
11–14	'Loads of truancy'	Living with mother and stepfather in East Kelby (father left when Richard was age 4)	**Street-based socializing** with friends, whilst truanting	Occasional shoplifting ('**leisure crime**') "I think I went off the rails with my Dad being away"	Cannabis use
14–16	**Re-engagement** with school: 5 (low grade) GCSEs	(Ditto)	Some disengagement from peer group	Reduced offending [Heroin arrives in East Kelby]	(Ditto)
16–19	'Typical' post-16 career: Youth Training schemes unemployment, short-term unskilled jobs, New Deal, unemployment	(Ditto)	(Ditto)	1st heroin use: "me and my friends thought we'd have a daft go at it [heroin] and before we knew it a few of us were [cold] turkeying and then we all were. Hooked. "	Attempts to desist, with methadone

19–20	Unemployed	**Ejected from family home** (accused of theft), sleeps rough, assaulted/ hospitalized, moves to homeless hostel	Immersed in new, heroin-using peer group at hostel	Accelerated rate of shop-lifting to fund drug use, increasingly **chaotic, acquisitive crime**, burglary, period on remand, release, further burglary and shoplifting, on remand then probation sentence.	Relapses to heroin – **addicted, daily use**
				"**You don't think about anything else at all. All you think is heroin** – where do you want to go for a mooch [to thieve], where to score a bag [purchase heroin], where to do it [to administer the drug]."	
	Aspires to return to college	Hopes to be re-united with family	Wants to dissociate from drug-using/ criminal associates	**Attempts to desist from offending**	Persisting with new, methadone programme
			"It's 'cos I don't occupy myself. No job to keep me busy. It does me head in just wandering around. Nothing to do. So I end up knocking around with me old mates. I just get back into it."		

worsening record of offending, had been imprisoned twice and, at the age of 20, was living in a bail hostel, struggling to maintain his commitment to a methadone programme and scratching around trying to find ways, beyond heroin, to fill tedious, directionless days. Questions can be asked about the descriptive purchase provided by the concept, but if anyone is 'socially excluded', Richard is. Cases like his represent perhaps the most intractable forms of social exclusion that were uncovered in the research.

What do these patterns of criminal and drug career tell us about popular theorizations of risk?

Firstly – to re-iterate an earlier point – although the research literature suggests a strong association between school truancy and delinquency (Graham and Bowling, 1995), we need to be wary of analyses that imply a tight, causal fit between dodging school and criminal offending (Social Exclusion Unit, 1997). For only a proportion of even those classed as frequent truants did truancy time signify the moment or opportunity to initiate delinquent activities. And whilst the majority (n. 16) of those with more sustained, criminal careers (n. 20) *had* been frequent school truants (and of these, most described at least one spell of school exclusion), a substantial minority (n. 14) of those classed as frequent truants (n. 40) reported no offending whatsoever. Whilst some frequent truants did enliven truant time with first forays into recreational drug use (Simpson, 2003) or petty offending, these often did not harden up into more sustained offending.

Secondly, the historical and spatial context in which youth transitions are made is crucial for setting the range of likely experiences and outcomes for young people. During the 1990s, parts of Teesside have become notorious for drug-related crime and a key focus of government interventions to tackle this problem (Home Office, 2003). Prior to the mid-1990s, it would have been difficult to locate any individuals who had the sort of transition described by Richard. In other words, new, imported risks bear down on young people's lives here; risks which were unknown just a few years earlier.

Of course, it would be foolish to argue that persistent youth offending is always and has always been rooted in drug dependency. Craine's (1997) ethnographic research shows how economically marginal transitions can readily generate minority 'alternative careers' of crime, regardless of any contact with 'poverty drugs'. The Teesside study documented the situation as it was found amongst the people interviewed, not as might have been the case in Kelby prior to the influx of heroin. Nevertheless, the form of drug–crime career displayed by people like Richard explains much of, and the most pernicious examples of, current youth offending in this locale. The implication of this argument is that in emphasizing childhood experiences and ingrained personality factors, most criminal career research underestimates the influence of *changing* community conditions (specific to particular places and times) and how these are encountered in *youth* transitions in generating the most serious forms of criminal career (Smith and McVie, 2003). If Richard had been born 10 years earlier, it is unlikely that his life would have turned out like it has.

Thirdly, the research struggled to identify any earlier single, individual or family-level factor that would predict confidently those who would follow 'delinquent' transitions: those with the most persistent, extensive later criminality could *not* "have been identified with reasonable accuracy at age 10" (Farrington, 1994, p. 566). The sample as a whole shared many socio-economic (i.e., low socio-economic class), educational (e.g., poor school performance) and family (e.g., parental separation, bereavement) risk factors. These were not, however, able to explain why a minority of individuals pursued criminal careers and a majority did not.[5] For instance, contrary to some theorizations of crime in poor neighbourhoods (e.g., Dennis, 1993; *The Guardian* 5 April 2001), the study found little co-relation between family type and later criminality. Only four (from 20) of those who reported frequent, longer-term offending were brought up in lone-parent families. Similarly, the majority of those counted as displaying persistent truancy came from intact families. Interviewing siblings who followed quite different paths confirmed our wariness about the 'actuarial positivism' present in some contemporary criminology (Young, 1999).[6] Many were called, but few were chosen. Long-term educational disengagement and engagement with street-based peer groups *was* a necessary condition for the evolution of serious criminal careers but it was not a *sufficient* condition.[7]

The same applies to involvement in more problematic drug use. The received wisdom in the UK drugs research literature is that recreational and dependent users are distinct, separate groups. The former are said to be "sociable, sensible, and morally aware as non-users" (Perri 6 *et al.*, 1997, p. 45); like most young people, they view "taking hard drugs and actually injecting as anathema: a Rubicon they will never cross" (Parker *et al.*, 1998b, p. 132). Dependent users of heroin are, on the other hand, "from the edges" (Parker *et al.*, 1998a): the "basic identi-kit of the most likely heroin user" would list "poor school performance and attendance, light parental supervision" and having grown up "at the wrong end of town" on "the poorest estates". Parker *et al.* conclude by saying that: "the least worst scenario is that heroin trying does not become accommodated within the far larger 'recreational' drugs scene but remains predominantly associated with *degrees of social exclusion*" (1998a, pp. 45–46, emphasis added).

The issue, though, for poor neighbourhoods of East Kelby is that the risk profile sketched by Parker and colleagues would match a large proportion of their young residents. They all experience 'degrees of social exclusion' yet a large minority were opposed to drug use *of any sort* (MacDonald and Marsh, 2002). For the largest minority, drug careers, for the present, extended only to recreational drugs. This and other studies suggest, however, that the Rubicon dividing recreational and dependent heroin use is being bridged by an apparently growing number of young people, like Richard, in poor areas of the north-east of England (Johnston *et al.*, 2000; Simpson, 2003).

Thus, many people who appeared to possess many of the requisite risk factors did *not* pursue full-blown criminal or drug-using careers. Qualitative, biographical interviews helped elucidate subjective explanations of this conundrum. They highlighted the significance of

---

[5]Risk factor theories tend to seek probabilistic, general associations between risks and later outcomes that might not be applicable to individual cases. Nevertheless, whilst academic proponents of risk factor approaches sometimes demur from using risk factors to predict individual behaviour, this is not always the case with some of the policy and practice outcroppings of risk theory. The offender risk assessment system (OASys) used by the UK Probation Service and the British government's programme of Youth Inclusion Projects do exactly this.

[6]In Farrington and Painter's (2004) study of offending amongst the brothers and sisters of the male offenders in the Cambridge Study in Delinquent Development, less than half of brothers (44%) had a conviction and less than an eighth of sisters (12%) had any record of offending, despite the fact - presumably - that these siblings shared many of the same risk factors as their offending brothers.

[7]The design of the research meant that it was unable to say anything precise about childhood behaviours, personality types or the sort of parenting that interviewees had received. It is possible that these risk factors might explain involvement in criminal careers amongst our sample. It is possible but unlikely. It is improbable that the increase in youth offending in Teesside in the 1990s and the forms of crime that underlay it can be explained by a sudden change in local parenting styles or an increase in the local preponderance of anti-social personality types (Smith and McVie, 2003).

contingent, unpredictable events and experiences in the creation of youth transitions of different sorts. Thus, although class, ethnicity and place united these interviewees, their subjective *experiences* of transition were different. The combined influence of school-to-work, family, housing, leisure, criminal and drug careers also meant that individual transitions were complex, fluid and unpredictable. Events and encounters in one sphere could have dramatic repercussions in another. Unpredictable critical moments had unpredictable consequences (Johnston *et al.*, 2000; Thomson *et al.*, 2002).[8]

Physical and mental ill health was very widespread amongst interviewees and their families, unsurprisingly so given what we know about the socio-spatial concentration of health inequalities (Macintyre *et al.*, 2002; Mitchell *et al.*, 2000; Tees Valley Joint Strategy Unit, 2002). Experiences of loss – particularly of bereavement and parental separation – proved to be especially important in shaping the course of individuals' lives thereafter. Again, though, *how* such events impact on transitions would be unknowable without the benefit of interviewees' *retrospective* biographical accounts. Seemingly following uneventful, conventional transitions until that point, a few interviewees highlighted family traumas as the moment when they started 'going off the rails'. For instance, learning her 'father' was not actually her father at the age of 11 was identified by Sarah as the 'critical moment' or 'turning point' (Hodkinson and Sparkes, 1997) that set in train a series of turbulent relationships with family members and later boyfriends, which in turn motivated a chaotic, nomadic housing career (MacDonald and Marsh, 2001). According to Jason, the onset of his long-running criminal career could be traced back to the separation of his parents, also when he was 11, and his father's ensuing alcoholism. Conversely, in Martin's case the death of his father and the suicide of his best friend caused him to re-double his commitment to local community work and to his job. Webster *et al.* (2004) show how these sorts of family traumas can – sometimes within the same biography – become the psychological triggers for the onset of *and* desistance from criminal and drug careers.

Summary and Conclusion

In making transitions in poor neighbourhoods, these interviewees collided with the numerous hardships that typify socially excluded places. Direct, cumulative experience of, *inter alia,* poverty, personal and family ill-health, criminal victimization, unemployment, poor schooling, problematic drug use, homelessness and so on undeniably affected the sort of lives they led. These were the sort of risks that affected youth transitions in these poor neighbourhoods. Exactly what sort of effects such experiences might have, at the level of the individual case, is much less certain. Transitions were contingent; buffeted by unanticipated critical moments, they were a complex set of twists and turns. A key conclusion of the study is, then, that transitions of whatever sort – whether they be more or less 'conventional' or 'delinquent' – do not roll on deterministically to foregone conclusions.

---

[8]For instance, critical moments that spurred desistance were of many sorts. Traumatic episodes sometimes caused people to re-orient their lives. Lisa used to be "in with a crowd getting into trouble and doing drugs" until she was raped by one of them. Zack explained how "the turning point" in his life was when "my best mate hung 'imself". He had "calmed down now", given up "all sorts of mad stuff" and committed most of his time to running an informal, voluntary youth group.

As such, it is not easy – or particularly helpful – to apply orthodox risk assessments and predictions to lives like these (Craine, 1997; Laub and Sampson, 2003 offer less deterministic theories of criminal career; Sampson and Laub, 1993). Experience of truancy, school disengagement, parental separation, low educational attainment, early offending and so on was common and widespread but the most serious forms of social exclusion – signified by long-term criminal and drug-using careers – were limited to a minority. Conversely, economic marginality in late teenage years and early adulthood – symbolized by recurrent episodes of 'poor work' and unemployment – was the preserve of all, despite differential levels of school engagement and educational qualification.

In conclusion, the value is stressed of more ethnographic, biographical, 'close-up' approaches to understanding the risks encountered and responded to by 'socially excluded' young people as they grow up in poor neighbourhoods. At the same time, however, the chapter has emphasized how individual youth transitions must be understood in relation to changing, place-specific and unequal 'structures of opportunity' (e.g., the opportunities and risks afforded by formal and informal labour markets, by drug and criminal markets, by educational provision and so on). These emphases suggest an approach that supplements the current academic and policy fascination with the twists and turns of individual careers and transitions with a more panoramic view of the social structural processes that create 'risk' and 'exclusion' for young people.

Further Reading

Coles, B. (2000) *Joined up youth research, policy and practice: An agenda for change?* Youth Work Press: Leicester. [As its title suggests, this book seeks to critically explore the connections between research, policy and practice in respect of young people. It provides a good review of recent youth research on particular topic areas, uses case study material drawn from youth work projects in Britain and gives an important statement of the key principles that should inform research, policy and practice in this field.]

Craine, S. (1997) The Black Magic Roundabout: Cyclical transitions, social exclusion and alternative careers. In MacDonald, R. (Ed.), *Youth, the 'underclass' and social exclusion.* Routledge: London. [Based on long-term, participant observation research, this chapter provides a rare example of an ethnographic, sociological attempt to understand the development of criminal careers from the perspective of young adults.]

Farrington, D. (1996) *Understanding and preventing youth crime.* Joseph Rowntree Foundation Social Policy Findings 93. Joseph Rowntree Foundation: York. www.jrf.org.uk/knowledge/findings/socialpolicy/SP93.asp [This is a short summary of findings, drawn from a larger report, available free of charge from the Joseph Rowntree Foundation. This report provides a useful statement of some of David Farrington's work on risk and criminal careers, including a summary of key risk factors.]

MacDonald, R. and Marsh, J. (2005) *Disconnected youth? Growing up in Britain's poor neighbourhoods.* Palgrave: Basingstoke. [This book provides a full account of the youth research upon which this chapter is based. Going beyond issues of risk, crime and economic marginality, it attempts to give an in-depth, close-up understanding of the realities of social exclusion for young adults in some of Britain's poorest neighbourhoods.]

Discussion Questions

1. On the basis of your own experience, thinking and reading, describe what you think may be the main 'risk' and 'protective' factors in respect of the development of individual criminal careers.
2. What are the key critical questions that this chapter asks in respect of orthodox risk factor approaches to criminal careers?
3. What are the strengths and what are the weaknesses of the Teesside research described in this chapter, particularly in terms of its ability to comment critically on risk factor approaches?
4. What sort of policy and practice interventions might be most effective in tackling the sort of criminal careers that the chapter describes?

Chapter 9

Adolescence, Risk and Resilience: A Conclusion

John Coleman

Senior Research Fellow, University of Oxford

Ann Hagell

Programme Director Adolescent Mental Health, Nuffield Foundation;
Editor, Journal of Adolescence

- ■ Introduction
- ■ Resilience: a slippery concept?
- ■ Resilience in the context of young people at risk
- ■ Interventions to enhance resilience

Introduction

In this book we have looked at a spectrum of disadvantage that might be experienced by adolescents in our society. In selecting the authors, and in providing a framework in which disadvantage may be understood, we have been guided by the literature on risk and resilience. This literature has a particular advantage for us, in that it emphasizes a positive perspective on the sorts of obstacles and difficulties outlined in this book. In this final chapter we want to focus on what might be called beating the odds – how young people can overcome adversity, and what we as professional adults can do to facilitate such a process.

We have deliberately used the subtitle *Against the odds* for this book because we wanted to focus on healthy aspects of young people's adaptation and development. However, resilience differs depending on the nature of risk, the extent of adversity, the types of protective factors

Adolescence, Risk and Resilience: Against the odds. John Coleman and Ann Hagell (eds.).
Published in 2007 by John Wiley & Sons, Ltd

operating in the environment and so on, and we need to keep in mind that resilience is a slippery concept. In recent years some writers have been critical of the way in which resilience has come to mean so many different things to different people (e.g., Evans and Pinnock, 2007; Olsson *et al.*, 2003). In this final chapter we will attempt to unpick the concept, and consider how it can be applied to the young people who have been described in this book.

Before we look in detail at the difficulties associated with the concept of resilience, there are some key points to hold in mind:

- Risk and resilience are closely linked. The nature of resilience displayed by an individual will only make sense if we take into account the risk side of the equation as well.
- It is rarely one risk, or one protective factor, that makes the difference. More often each risk adds to the level of adversity, just as each protective factor bolsters resilience in a cumulative fashion.
- Risks differ in their nature and in their effects. Long-term chronic risk is different from acute trauma.
- Experiencing some degree of risk for a young person may be positive, indeed may even be protective against later adversity. Pearce (Chapter 4) challenges us to consider whether resilience can develop at all without exposure to risk. This is an important question, yet most authors see risk and resilience as related concepts.
- We should remember the distinction made in the first chapter between the different concepts of risk. Risk can mean adversity, but it can also mean potentially harmful behaviour. Some argue that certain sorts of behaviour should be called 'experimental' rather than risky, as for example, in getting drunk or smoking cannabis. Risk is also used in the phrases 'at risk', meaning vulnerable, and 'posing a risk', as in challenging to adults.

With these thoughts in mind, we will now turn to an exploration of the problems associated with the concept of resilience.

Resilience: A Slippery Concept?.

Resilience as a Process

As we have noted, resilience is both widely used and open to many different interpretations. We will now look at some of the difficulties that have been raised in making best use of this concept. A good place to start is with the definition of the concept. What does resilience mean? Is it a personality trait, or a process? Does it reside in the individual, or in the family or community? Are there many different types of resilience? And if so, what are they? Would something be called resilience in one context, but not in another? Does resilience change over the life span? Is it always a positive concept, or can it have negative connotations?

Olsson *et al.* (2003) make an important point when they indicate that resilience can apply to outcomes or to processes, and that it is essential to keep these two distinct. Thus the concept of resilience can be used to consider the types of behaviour, the psycho-social outcomes, seen in young people who have been exposed to adversity. Here one might be considering educational performance, stability of relationships, avoidance of criminal behaviour, or other measures of 'good' functioning. A major problem with this approach is that there are numerous possible measures of outcome, and therefore numerous possible indices of resilience. On the other hand, studies that look at processes are more likely to be interested in the ways in which risk and protective factors interact. In this latter approach there is less of a concern with outcome, and more of a focus on how the spectrum of risks and protective factors interact to produce adaptation to particular circumstances. This is a view which is stressed in Rutter's recent papers (Rutter, 2003, 2006a), where he underlines the role of genetic and physiological as well as psychological factors in determining resilience.

The distinction between process and outcome is particularly important when considering, for example, young people growing up in deprived, impoverished communities. In such circumstances a commonly identified outcome, such as avoidance of substance misuse, or good school performance, may not be as important as the development of optimism or pro-social behaviour. If we look at the young person by taking into account not only the range of adversities, but also the potential strengths of the individual, this will produce a more process-oriented view of resilience. This point is one which is emphasized by many authors here, including Hagell (Chapter 7) and MacDonald (Chapter 8).

This takes us on to the question of whether the use of the concept of resilience can have any disadvantages. It is certainly the case that if resilience is seen as a personality attribute, then the opportunity arises to perceive those who do not overcome adversity as somehow lacking in some essential quality. Luthar and Zelazo (2003) make the point that the resilience paradigm, as they call it, can foster a 'blame' perspective. They worry that the use of resilience in this context may lead some adults to believe that, if some young people who are exposed to serious adversity are able to succeed in life, then there must be something wrong with those who do not succeed. The less fortunate ones either lack some important personality characteristic, or they have not made sufficient effort to overcome disadvantage. As these authors point out, there is much that can be done to avoid any such notion, but it is as well to be aware of it.

This is a useful moment to raise the question of the value judgements that underlie the use of the concept of resilience. As we have noted above, while resilience may seem at first sight to be a wholly positive notion, it is possible to imagine ways in which the concept could be used to discriminate or blame young people. There is also another dimension to this. Is it the case that resilience is always healthy? Could there be such a thing as unhealthy coping? Here again Olsson *et al.* (2003) provide some useful examples. What about a young person who is experiencing high levels of disadvantage or adversity over a long period of time? It could be argued that to display distressed emotions in response to this experience shows resilience, whilst to deny or avoid emotion would be a less 'healthy' response. As these authors put it: "Considerable data exist suggesting that young people functioning well under high stress often show higher levels of emotional distress compared to their low stress peers" (Olsson *et al.*, 2003, p. 3).

To conclude this section, and to summarize our views on resilience, we can note that:

- Resilience is not a stable personality characteristic, but a process. It arises as a result of an interaction between risk and protective factors.
- Resilience is often seen as an outcome, but this is misleading. Good school performance, or avoidance of crime, is an outcome. Resilience is not something people have or do not have, but rather it is a response to difficult circumstances.
- There are many different types of resilience, depending on the particular individual. Some types of resilience may be considered more 'healthy' than others, but it will depend on the situation of the individual.
- Resilience is not static; it can change over the life span. It may not be apparent at one stage, but may then develop at another stage because of the availability of protective factors.

- We have to be careful not to 'blame' people if they are seen to be less resilient than others. Resilience is not to do with value judgements, but rather with an understanding of the individual's response to a complex set of positive and negative circumstances.

Gender and Culture

Further interesting questions arise when we consider how resilience relates to gender and culture. Is resilience the same for boys and girls? Are there different protective factors operating for different cultural or ethnic groups?

Readers may have noticed that in the course of this book there has so far been no discussion as to whether gender or ethnic background might operate as either a risk or a protective factor. We will now briefly explore both these individual characteristics in the light of our investigation of risk and resilience.

Turning first to gender, there are a wide range of behavioural outcomes which might lead to speculation on this question. It is well known from the mental health literature that males externalize their difficulties, whilst females are more likely to internalize them. In the context of this book we know that rates of completed suicide are four times higher in young men than in young women, whilst self-harming behaviours are much more frequent in young women. Anti-social behaviour and conduct disorder are seen more often in males, whilst depression and other affective disorders occur more often in females. All research on worry and anxiety shows that girls worry more than boys (Balding, 2006). What do these differences tell us? In the first place they certainly do not indicate that one gender is more at risk than the other. What they do tell us, however, is that when faced with stress or adversity boys and girls, young men and young women, are likely to respond with a different range of behaviours.

As Frydenberg and Lewis (1993) put it in the title of their paper on stress and coping among male and female adolescents: *Boys play sport and girls turn to others*. Of course the situation is somewhat more complex than this, but it is clear from a body of research on this topic (see Coleman and Hendry, 1999) that, broadly speaking, males and females choose different coping strategies when faced with stress. Males make more use of active coping, being more inclined to go out and meet the problem head-on, and more often using aggressive or confrontational techniques to deal with interpersonal difficulties. In addition, a number of studies have shown that men are more likely than women to use denial in response to adversity.

By contrast, it is consistently reported that girls are more affected by stress than boys and are more likely to disclose a greater number of stressful events in their lives. Girls see setbacks and adversities as more threatening than boys, and are more likely to expect the worst in stressful situations. In Seiffge-Krenke's (1995) study girls, in comparison with boys, saw identical stressors as four times more threatening. In terms of coping with stress, females use social support much more than males, but this also exposes them to added vulnerability. If the very relationships on which they depend, especially those with a parent or partner, are the cause of distress then the support on which they depend is rendered unavailable.

As far as resilience is concerned, we can conclude from the above that males and females may be affected by a somewhat different range of protective factors, with social support playing a greater role for girls than for boys. However, the literature is far from clear about how exactly this process works. A number of studies on the impact of divorce have shown that boys appear to be more affected by family upheaval than girls (Hetherington, 1989). On the other hand, many studies of adversity have found no differences between males and females in their levels of resilience. This finding is best exemplified in the landmark research carried out in New Zealand by Fergusson and Lynskey (1996), who concluded: "(In this study)…there was no significant relationship between gender and adolescent resilience" (p. 287).

When we look at ethnicity we find a similarly confusing picture. On the one hand, we can point to various risk behaviours that may be associated with particular cultural backgrounds. It has, for example, been claimed that Asian young women in Britain are more likely to harm themselves through self-poisoning than their white peers (Williams, 1995). However, any research in this field is open to question because of possible bias in assessment and reporting, as well as differences in the understanding of mental health across cultures.

Other risks associated with particular ethnic groups include possible higher rates of mental disorder in black African and black Caribbean 11- to 15-year-olds (Melzer, 2000), and early unprotected sexual activity among black Caribbean young men and young women (Testa and Coleman, 2006). In terms of lone parent families there are significantly greater numbers of children and young people coming from black Caribbean backgrounds who grow up in such families, while significantly fewer young people of Asian background experience such family types (Coleman and Schofield, 2007). In addition to all this there is the probability that racism itself can act as a risk factor, creating stress and adversity for young people from any minority background.

As with gender, however, we have to be very cautious indeed about assuming that any one cultural or ethnic background involves a higher degree of risk than any other background. What is most likely is that each culture has a different pattern of risk, as well as having different factors that promote resilience. We noted in Chapter 1 the suggestion that while one parenting style might be appropriate for low-risk suburban environments, another parenting style (a more authoritarian style) might be more appropriate for a high-risk inner urban environment. Young people from ethnic minority backgrounds are more likely to be living in inner city environments, and therefore a stricter, more authoritarian parenting style may prove to be more protective for them (Cauce *et al.*, 2003; Coleman and Hendry, 1999).

It is encouraging to see that, in the United States at least, there has been a growing interest in studying resilience and positive adaptation among minority young people (Lerner *et al.*, 2002; Werner and Smith, 2001). Interestingly, many of the studies reviewed in these publications highlight protective factors that are similar to those found in white populations. Family factors are particularly salient for those from minority backgrounds, especially as many of these young people have substantial adversities to overcome. However, as we have noted all along, resilience is a complex concept and can only be understood as a dynamic process rather than a simple outcome.

This is well illustrated in recent research by Ong *et al.* (2006), who studied educational outcomes among young people from Hispanic backgrounds. Their findings highlighted the role of parental support as a central protective mechanism, but this variable interacted with others. They noted that what was called 'ethnic identity' also played a part in facilitating positive outcomes. Ethnic identity involved both a wish to explore one's own background, as well as a commitment to one's own particular ethnic group. Once again we can see how resilience develops, not just from a combination of protective factors but from factors which are appropriate to the circumstances of the individual.

Strengths and Weaknesses of the Medical Model

Many authors have pointed out that much of the thinking behind notions of both risk and resilience has been influenced by a simple version of the medical model. Sameroff *et al.*

(2003) make the point that the term 'risk factors' arose in the early epidemiological research which was trying to establish the causes of heart disease. Results from these studies showed that no one factor was either necessary or sufficient. Thus obesity, lack of exercise and smoking all made significant contributions, but for any one individual the pattern of risk factors differed according to the circumstances. However, even this acknowledgement of the interactive effect of various risk factors is far too simple an explanation for the types of behaviours we have been considering in this book. While it could be argued that the 'risk factor' concept has been helpful in some ways, it can also be seen that it may well have encouraged an oversimplified, outcome-based view of resilience.

Another example of the application of the medical model has been highlighted by Olsson *et al.* (2003) in their discussion of Rutter's ideas about 'steeling experiences'. These ideas again stem essentially from a medical concept, the concept of inoculation. Thus we know that giving someone a very small dose of a virus, such as the smallpox virus, increases their immunity to future re-infection. It may be that exposure to stress can teach people to be resilient. However, is this necessarily an appropriate model to apply to psychological processes? As Olsson *et al.* put it: "There is nothing about exposure to adversity that necessarily toughens one up" (2003, p. 7). We simply do not know whether it is true that small doses of adversity enhance resilience. In fact, resilience may indeed be strongest in those who have experienced close and secure attachments, and have not had to deal with loss, rejection or trauma. More research is needed to tackle these questions.

It may be that a model based on the notion of an accumulation of protective factors could more closely represent the underlying development of resilience. In other words, it could be argued that the more protective factors you have experienced, the more you will have to draw on when things get difficult. If we develop this notion further we can see that those who have had trusting relationships with parents and other important figures, and whose social circumstances provide a range of resources, may be more resilient than those who lack such resources. However, we have to be careful, as even this notion may be too simple. Olsson *et al.* (2003) make the point that when we consider 'steeling experiences' we have to keep in mind the dosage, as well as the timing and the existence of other buffering factors. Mild adversity in a situation where there are supports available may well lead to the development of new skills, and an enhanced self-concept. On the other hand, more powerful adversity experienced in a situation where there are few supports to buffer the impact could be very damaging.

We have raised this question of the place of the medical model in concepts of risk and resilience because this is a subject where there is still much that is unclear. Where concepts from one field of study are applied to another there is always room for misunderstanding, and as we have seen we have a long way to go before we can claim to have answered all the questions that apply to the notion of resilience. We will now turn to look at the ways that authors in this book have applied ideas about resilience to their particular fields.

Resilience in the Context of Young People at Risk

In reading the chapters in this book it becomes apparent that there are both similarities and differences between the authors in the ways they make use of the concept of resilience. There is certainly overlap between some of the chapters, but there are also many examples of authors looking at resilience from different perspectives. Taking the family first it will be apparent that, throughout the literature on risk and resilience, one conclusion that is agreed by all has to do with the key role played by parenting as both a risk and a protective factor. O'Brien and Scott (Chapter 2) make this point in no uncertain terms. The family offers a range of positive experiences, including of course love and affection, the quality of child care, stability, effective parenting styles, engagement and involvement in the life of the child or young person, as well as the material resources and social capital available in the family environment. Where these positive characteristics of family life are missing it will be obvious that children are likely to be at risk. In addition, O'Brien and Scott highlight three major risk factors: poverty, ineffective parenting styles and social exclusion, where it applies to parents.

There is a strong emphasis in Chapter 2 on the role of social capital as a protective factor, and it is worth noting that this is not something that other authors explore in any detail. By social capital in this context is meant a range of non-material resources that are available to influence the outcomes for children and young people. One example would be the quality of relationships within the family, including communication patterns, shared activities and so on. Other features of what is normally called social capital include the family's networks and contacts, their values, attitudes and opinions, and the range of supports that can be drawn up by family members in times of difficulty. The research by Pilling (1990) on educational achievement in disadvantaged circumstances highlights the role of social capital very well. In this research the key protective variables included parental interest and involvement, as well as high parental aspirations despite economic disadvantage.

Another approach to resilience can be seen in the three chapters dealing with disability, mental health and substitute care. In all three chapters the authors share a view of risk and resilience that highlights the disadvantage of stigma, and stresses the importance of developing a sense of agency in young people in order to overcome their adversities. Taking Mills and Frost (Chapter 3) first, their concern is with young people living in either residential or foster care. In this context the authors argue that such young people will be exposed to numerous risk factors, including of course disruption to family stability, as well as the possibility of having parents who have themselves experienced major disadvantage. Mills and Frost are particularly concerned to stress the importance of recognizing the young teenager's own strengths and capabilities, and finding ways of allowing these to develop. They believe that resilience can be encouraged through a tailored, individual and holistic approach to young people.

In Chapter 5, Vostanis explores the variety of mental health problems that may be experienced by adolescents, and he too stresses the importance of combating any stigma associated with mental disorder. Where resilience is concerned, Vostanis underlines the role of agency in the development of resources which may allow young people to recover and re-adjust following a period of mental ill-health. As he notes, a time of treatment or hospitalization may lead young people to feel that they have no agency, and that their fate is in the hands of doctors and other medical personnel. Resilience can be fostered through work which encourages adolescents to take control of their daily lives, and to rediscover the skills and resources they have available to them.

Stalker (Chapter 6) makes very similar points, although her concern is with disability. As she says, one of the most difficult things for young people with a disability is the issue of difference, of being considered an 'impaired person' who cannot do certain things and has to be treated with care and caution. This aspect of stigma is of major importance to such young people. This also links to the problem of over-protection, and the consequence that adolescents with a disability are often prevented from experiencing ordinary risk-taking behaviour. Stalker underlines the importance of adults being able to recognize the abilities and strengths of young people, and allow them to develop these in an appropriate manner. Resilience cannot grow in the context of disability unless young people are seen as individuals, with the capacity to achieve and mature.

It is of interest to note that the approach taken by these three chapters (Chapters 3, 5 and 6) does differ from that taken by Hagell (Chapter 7) and MacDonald (Chapter 8). Whilst the three we have just summarized emphasize the importance of stigma, and see resilience as coming from the development of personal characteristics such as agency, the next group of chapters focuses more on reducing the impact of risk, and on the influence of community factors on young people who experience adversity. Hagell (Chapter 7) makes this point when she argues for a need to reduce the focus on individual factors, and to recognize that offending has many different antecedents, only some of which can be traced back to the characteristics of the young person. As she states: "It is the role of the community that matters". By saying this she is underlining the point that we cannot expect resilience to develop among young people who may have had lifelong experiences of adversity unless their communities are willing to support them.

Hagell also points to the fact that many, if not most, of the young people who may become involved in anti-social behaviour will themselves be vulnerable, and will have been exposed to many adversities. They may have been victims themselves, they may have experienced abuse, trauma or rejection, and they will be likely to have substance misuse or mental health problems. Thus resilience for such young people can only be understood in the context of the hurdles that have to be overcome. The key task will be to reduce the impact of risk, either by offering new opportunities, or by developing new skills so that the risk environment can be minimized or avoided. Finally, Hagell points out the developmental nature of resilience. Resilience is not static. It may not be available to the individual at one stage of life, and yet may become possible at another stage if protective factors are in place.

MacDonald's argument follows similar lines. As he notes in Chapter 8, there are many problems with the discourse of risk as it applies to very disadvantaged or socially excluded young people. He points out that almost all the young people who have been involved in his research have been exposed to a wide variety of risks, and yet each has responded in an individual manner to his or her circumstances. In his view the life course of these young people can only be understood from a biographical, long-term perspective, linking to Hagell's point about resilience not being set in stone at any one life stage. MacDonald's major concern has to do with two risks – those of economic exclusion and of criminal involvement.

His studies allow for an exploration of the roles of historical and social context in an understanding of both risk and resilience. He stresses the variability among young people in their response to transitions, and notes the key part that opportunity plays in providing routes out of hardship. For MacDonald the role of individual factors in the development of resilience, while important, is less salient than the role of factors originating in the community.

We turn lastly to Chapter 4 by Pearce on sex and risk. In this chapter the author, after discussing how the sexual behaviour of young people can lead to risks of various types, then goes on to outline some of the ways that resilience can be facilitated in the context of sexual exploitation. Here Pearce suggests four areas for consideration:

• Strengthening psycho-social development, through the development of personal awareness, exploring and understanding trusting relationships, and the development of insight.

- Finding ways of supporting cognitive development, through showing the young person how to obtain useful information, learn about out-of-school education and engage in creative arts activities.
- Exploring and strengthening personal values, through enhanced self-esteem and independence.
- Helping young people become more perceptive about the social environment, by learning about community resources, health and other services, and by finding out about supportive adults in the locality.

This approach, offering many useful suggestions to practitioners, may be compared with the one outlined by Mills and Frost (Chapter 3) where they look at young people in care through the lens of the Every Child Matters agenda, and ask how the five outcomes can be used to promote resilience in the looked-after population. Considering, for example, the outcome 'Be Healthy', they discuss how this can be applied in the care situation. They ask how staff can focus on each of the outcomes to press for more resources and better services for this group in furtherance of the Every Child Matters agenda.

In this section we have looked at each chapter, and considered how the various authors have understood the notions of risk and resilience with reference to their own particular populations or areas of expertise. As we have noted, there is much overlap, but also some striking differences between the approaches. These similarities and differences are instructive, and they help us see how ideas about risk and resilience are used in different settings. They show the importance of the concept of resilience, but they also make concrete some of the concerns and difficulties which relate to these topics, which we have discussed in some detail in the earlier parts of this concluding chapter.

Interventions to Enhance Resilience

This last section is about ways that we might encourage successful outcomes with young people who have experienced significant adversity. Many young people do exceptionally well, even though the odds are stacked against them. How do they do this? Much is to do with the individuals themselves, or with their families and communities, but there are many things that professional adults can do too to assist in this process. Promoting resilience is not easy, and it requires sensitivity and flexibility. It often requires much time and effort, and it is helpful for adults to hold on to a conviction that risk does not necessarily lead to poor outcomes.

Luthar (2003) writes about a resilience framework for policy and practice, in which she suggests a mission, a model, measures that can be taken and some methods that may lead to the enhancement of resilience. In summary, these are as follows (p. 17).

- **Mission:** to frame goals in positive terms.
- **Model:** include positive predictors and outcomes in all models of change.
- **Measures:** in all assessments make sure the positives as well as the negatives are included.
- **Methods:** always consider multiple strategies based on models of resilience.

These ideas are very helpful, and they underline our views about the benefits of the use of a concept of resilience. We have stated that one of the most powerful benefits stemming from the use of resilience is that it makes it difficult to ignore the strengths of an individual. The use of resilience is a way of keeping hold of a positive perspective, and of ensuring that it is not just troubles and difficulties that are to the fore, but the opportunities and capabilities too.

In Chapter 1 we outlined three strategies for the reduction of risk, and the enhancement of resilience. These are:

1. Reducing the young person's exposure to risk.
2. Interrupting the chain reaction of negative events that can be associated with particular types of adversity.
3. Enhancing protective factors.

In our review of the suggestions made by the authors in this book it will be apparent that these are the key strategies in use in many different situations. Thus the promotion of a sense of agency, and the development of cognitive and psycho-social skills, fall into the category of enhancing protective factors. Reducing the young person's exposure to risk might, for example, involve the planning of more permanent placements for those in care, or organizing better after-care arrangements for those who are discharged from custody. One might imagine that interrupting the chain reaction of negative events in the case, for example, of young people with a disability or a mental health problem might be put in place by planning new, imaginative approaches to treatment and care.

Of course these three strategies are not the only ones suggested by Rutter (1987) and by Newman and his colleagues (2004). Some other strategies outlined by authors such as these include positive cognitive processing of negative events, providing compensatory experiences that counter the risk effect, facilitating a positive chain reaction following a good or self-enhancing experience, and finally reducing the impact of risk by putting buffering factors in place at appropriate times.

In conclusion, our belief, which has run through the text from the beginning, is that professional adults will achieve far more for young people who experience adversity if they emphasize the strengths and capabilities rather than the weaknesses. We take the view that it is possible to enhance resilience, and we have outlined here some of the strategies which are available to us all in our work with adolescents who are at risk. Not all the strategies will work, and not all will necessarily be appropriate. However, the very fact that there are strategies to enhance resilience, and that these can be applied to the young people who have been the focus of this book, should prove encouraging to all who are concerned with adolescents at risk.

References

A National Voice (2004) *There's no place like home.* www.anationalvoice.org

AACAP (1998) Practice parameters for the assessment and treatment of children and adolescents with depressive disorders. *Journal of the American Academy of Child and Adolescent Psychiatry* **37**(10): 63S–83S.

Action on Aftercare Consortium (2004) In Allard, A., Fry, E. and Sufian, J. (Eds), *Setting the agenda: What's left to do in leaving care.* NCH: London.

Adam, B., Beck, U. and Van Loon, J. (2000) *The risk society and beyond: Critical issues for social theory.* Sage: London.

Aggleton, P., Hurry, J. and Warrick, I. (2000) *Young people and mental health.* John Wiley & Sons, Ltd: Chichester.

Ainley, P. (1991) *Young people leaving home.* Cassell: London.

Alder, C. and Worrall, A. (2004) *Girls' violence: Myths and realities.* SUNNY Press: New York.

Allatt, P. (1993) Becoming privileged: The role of family processes. In Bates, I. and Riseborough, G. (Eds), *Youth and inequality.* Open University Press: Milton Keynes.

Allatt, P. and Yeandle, S. (1992) *Youth unemployment and the family: Voices of disordered times.* Routledge: London.

Anderson, L., Vostanis, P. and Spencer, N. (2004) Health needs of young offenders. *Journal of Child Health Care* **8**: 149–164.

Appleyard, K., Egeland, B., Van Dulmen, M. and Sroufe, A. (2005) When more is not better: The role of cumulative risk in child behavior outcomes. *Journal of Child Psychology and Psychiatry* **46**: 235–245.

Aries, P. (1962) *Centuries of childhood.* Vintage: New York.

Armstrong, C., Hill, M. and Secker, J. (2000) Young people's perceptions of mental health. *Children and Society* **14**: 60–72.

Armstrong, D. (2003) Pathways into and out of crime: Risk, resilience and diversity. *ESRC Research Priority Network Conference*, University of Sheffield.

Audit Commission (2004) *Services for disabled children – A review of services for disabled children and their families.* http://www.audit-commission.gov.uk/reports/NATIONAL-REPORT.asp?CategoryID.

Baker, K. and Donelly, M. (2001) The social experiences of children with disability and the influence of environment: A framework for intervention. *Disability and Society* **16**(1): 71–85.

Balding, J. (2006) Young people in 2005. Exeter Health Education Unit, Exeter University: Exeter.

Ball, S., Maguire, M. and Macrae, S. (2000) *Choice, pathways and transitions post-16: New youth, new economies in the global city.* Routledge/Falmer: London.

Barrett, H. and Tasker, F. (2001) Growing up with a gay parent: Views of 101 gay fathers on their sons' and daughters' experiences. *Educational and Child Psychology* **18**: 62–77.

Adolescence, Risk and Resilience: *Against the odds.* John Coleman and Ann Hagell (eds.).
Published in 2007 by John Wiley & Sons, Ltd

Bebbington, A. and Miles, J. (1989) The background of children who enter local authority care. *British Journal of Social Work* **19**(5): 349–368.

Beck, U. (1992) *Risk society: Towards a new modernity.* Sage: London.

Becker, H. (1963) *Outsiders: Studies in the sociology of deviance.* Free Press: Glencoe.

Beinart, S., Anderson, B., Lee, S. and Utting, D. (2002) *Youth at risk? A national survey of risk factors, protective factors and problem behaviour among young people in England, Scotland and Wales.* Communities that Care: London.

Benard, B., Marshall, K. (2001) *Protective factors in individuals, families and schools: National Longitudinal Study on Adolescent Health Findings.* National Resilience Resource Center, University of Minnesota: Minnesota.

Beresford, B. (1994) *Positively parents: Caring for a severely disabled child.* HMSO/SPRU: London.

Berger, P. and Berger, B. (1972) *Sociology: A biographical approach.* Basic Books: New York.

Bergman, M.M. and Scott, J. (2001) Young adolescents' well-being and health-risk behaviours: Gender and socio-economic differences. *Journal of Adolescence* **24**: 183–197.

Beynon, H., Hudson, R. and Sadler, D. (1994) *A place called Teesside.* Edinburgh University Press: Edinburgh.

Bhrolcháin, M., Chappell, R., Diamond, I. and Jameson, C. (2000) Parental divorce and outcomes for children: Evidence and interpretation. *European Sociological Review* **16**: 67–91.

Biehal, N., Clayden, J., Stein, M. and Wade, J. (1995) *Moving on.* HMSO: London.

Birchwood, M., Todd., P. and Jackson, C. (1998) Early intervention in psychosis: The critical period hypothesis. *British Journal of Psychiatry* **172** (Suppl. 33): 53–59.

Block, J.H., Block, J. and Gjerde, P.F. (1986) The personality of children prior to divorce: A prospective study. *Child Development* **57**: 827–840.

Bourdieu, P. (1986) The forms of capital. In Richardson, J.E. (Ed.), *Handbook of theory of research for the sociology of education.* Greenwood Press: New York.

Bourdieu, P. and Passeron, J.C. (1977) *Reproduction in education, society and culture.* Sage: London.

Bradshaw, J. (2002) Child poverty and child outcomes. *Children and Society* **16**: 131–140.

Brannen, J. (1999) Reconsidering children and childhood: Sociological and policy perspectives. In Silva, E.B. and Smart, C. (Eds), *The new family?* Sage: London; pp. 143–158.

Britton, L., Chatrick, B., Coles, B., Craig, G., Hylton, C. and Mumtaz, S. (2002) *Missing Connexions.* Policy Press: Bristol.

Brown, G.W. and Harris, T.O. (1989) *Life events and illness.* Guilford Press: New York.

Brown, P. (1987) *Schooling ordinary kids.* Tavistock: London.

Brown, P. and Scase, R. (1991) Social change and economic disadvantage. In Brown, P. and Scase, R. (Eds), *Poor work: Disadvantage and the division of labour.* Open University Press: Milton Keynes.

Bynner, J. (2001) Childhood risks and protective factors in social exclusion. *Children and Society* **15**: 285–301.

Bynner, J. and Parsons, S. (2002) Social exclusion and the transition from school to work: The case of young people not in education, employment or training. *Journal of Vocational Behaviour* **60**: 289–309.

Byrne, D. (1999) *Social exclusion.* Open University Press: Milton Keynes.

Callaghan, J., Young, B., Pace, F. and Vostanis, P. (2003) Mental health support for youth offending teams: A qualitative study. *Health and Social Care in the Community* **11**: 55–63.

Cameron, L. and Murphy, J. (2001) Views of young adults at the time of transition. *Communication Matters* **15**(1): 31–32.

Carlen, P., Gleeson, D. and Wardhaugh, J. (1992) *Truancy: The politics of compulsory schooling.* Open University Press: Buckingham.

Carr, A. (2000) *What works with children and adolescents?* Routledge: London.

Catan, L. (2004) *Becoming adult: Changing youth transitions in the 21st century: A synthesis of findings from the ESRC Research Programmes.* Youth, Citizenship and Social Change 1998–2003. Trust for the Study of Adolescence: Brighton.

Cauce, A.-M., Stewart, A., Rodriguez, M., Cochran, B. and Ginzler, J. (2003) Overcoming the odds? Adolescent development in the context of urban poverty. In Luthar, S. (Ed.), *Resilience and vulnerability*. Cambridge University Press: Cambridge.

Cavet, J. (1998) Leisure and friendship. In Robinson, C. and Stalker, K. (Eds), *Growing up with disability*. Jessica Kingsley Publishers: London.

Center for Longitudinal Studies (2005) *CLS Briefing November 2005: Parenting*. http://www.cls.ioe. ac.uk/downloads/CLSBriefing_Parenting.pdf

Chamberlain, P. (2003) The Oregon Multidimensional Treatment Foster Care model: Features, outcomes, and progress in dissemination. In Schoenwald, S. and Henggeler, S. (Series Eds), Moving evidence-based treatments from the laboratory into clinical practice. *Cognitive and Behavioral Practice* **10**(4): 303–312.

Chamberlayne, P., Rustin, M. and Wengraf, T. (2002) (Eds) *Biography and social exclusion in Europe*. Policy Press: Bristol.

Chase, E. and Stratham, J. (2005) Commercial sexual exploitation of children and young people in the UK – A review. *Child Abuse Review* **14**: 4–25.

Cliffe, D. and Berridge, D. (1991) *Closing children's homes: An end to residential care?* National Children's Bureau: London.

Coleman, J. (1988) Social capital in the creation of human capital. *American Journal of Sociology* **94**: 95–120.

Coleman, J. and Hendry, L. (1999) *The nature of adolescence*, 3rd edn. Routledge: London.

Coleman, J. and Roker, D. (2001) *Supporting parents of teenagers: A handbook for professionals*. Jessica Kingsley Publishers: London.

Coleman, J. and Schofield, J. (2005) *Key data on adolescence, 2005*. Trust for the Study of Adolescence: Brighton.

Coleman, J. and Schofield, J. (2007) *Key data on adolescence, 2007*. Trust for the Study of Adolescence: Brighton.

Coleman, L. and Cater, S. (2005) Underage 'risky' drinking: Motivations and outcomes. Joseph Rowntree Foundation: York and Trust for the Study of Adolescence: Brighton.

Coles, B. (1995) *Youth and social policy*. UCL Press: London.

Coles, B. (2000) *Joined up youth research, policy and practice: An agenda for change?* Youth Work Press: Leicester.

Collishaw, S., Maughan, B., Goodman, R. and Pickles, A. (2004) Time trends in adolescent mental health. *Journal of Child Psychology and Psychiatry* **45**: 1350–1362.

Compas, B. (1995) Promoting successful coping during adolescence. In Rutter, M. (Ed.), *Psychosocial disturbances in young people*. Cambridge University Press: Cambridge.

Compas, B., Orosan, P. and Grant, K. (1993) Adolescent stress and coping: implications for psychopathology in adolescence. *Journal of Adolescence* **16**: 331–349.

Conger, R.D., Ge, X., Elder, G.H., Lorenz, F. and Simons, R. (1994) Economic stress, coercive family process, and developmental problems of adolescents. *Child Development* **65**: 541–561.

Connors, C. and Stalker, K. (2003) *The views and experiences of disabled children and their siblings: A positive outlook*. Jessica Kingsley Publishers: London.

Cooper, A. and Lousada, J. (2005) *Borderline welfare: Feeling and fear of feeling in modern welfare*. Karnac Books: London.

Craine, S. (1997) The Black Magic Roundabout: Cyclical transitions, social exclusion and alternative careers. In MacDonald, R. (Ed.), *Youth, the 'underclass' and social exclusion*. Routledge: London.

Crow, I., France, A., Hacking, S. and Hart, M. (2004) *Does Communities that Care Work? An evaluation of a community-based risk prevention programme in three neighbourhoods*. Joseph Rowntree Foundation: York. Downloadable summary on the JRF website at www.jrf.org.uk/knowledge/findings/socialpolicy/n14.asp

Cunningham-Burley, S. and Coates, N. (2005) *Poverty and disability: A focus on families with disabled children*. Briefing Paper for Scottish Executive Social Inclusion Division, University of Edinburgh, Centre for Research on Families and Relationships.

Currie, C. (2004) (Ed.) *Health behaviour in school-aged children (HBSC) study: International report for the 2001/2002 survey*. WHO: Geneva, Switzerland.

Cusick, L., Martin, A. and May, T. (2003) *Vulnerability and involvement in drug use and sex work*. HOR 268. Home Office: London.

Daniel, B. and Wassell, S. (2002) *Assessing and promoting resilience in vulnerable children*. Jessica Kingsley Publishers: London.

Davis, J., Watson, N. and Cunningham-Burley, S. (2000) Learning the lives of disabled children: A reflexive approach. In Christiensen, P. and James, A. (Eds), *Research with children: Perspectives and practices*. Falmer Press: London.

Dean, J. (2003) *Unaddressed: The housing aspirations of young disabled people in Scotland*. Joseph Rowntree Foundation: York.

Dennis, N. (1993) *Rising crime and the dismembered family*. Institute of Economic Affairs: London.

Department for Education and Skills (2003) *Every child matters*. DfES: London.

Department of Health (1998) *Caring for children away from home: Messages from research*. John Wiley & Sons, Ltd: Chichester.

Department of Health (2000) *Me, survive, out there?* DoH: London.

Department of Health (2004) *National service framework for children, young people and maternity services: The mental health and psychological well-being of children and young people*. HMSO: London.

Department of Health/Home Office (2000) *Safeguarding children involved in prostitution*. HMSO: London.

Department of the Environment, Transport and the Regions (2000) *Index of multiple deprivation*. DETR: London.

Department for Education and Skills (2004) *Sex and relationship guidance* (update). www.dfes.gov.uk

Dishion, T.J. and McMahon, R.J. (1998) Parental monitoring and the prevention of child and adolescent problem behavior: A conceptual and empirical formulation. *Clinical Child and Family Psychology Review* **1**: 61–75.

Dishion, T.J., Poulin, F. and Medici Skaggs, N. (2000) The ecology of premature adolescent autonomy: Biological and social influences. In Kerns, K.A., Contreras, J. and Neal-Barrett, A.M. (Eds), *Explaining associations between family and peer relationships*. Praeger: Westport, CT; pp. 27–45.

Dishion, T.J., Nelson, S.E. and Kavanagh, K. (2003) The family check-up with high-risk young adolescents: Preventing early-onset substance use by parent monitoring. *Behavior Therapy* **34**: 553–571.

Dogra, N., Vostanis, P., Abuateya, H. and Jewson, N. (2005) Understanding of mental health and mental illness by Gujarati young people and their parents. *Diversity in Health and Social Care* **2**: 91–97.

Douglas, M. (1982) *Risk and culture: An essay on the selection of technological and environmental dangers*. University of California Press: Berkeley.

Douvan, E. and Adelson, J. (1966) *The adolescent experience*. John Wiley & Sons, Inc.: New York.

Duncan, G. and Brooks-Gunn, J. (1997) Income effects across the life span: Integration and interpretation. In Duncan, G. and Brooks-Gunn, J. (Eds). *Consequences of growing up poor*. Russell Sage Foundation: New York.

Dunn, J. and Plomin, R. (1990) *Separate lives: Why siblings are so different*. Basic Books: New York.

Emerson, E. (2003) The prevalence of psychiatric disorders in children and adolescents with and without developmental disabilities. *Journal of Intellectual Disability Research* **47**: 51–58.

Ennew, J. (2002) Outside childhood: Street children's rights. In Franklin, B. (Ed.), *The new handbook of children's rights*. Routledge: London.

Epps, K. (2006) 'Hard to place' children and young people: A commentary on past, present and future approaches to care and treatment. In Hagell, A. and Jeyarajah-Dent, R. (Eds), *Children who commit acts of serious interpersonal violence: Messages for best practice.* Jessica Kingsley Publishers: London.

Ermisch, J. and Francesconi, M. (2001) *The effect of parents' employment on children's lives.* Family Policy Studies Centre for the Joseph Rowntree Foundation: London.

ESRC (2004) *Pathways into and out of crime: Risk, resilience and diversity: Research Priority Network.* University of Sheffield: Sheffield.

Evans, R. and Pinnock, K. (2007) Promoting resilience and protective factors in the Children's Fund. *Journal of Children and Poverty* **13**: 21–32.

Farmer, E., Moyers, S. and Lipscombe, J. (2004) *Fostering adolescents.* Jessica Kingsley Publishers: London.

Farrell, C. (1978) *My mother said: The way young people learned about sex and birth control.* Routledge: London.

Farrington, D. (1994) Human development and criminal careers. In Maguire, M., Morgan, R. and Reiner, R. (Eds), *Oxford Handbook of Criminology.* Oxford University Press: Oxford.

Farrington, D. (1996) *Understanding and preventing youth crime.* Joseph Rowntree Foundation Social Policy Findings 93. Joseph Rowntree Foundation: York.

Farrington, D. and Painter, K. (2004) *Gender differences in offending: Implications for risk-focused prevention.* Home Office Online Report 09/04. Home Office: London.

Fawcett, B., Featherstone, B. and Goddard, J. (2004) *Contemporary child care policy and practice.* Palgrave Macmillan: Basingstoke.

Featherstone, B. (2004) *Family life and family support.* Palgrave: London.

Fergusson, D. and Horwood, L. (2003) Resilience to childhood adversity: results of a 21 year study. In Luthar, S. (Ed.), *Resilience and vulnerability.* Cambridge University Press: Cambridge.

Fergusson, D. and Lynskey, M. (1996) Adolescent resiliency to family adversity. *Journal of Child Psychology and Psychiatry* **37**: 281–292.

Fergusson, D., Horwood, J. and Lynskey, M. (1994) The childhoods of multiple problem adolescents: a 15-year longitudinal study. *Journal of Child Psychology and Psychiatry* **35**: 1123–1140.

Ferri, E. and Smith, K. (2003) Family life. In Ferri, E., Bynner, J. and Wadsworth, M. (Eds), *Changing Britain, changing lives: Three generations at the turn of the century.* Institute of Education: London; pp. 133–147.

Finkelstein, V. (1993) Disability: A social challenge or an administrative responsibility? In Swain, J., Finkelstein, V., French, S. and Oliver, M. (Eds), *Disabling barriers – enabling environments.* Sage: London.

Fleitlich-Bilyk, B. and Goodman, R. (2004) Prevalence of child and adolescent psychiatric disorders in southeast Brazil. *Journal of the American Academy of Child and Adolescent Psychiatry* **43**: 727–734.

Fonagy, P. (with Target, M., Cottrell, D., Phillips, J. and Kurtz, Z.) (2002) *What works for whom? A critical review of treatments for children and adolescents.* Guilford: New York.

Foundation for People with Learning Disabilities (2002) *Count Us In: The report of a committee of enquiry into meeting the mental health needs of young people with learning disabilities.* The Foundation for People with Learning Disabilities: London.

Frost, N., Mills, S. and Stein, M. (1999) *Understanding residential care.* Ashgate: Aldershot.

Frydenberg, E. and Lewis, R. (1993) Boys play sport and girls turn to others: Age, gender and ethnicity as determinants of coping. *Journal of Adolescence* **16**: 253–266.

Furstenberg, F. and Hughes, M. (1995) Social capital and successful development among at-risk youth. *Journal of Marriage and Family* **57**: 580–592.

Garmezy, N. and Rutter, M. (1983) (Eds) *Stress, coping and development in children.* McGraw-Hill: New York.

Gest, S., Reed, M. and Masten, S. (1999) Measuring developmental changes in exposure to adversity. *Development and Psychopathology* **11**: 171–192.

Giddens, A. (1990) *The consequences of modernity.* Polity Press: Cambridge.

Gillberg, C. (1995) *Clinical child neuropsychiatry.* Cambridge University Press: Cambridge.

Gilligan, R. (1999) Enhancing the resilience of children in public care by mentoring their talent and interests. *Child and Family Social Work* **4**(3): 187–196.

Gilligan, R. (2001) *Promoting resilience: A resource guide on working with children in the care system.* British Association for Adopting and Fostering: London.

Gittens, D. (1998) *The child in time.* Macmillan: Basingstoke.

Goldson, B., Lavalette, M. and McKechnie, J. (2002) (Eds) *Children, welfare and the state.* Sage: London.

Goldstein, S. and Brooks, S.R. (2005) *Handbook of resilience in children.* Kluwer Academic Press: New York.

Golombok, S. (2000) *Parenting: What really counts?* Routledge: London.

Golombok, S. and Tasker, F. (1996) Do parents influence the sexual orientation of their children? Findings from a longitudinal study of lesbian families. *Developmental Psychology* **32**: 3–11.

Gowers, S. and Bryant-Waugh, R. (2004) Management of child and adolescent eating disorders: the current evidence base and future directions. *Journal of Child Psychiatry and Psychology* **45**: 63–83.

Graham, J. and Bowling, B. (1995) *Young people and crime.* Home Office Research Study 145. HMSO: London.

Green, H. *et al.* (2005) *Mental health of children and young people in Britain, 2004.* Office for National Statistics: London.

Gregg, P., Harkness, S. and Machin, S. (1999) *Children's development and family incomes.* Joseph Rowntree Foundation: York.

Gurney, A. (2000) Risk management. In Davies, M. (Ed.), *The Blackwell Encyclopaedia of Social Work.* Blackwell: Oxford.

Hagell, A. (2003) *Understanding and challenging youth offending.* Research in Practice Quality Protects Briefing No. 8. Department of Health, Research in Practice and Making Research Count: London. Available at www.rip.org.uk

Hagell, A., Hazel, N. and Shaw, C. (2000) *Evaluation of Medway Secure Training Centre.* Home Office Research, Development and Statistics Directorate: London.

Halpern, C., Young, M., Waller, M., Martin, S. and Kupper, L. (2004) Prevalence of partner violence in same-sex romantic and sexual relationships in a national sample of adolescents. *Journal of Adolescent Health* **35**: 124–131.

Harper, Z. and Scott, S. (2005) *Meeting the needs of sexually exploited young people in London.* Barnardo's: Essex.

Harrikson, S., Rickert, V. and Wiemann, C. (2002) Prevalence and patterns of intimate partner violence among adolescent mothers during the postpartum period. *Archives of Pediatrics and Adolescent Medicine* **157**(4): 325–330.

Hawkins, J. et al. (1999) Preventing adolescent health-risk behaviors by strengthening protection during childhood. *Archives of Pediatric Medicine* **153**: 226–234.

Hawton, K., Hall, S., Simkin, S., Bale, L., Bond, A., Codd, S. and Stewart, A. (2003) Deliberate self-harm in adolescents: A study of characteristics and trends in Oxford, 1999–2000. *Journal of Child Psychology and Psychiatry* **44**: 1191–1198.

Hayden, C. (2003) Exclusion or inclusion? *Social Policy Association Conference*, University of Teesside, 15–17 July 2003.

Hayden, C., Goddard, J., Gorin, S. and Van Der Speck, N. (1999) *State child care.* Jessica Kingsley Publishers: London.

Hayward, R. and Sharp, C. (2005) *Young people, crime and antisocial behaviour: Findings from the 2003 Crime and Justice Survey.* Home Office Findings No. 245. Research, Development and Statistics Directorate, Home Office: London. Downloadable from www.homeoffice.gov.uk/rds/pdfs05/r245.pdf/

Health Advisory Service (1995) *Child and adolescent mental health services.* HMSO: London.

Heaven, P.C.L. (1994) *Contemporary adolescence: A social psychological approach.* Macmillan: Basingstoke.

Hebdige, D. (1979) *Subculture.* Routledge: London.

Hebdige, D. (1988) *Hiding in the light.* Comedia/Routledge: London.

Hendry, L.B., Shucksmith, J., Love, J.G. and Glendinning, A. (1993) *Young people's leisure and life-styles.* Routledge: London.

Henggeler, S.W., Clingempeel, W.G., Brondino, M.J. and Pickrel, S.G. (2002) Four-year follow-up of multisystemic therapy with substance-abusing and substance-dependent juvenile offenders. *Journal of the American Academy of Child and Adolescent Psychiatry* **41**(7): 868–874.

Heslop, P., Mallett, R., Simons, K. and Ward, L. (2001) *Bridging the divide: The experiences of young people with learning difficulties and their families at transition.* Norah Fry Research Centre, University of Bristol.

Hess, L. (1995) Changing family patterns in Western Europe: Opportunities and risk factors for adolescent development. In Rutter, M. and Smith, D. (Eds), *Psychosocial disorders in young people: Time trends and their causes.* John Wiley & Sons, Ltd: Chichester.

Hetherington, E. (1989) Coping with family transition: winners, losers and survivors. *Child Development* **60**: 1–14.

Hill, J. and Maughan, B. (2001) (Eds) *Conduct disorders in childhood and adolescence.* Cambridge University Press: Cambridge.

Hill, M. (1999) *Signposts in fostering.* British Association for Adoption and Fostering: London.

Hills, J., Le Grand, J. and Piachaud, D. (2002) (Eds) *Understanding social exclusion.* Oxford University Press: Oxford.

Hochschild, A. (1997) *The time bind: When work becomes home and home becomes work.* Metropolitan Books: New York.

Hodkinson, P. and Sparkes, A. (1997) Careership: A sociological theory of career decision making. *British Journal of Sociology of Education* **18**(1): 29–44.

Hoggart, L. (2006) Risk: Young women and sexual decision-making [55 paragraphs]. *Forum Qualitative Sozialforschung/Forum: Qualitative Social Research* [on-line journal] **7**(1), Art. 28. Available at: http://www.qualitative-research.net/fqs-texte/1-06/06-1-28-e.htm

Holland, J., Ramazanoglu, C. and Sharpe, S. (1993) *Wimp or gladiator: Contradictions in acquiring masculine sexuality.* WRAP/MRAP Paper 9. Tufnell Press: London.

Holloway, W. and Valentine, G. (2001) (Eds) *Children's geographies.* Routledge: London.

Home Office (2003) Government cracking crime in 'Kelby'. *Press Release,* www.drugs.gov.uk/news [accessed 1 September 2003].

Home Office (2004) *Confident communities in a secure Britain: The Home Office Strategic Plan 2004-8.* CM 6287. Home Office: London.

Home Office (downloaded 25 November 2006) http://www.homeoffice.gov.uk/anti-social-behaviour/

Howard, S., Dryden, J. and Johnson, B. (1999) Childhood resilience: Review and critique of literature. *Oxford Review of Education* **25**(3): 307–323.

Hughes, B., Russell, R. and Paterson, K. (2005) Nothing to be had 'off the peg': Consumption, identity and the immobilization of young disabled people. *Disability and Society* **20**(1): 3–18.

Hussain, Y., Atkin, K. and Waqar, A. (2001) *South Asian disabled young people and their families.* Policy Press: Bristol.

Hutson, S. and Jenkins, R. (1989) *Taking the strain: Families, unemployment and the transition to adulthood.* Open University Press: Milton Keynes.

Huurre, T., Aro, H., Rahkonen., O. and Komulainen, E. (2006) Health, lifestyle, family and school factors in adolescence: Predicting adult educational level. *Educational Research* **48**(1): 41–53.

Ingoldsby, E. and Shaw, D.S. (2002) Neighborhood contextual factors and the onset and progression of early-starting antisocial pathways. *Clinical Child and Family Psychology Review* **5**: 21–55.

Irwin, C.E. Jr. and Millstein, S.G. (1986) Biopsychosocial correlates of risk-taking behaviours during adolescence. *Journal of Adolescent Health Care* **7**: 82–96.

Istance, D., Rees, G. and Williamson, H. (1994) *Young people not in education, training or employment in South Glamorgan*. South Glamorgan Training and Enterprise Council/University of Wales: Cardiff.

Jackson, S. (2000) Resilience. In Davies, M. (Ed.), *The Blackwell Encyclopaedia of Social Work*. Blackwell: Oxford.

Jackson, S. (2001) (Ed.) *No one ever told us school matters*. British Association for Adoption and Fostering: London.

Jackson, S. and Goossens, L. (2006) (Eds) *Handbook of adolescent development*. Psychology Press: Hove, Sussex.

James, A., Jenks, C. and Prout, A. (1998) *Theorising childhood*. Polity Press: Cambridge.

Jessor, R. and Jessor, S. (1977) *Problem behaviour and psychosocial development: a longitudinal study of youth*. Academic Press: New York.

Jessor, R., Turbin, M.S., Costa, F.M., QiDong, H.Z. and Wang, C. (2003) Adolescent problem behaviour in China and the United States: A cross national study of psychosocial protective factors. *Journal of Research on Adolescence* **13**: 329–360.

Johnston, L., MacDonald, R., Mason, P., Ridley, L. and Webster, C. (2000) *Snakes & ladders: Young people, transitions & social exclusion*. Policy Press: Bristol.

Jones, G. (1995) *Leaving home*. Open University Press: Milton Keynes.

Joshi, H. and Verropoulou, G. (2000) *Maternal employment and child outcomes: Analysis of two birth cohorts*. The Smith Institute: London.

Joshi, H., Cooksey, E., Wiggins, R., McCulloch, A., Verropoulou, G. and Clarke, L. (1999) Diverse family living situations and child development. A multi-level analysis comparing longitudinal information from Britain and the United States. *International Journal of Law and Social Policy* **13**: 293–314.

Kaestle, C. and Halpern, C. (2005) Sexual intercourse precedes partner violence in adolescent romantic relationships. *Journal of Adolescent Health* **36**: 386–392.

Kelley, P., Hood, S. and Mayall, B. (1998) Children, parents and risk. *Health and Social Care in the Community* **6**(1): 16–24.

Kiernan, K.E. (1992) The impact of family disruption in childhood on transitions in young adulthood. *Population Studies* **46**: 213–221.

Kiernan, K.E. (1996) Lone motherhood, employment and outcomes for children. *International Journal of Law, Policy and the Family* **10**: 233–249.

Langan, J. (1999) Assessing risk in mental health. In Parsloe, P. (Ed.), *Risk assessment in social care and social work*. Jessica Kingsley Publishers: London.

Laub, J. and Sampson, R. (2003) *Shared beginnings, divergent lives: Delinquent boys to aged 70*. Harvard University Press: Cambridge, MA.

Lawson, J. (1996) A framework of risk assessment and management for older people. In Kemshall, H. and Pritchard, J. (Eds), *Good practice in risk assessment and risk management*, Vol. 1. Jessica Kingsley Publishers: London.

Lee, S. (2002) Gender, ethnicity and vulnerability in young women in local authority care. *British Journal of Social Work* **32**: 907–922.

Leonard, M. (2005) Children, childhood and social capital: Exploring the links. *Sociology* **39**: 605–622.

Lerner, R., Jacobs, F. and Wertlieb, D. (2002) *Handbook of applied developmental science*, Vol. 1. Sage Publications: New York.

Leventhal, T. and Brooks-Gunn, J. (2000) The neighborhoods they live in: The effects of neighborhood residence on child and adolescent outcomes. *Psychological Bulletin* **26**: 309–337.

Levitas, R. (1998) *The inclusive society? Social exclusion and New Labour*. Macmillan: Basingstoke.

Loeber, R. and Stouthamer-Loeber, M. (1986) Family factors as correlates and predictors of juvenile conduct problems and delinquency. In Tonry, M. and Morris, N. (Eds), *Crime and justice*, Vol. 7. University of Chicago Press: Chicago.

Logan, J., Kershaw, S., Karban, K., Mills, S., Trotter, J. and Sinclair, M. (1996): *Confronting prejudice Lesbian and gay issues in social work education.* Arena: Aldershot.

Luthar, S. (2003) (Ed.) *Resilience and vulnerability.* Cambridge University Press: Cambridge.

Luthar, S. and Zelazo, L. (2003) Research on resilience: An integrative review. In Luthar, S. (Ed.), *Resilience and vulnerability.* Cambridge University Press: Cambridge.

MacDonald, R. (1997) Youth, social exclusion and the millennium. In MacDonald, R. (Ed.), *Youth, the 'underclass' and social exclusion.* Routledge: London.

MacDonald, R. (2006) Social exclusion, youth transitions and criminal careers: Five critical reflections on risk. *Australian and New Zealand Journal of Criminology* **39**(3): 371–383.

MacDonald, R. and Marsh, J. (2001) Disconnected youth? *Journal of Youth Studies* **4**(4): 373–391.

MacDonald, R. and Marsh, J. (2002) Crossing the Rubicon: Youth transitions, poverty drugs and social exclusion. *International Journal of Drug Policy* **13**: 27–38.

MacDonald, R. and Marsh, J.(2005) *Disconnected youth? Growing up in Britain's poor neighbourhoods.* Palgrave: Basingstoke.

MacDonald, R. and Shildrick, T. (2007) Street corner society: Leisure careers, youth (sub)culture and social exclusion. *Leisure Studies,* **26**(3): 339–355.

Macintyre, S., MacIver, S. and Sooman, A. (2002) Area, class and health: Should we be concentrating on places or people? In Nettleton, S. and Gustaffson, U. (Eds), *The Sociology of Health and Illness Reader.* Polity Press: Cambridge.

Masten, A. and Powell, J. (2003) A resilience framework for research, policy and practice. In Luthar, S. (Ed.), *Resilience and vulnerability.* Cambridge University Press: Cambridge.

McAuley, C., Knapp, M., Beecham, J., McCurry, N. and Sleed, M. (2004) *Young families under stress: Outcomes and costs of Home-Start support.* Joseph Rowntree Foundation: York.

McDermott, P. (1996) A nationwide study of developmental and gender prevalence for psychopathology in childhood and adolescence. *Journal of Abnormal Child Psychology* **24**: 53–66.

McKeganey, N. and Barnard, M. (1992) *Sex work on the streets.* Blackwell: London.

Meetoo, V. and Mirza, H. (2007) Lives at risk: Multiculturalism, young women and 'honour' killings. In Thom, B., Sales, R. and Pearce, J. (Eds), *Growing up with risk.* Policy Press: Bristol.

Melrose, M. and Barrett, D. (2004) (Eds) *Anchors in floating lives: Interventions with young people sexually abused through prostitution.* Russell House Publishing: Lyme Regis.

Meltzer, H., Gatward, R., Goodman, R. and Ford, T. (2000) *The mental health of children and adolescents in Great Britain.* HMSO: London.

Mental Health Foundation (1999) *Bright futures: promoting children and young people's mental health.* Mental Health Foundation: London.

Merton, B. (1998) *Finding the missing.* Youth Work Press: Leicester.

Michaud, P.-A. (2006) Adolescents and risks: Why not change our paradigm? *Journal of Adolescent Health* **38**: 481–483.

Miller, D. (2003) Disabled children and abuse. In *"It doesn't happen to disabled children": Child protection and disabled children.* Report of the National Working Group on Child Protection and Disability.

Mills, S. (1998) Exploring perceptions of risk in residential child care. Unpublished M.A. Dissertation, University of Bradford.

Mitchell, R., Shaw, M. and Dorling, D. (2000) *Inequalities in life and death: What if Britain were more equal?* Policy Press: Bristol.

Moore, S. and Rosenthal, D. (2006) *Sexuality in adolescence: Current trends.* Routledge: London.

Morris, J. (2002) *Young disabled people moving into adulthood,* Foundations 512. Joseph Rowntree Foundation: York. www.jrf.org.uk

Morrow, V. and Richards, M. (1996) *Transitions to adulthood: A family matter?* Joseph Rowntree Foundation: York.

Murray, P. (2000) Disabled children, parents and professionals: Partnership on whose terms? *Disability and Society* **15**(4): 683–698.

NACRO (2006) *Youth Crime Briefing: Some facts about children and young people who offend – 2004.* NACRO: London. Downloadable from www.nacro.org.uk

National Working Group on Child Protection and Disability (2003) "*It doesn't happen to disabled children": Child protection and disabled children.* NSPCC: London. See also www.nspcc.org.uk

Newman, T. (2002) Promoting resilience in children and young people during periods of transition. Scottish Executive: Edinburgh. Available at: http://www.scotland.gov.uk/library5/education/ic78-00.asp

Newman, T. (2004) *What works in building resilience?* Barnado's: Essex.

NHS Health Scotland (2005) *Young people's attitudes towards gendered violence – August 2005.* NHS Health Scotland: Edinburgh.

Nuffield Foundation (2004) *Time trends in adolescent well-being.* Briefing paper. Nuffield Foundation: London (www.nuffieldfoundation.orgamh)

O'Brien, M. and Jones, D. (1999) Children, parental employment and educational attainment. *Cambridge Journal of Economics* **23**: 599–621.

Oliver, M. (1990) *The politics of disablement.* Macmillan: Basingstoke.

Olsson, C., Bond, L., Burns, J., Vella-Brodrick, D. and Sawyer, S. (2003) Adolescent resilience: A concept analysis. *Journal of Adolescence* **26**: 1–11.

Ong, A., Phinney, J. and Dennis, J. (2006) Competence under challenge: Exploring the protective influence of parental support and ethnic identity in Latino college students. *Journal of Adolescence* **29**: 961–980.

Osler, A., Street, C., Lall, M. and Vincent, K. (2002) *Not a problem? Girls and school exclusion.* National Children's Bureau: London.

Page, R. and Clarke, G. (1976) *Young people in care speak out.* National Children's Bureau: London.

Palmer, T. and Stacey, L. (2004) *Just one click.* Barnardo's: Essex.

Parker, H., Bury, C. and Eggington, R. (1998a) *New heroin outbreaks amongst young people in England and Wales.* Police Research Group, Paper 92. Home Office: London.

Parker, H., Aldridge, J. and Measham, F. (1998b) *Illegal leisure.* Routledge: London.

Patterson, C.J. (1996) Lesbian and gay parenthood. In Bornstein, M.H. (Ed.), *Handbook of parenting.* Lawrence Erlbaum Associates: Hillsdale, NJ; pp. 255–274.

Patterson, G. (1982) *Coercive family processes.* Castalia: Eugene, OR.

Pavis, S. and Cunningham-Burley, S. (1999) Male youth street culture: Understanding the context of health-related behaviours. *Health Education Research* **14**(5): 583–596.

Pearce, J. (2006) Who needs to be involved in safeguarding sexually exploited young people? *Child Abuse Review* **5**(5): 326–341.

Pearce, J. (2007) Risk and resilience: A focus on sexually exploited young people. In Thom, B., Sales, R. and Pearce, J. (Eds), *Growing up with risk.* Policy Press: Bristol.

Pearce, J.J. (with Williams, M. and Galvin, C.) (2002) *It's someone taking a part of you: A study of young women and sexual exploitation.* National Children's Bureau: London.

Pearson, G. (1983) *Hooligan: A history of respectable fears.* Macmillan: London.

Perri 6 *et al.* (1997) *The substance of youth: The role of drugs in young people's lives today.* Joseph Rowntree Foundation: York.

Phillips, M. (2004) Childhood's lost idyll. *Daily Mail*, 14 September 2004 [Online]. Available at: http://www.melaniephillips.com/articles-new/?p=254 (13 October 2006).

Phoenix, J. (2002) In the name of prostitution: Youth prostitution policy reforms in England and Wales. *Critical Social Policy* **22**(2): 353–375.

Pilling, D. (1990) *Escape from disadvantage.* The Falmer Press: London.

Pinderhughes, E.E., Nix, R., Foster, E.M. and Jones, D. (2001) The Conduct Problems Prevention Research Group. Parenting in context: Impact of neighborhood poverty, residential stability, public services, social networks, and danger on parental behaviors. *Journal of Marriage and the Family* **63**: 941–953.

Pitts, J. (1997) Causes of youth prostitution, new forms of practice and political responses. In Barrett, D. (Ed.), *Child prostitution in Britain: Dilemmas and practical responses*. The Children's Society: London; pp. 139–158.

Prince's Trust (2004) *Looking beyond the label*. The Prince's Trust: London.

Raffe, D. (2003) *Young people not in education, training or employment*. Special CES Briefing no. 29. Centre for Educational Sociology: Edinburgh.

Richards, M. and Vostanis, P. (2004) Interprofessional perspectives on mental health services for young people 16–19 years. *Journal of Interprofessional Care* **18**: 115–128.

Ridge, T. (2002) *Childhood poverty and social exclusion: From a child's perspective*. Policy Press: Bristol.

Roberts, H., Liabo, K., Lucas, P., DuBois, D. and Sheldon, T. (2004) Mentoring to reduce antisocial behaviour in childhood. *British Medical Journal* **328**: 512–514. Downloadable at www.bmj.bmjjournals.com/cgi/content/full/328/7438/512

Roberts, K. (1995) *Youth and employment in modern Britain*. Open University Press: Milton Keynes.

Robins, L. and Rutter, M. (1990) *Straight and devious pathways from childhood to adulthood*. Cambridge University Press: Cambridge.

Rodham, K., Brewer, H., Mistral, W. and Stallard, P. (2006) Adolescents' perception of risk and challenge: A qualitative study. *Journal of Adolescence* **29**: 261–272.

Roker, D. (1998) *Worth more than this: Young people growing up in poverty*. Trust for the Study of Adolescence: Brighton.

Ronka, A., Oravala, S. and Pulkinner, L. (2002) "I met this wife of mine, and things got on to a better track". Turning points in risk development. *Journal of Adolescence* **25**: 47–64.

Russell, P. (1996) Children with disabilities. In Kemshall, H. and Pritchard, J. (Eds), *Good practice risk assessment and risk management*, Vol. 1. Jessica Kingsley Publishers: London.

Rutherford, A. (1986) *Growing out of crime: society and young people in trouble*. Penguin Books: Middlesex.

Rutter, M. (1985) Resilience in the face of adversity: Protective factors and resistance to psychiatric disorders. *British Journal of Psychiatry* **147**: 589–611.

Rutter, M. (1987) Psychological resilience and protective mechanisms. *American Journal of Orthopsychiatry* **57**: 316–331.

Rutter, M. (2003) Genetic influences on risk and protection: Implications for understanding resilience. In Luthar, S. (Ed.), *Resilience and vulnerability*. Cambridge University Press: Cambridge.

Rutter, M. (2006a) Implications of resilience concepts for scientific understanding. *Annals of the New York Academy of Science* **1094**: 1–12.

Rutter, M. (2006b) Is Sure Start an effective intervention? *Child and Adolescent Mental Health* **11**(3): 135–141.

Rutter, M. and Smith, D.J. (1995) (Eds) *Psychosocial disorders in young people: Time trends and their causes*. John Wiley & Sons, Ltd: Chichester.

Rutter, M., Graham, P., Chadwick, O. and Yule, W. (1976) Adolescent turmoil: Fact or fiction? *Journal of Child Psychology and Psychiatry* **17**: 35–56.

Rutter, M., Dunn, J., Plomin, R., Simonoff, E., Pickles, A., Maughan, B., Ormel, J., Meyer, J. and Eaves, L. (1997a) Integrating nature and nurture: Implications of person–environment correlations and interactions for developmental psychopathology. *Developmental Psychopathology* **9**(2): 335–364.

Rutter, M., Maughan, B., Meyer, J., Pickles, A., Silberg, J., Simonoff, E. and Taylor, E. (1997b) *Heterogeneity of anti-social behaviour: Causes, continuities and consequences*. In Dienstbier,

R. and Osgood, D. (Eds), Nebraska Symposium on Motivation: Vol. 44. University of Nebraska Press: Lincoln, NE.

Rutter, M., Giller, H. and Hagell, A. (1998) *Antisocial behaviour by young people.* Cambridge University Press: Cambridge.

Sameroff, A., Gutman, L. and Peck, S. (2003) Adaptation among youth facing multiple risks: Prospective research findings. In Luthar, S. (Ed.), *Resilience and adversity.* Cambridge University Press: Cambridge.

Sampson, R. and Laub, J. (1993) *Crime in the making: Pathways and turning points through life.* Harvard University Press: Cambridge, MA.

Sanders, T. (2005) *Sex work. A risky business.* Willan Publishing: Devon.

Santisteban, D.A., Coatsworth, J.D., Perez-Vidal, A., Kurtines, W.M., Schwartz, S., Laperriere, A. and Szapocznik, J. (2003) The efficacy of brief strategic structural family therapy in modifying Hispanic adolescent behavior problems and substance abuse. *Journal of Family Psychology* **17**: 121–133.

Savin-Williams, R.C. and Diamond, L. (2001) Sexual identity trajectories among sexual minority youths: Gender comparisons. *Archives of Sexual Behaviour* **29**: 419–440.

Schoon, I. and Bynner, J. (2003) Risk and resilience in the life course: Implications for interventions and social policies. *Journal of Youth Studies* **6**: 21–31.

Schoon, I. and Parsons, S. (2002) Competence in the face of adversity: The influence of early family environment and long-term consequences. *Children and Society* **16**: 260–272.

Schutt, N. (2006) *Domestic violence in adolescent relationships.* Safer Southwark Partnerships: London.

Scott, J. (2004a) Family, gender, and educational attainment in Britain: A longitudinal study. *Journal of Comparative Family Studies* **35**: 529–540.

Scott, J. (2004b) Children's families. In Scott, J., Treas, J. and Richards, M. (Eds), *The Blackwell companion to the sociology of families.* Blackwell: Oxford; pp. 109–125.

Scott, J. and Chaudhary, C. (2003) *Beating the odds: Youth and family disadvantage.* Youth, Citizenship and Social Change: An ESRC Research Programme. National Youth Agency: Leicester.

Seiffge-Krenke, L. (1995) *Stress, coping and relationships in adolescence.* Lawrence Erlbaum Associates: Mahwah, NJ.

Sharland, E. (2005) Young people, risk taking and risk making: Some thoughts for social work. *British Journal of Social Work*, BJSW advance/access published online 17 October, 2005, doi:10.1093/bjsw/bch254.

Shaw, C. (1998) *Remember my messages: the experiences and views of 2000 children in public care in the UK.* Who Cares Trust: London.

SHS (Scottish Human Services) Trust (2002) *Real choices: A participatory action research project involving young people with learning difficulties who are about to leave school.* SHS Trust: Edinburgh.

Silva, E.B. and Smart, C. (1999) (Eds) *The new family?* Sage: London.

Simpson, D. and Cieslik, M. (2000) Expanding study support nationally: Implications from an evaluation of the East Middlesbrough Education Action Zone's programme. *Educational Studies* **26**(4): 503–515.

Simpson, M. (2003) The relationship between drug use and crime: A puzzle inside an enigma. *International Journal of Drug Policy* **14**: 307–319.

Sinclair, I., Wilson, K. and Gibbs, I. (2004a) *Foster placements: Why they succeed and why they fail.* Jessica Kingsley Publishers: London.

Sinclair, I., Wilson, K. and Gibbs, I. (2004b) *Foster carers: Why they stay and why they leave.* Jessica Kingsley Publishers: London.

Skelton, T. (2002) Research on youth transitions: Some critical interventions. In Cieslik, M. and Pollock, G. (Eds), *Young people in risk society: The restructuring of youth identities and transitions in late modernity.* Ashgate: Aldershot.

Skinner, T., Hester, M. and Malos, E. (2005) (Eds) *Researching gender violence: Feminist methodology in action*. Willan Publishing: Devon.

Smart, C. (1999) The 'new' parenthood: Fathers and mothers after divorce. In Silva, E.B. and Smart, C. (Eds), *The new family?* Sage: London; pp. 100–114.

Smart, C. and Neale, B. (1999) *Family fragments?* Polity Press: Cambridge.

Smith, D. and McVie, S. (2003) Theory and method in the Edinburgh Study of Youth Transitions and Crime. *British Journal of Criminology* **43**: 169–195.

Smith, K. and Leon, L. (2001) *Turned upside down: Developing community-based crisis services for 16–25-year-olds experiencing a mental health crisis*. Mental Health Foundation: London.

Social Care Institute for Excellence (2005) *Resilience resource guide*. www.scie.org.uk

Social Exclusion Unit (1997) *Tackling truancy*. Social Exclusion Unit: London.

Social Exclusion Unit (1998) *Bringing Britain together: A national strategy for neighbourhood renewal*. Social Exclusion Unit: London.

Social Exclusion Unit (1999) *Bridging the gap*. Social Exclusion Unit: London.

Stattin, H. and Kerr, M. (2000) Parental monitoring: A reinterpretation. *Child Development* **71**: 1072–1085.

Stein, M. (2005) *Overcoming the odds: Resilience and young people leaving care*. Joseph Rowntree Foundation: York.

Stein, M. and Carey, K. (1986) *Leaving care*. Blackwell: Oxford.

Sullivan, A. (2001) Cultural capital and educational attainment. *Sociology* **35**: 893–912.

Swain, J., French, S., Barnes, C. and Thomas, C. (2004) *Disabling barriers, enabling environments*, 2nd edn. Sage: London.

Szapocznik, J. and Coatsworth, J.D. (1999) An ecodevelopmental framework for organizing risk and protection for drug abuse: A developmental model of risk and protection. In Glantz, M. and Hartel, C.R. (Eds), *Drug abuse: Origins and interventions*. American Psychological Association: Washington, DC; pp. 331–366.

Taylor, C. and Dogra, N. (2002) Adolescent perceptions of mental health services and mental health. *Community Care*, 19–25 September, pp. 42–43.

Taylor, H., Vostanis, P., Stuttaford, M. and Broad, B. (2004) *Evaluation of mental health service provision for young homeless people in Foyers*. Report, Leicester University.

Tees Valley Joint Strategy Unit (2002) *Births and deaths for borough wards in 'Kelby'*. www.teesvalley-jsu.gov.uk/private/n114312.txt [accessed 3/10/03].

Testa, A. and Coleman, L. (2006) *Sexual health knowledge, attitudes and behaviours among Black and Minority ethnic youth in London*. Trust for the Study of Adolescence: Brighton.

Thabet, A.A., Stretch, D. and Vostanis, P. (2000) Child mental health problems in Arab children. *International Journal of Social Psychiatry* **46**: 266–280.

Thomas, C. (1999) *Female forms: Understanding and experiencing disability*. Open University Press: Buckingham.

Thomson, R., Bell, R., Holland, J., Henderson, S., McGrellis, S. and Sharpe, S. (2002) Critical moments: Choice, chance and opportunity in young people's narratives of transition. *Sociology* **36**(2): 335–354.

Treasure, J. and Schmidt, U. (2003) Treatment overview. In Treasure, J., Schmidt, U. and Van Furth, E. (Eds), *Handbook of eating disorders*, 2nd edn. John Wiley & Sons, Ltd: Chichester; pp. 207–217.

Triseliotis, J., Borland, M. and Hill, M. (2000) *Delivering foster care*. British Association of Adoption and Fostering: London.

Troiden, R.R. (1989) The formation of homosexual identities. In Herdt, G. (Ed.), *Gay and lesbian youth*. Hanworth Press: New York.

Trommsdorff, G. (2000) Subjective experience of social change in individual development. In Bynner, J. and Silbereisen, R.K. (Eds), *Adversity and challenge in the life course in the new Germany and England*. Macmillan: Basingstoke.

United Nations (1989) *Convention on the Rights of the Child.* United Nations Children's Fund: Geneva.

UPIAS (1976) *Fundamental principles of disability.* UPIAS: London.

Utting, W. (1991) *Children in public care.* HMSO: London.

Utting, W. (1997) *People like us.* TSO: London.

Valentine, G. (1996) Angels and devils: Moral landscapes of childhood. *Society and Space* **14**: 581–599.

Valentine, G., Skelton, T. and Butler, R. (2002) The vulnerability and marginalisation of lesbian and gay youth. *Youth and Policy* **75**: 4–29.

Vostanis, P. (2004) Impact, psychological sequalae and management of trauma affecting children. *Current Opinion in Psychiatry* **17**: 269–273.

Vostanis, P. (2005) Patients as parents and young people approaching adulthood: How should we manage the interface between mental health services for young people and adults? *Current Opinion in Psychiatry* **18**: 449–454.

Vostanis, P., Meltzer, H., Goodman, R. and Ford, T. (2003) Service utilisation by children with conduct disorders. *European Child and Adolescent Psychiatry* **12**: 231–238.

Walker, J., Simpson, B. and McCarthy, P. (1991) *The housing consequences of divorce.* Housing Research Findings No. 25. Joseph Rowntree Foundation: York.

Ward, J. and Patel, N. (2005) Broadening the discussion on 'sexual exploitation': Ethnicity, sexual exploitation and young people. *Child Abuse Review* **15**(5): 341–351.

Watson, N., Shakespeare, T., Cunningham-Burley, S., Barnes, C., Corker, M., Davis, J. and Priestley, M. (2000) *Life as a disabled child: A qualitative study of young people's experiences and perspectives.* www.regard.co.uk

Webster, C., Simpson, D., MacDonald, R., Abbas, A., Cieslik, M., Shildrick, T. and Simpson, M. (2004) *Poor transitions: Social exclusion and young adults.* Policy Press: Bristol.

Webster, C., MacDonald, R. and Simpson, M. (2006) Predicting criminality? *Youth Justice* **6**(1): 7–22.

Weeks, J., Donovan, C. and Heaphy, B. (1999) Everyday experiments: Narratives of non-heterosexual relationships. In Silva, E.B. and Smart, C. (Eds), *The new family?* Sage: London; pp. 83–99.

Wellings, K. *et al.* (2001) Sexual behaviour in Britain: Early heterosexual experience. *The Lancet* **358**: 1843–1850.

Werner, E.E. (1989) Vulnerability and resiliency: A longitudinal perspective. In Brambring, M., Losel, F. and Skowronek, H. (Eds), *Children at risk: Assessment, longitudinal research and intervention.* Walter de Gruyter: Berlin.

Werner, E. and Smith, R. (1982) *Vulnerable but invincible: A study of resilient children.* McGraw-Hill: New York.

Werner, E. and Smith, R. (1992) *Overcoming the odds: High risk children from birth to adulthood.* Cornell University Press: New York.

Werner, E. and Smith, R. (2001) *Journeys from childhood to mid-life: Risk, resilience and recovery.* Cornell University Press: New York.

West, A. (2002) Childhood and children's rights in China. In Franklin, B. (Ed.), *The new handbook of children's rights.* Routledge: London.

West, P. and Sweeting, H. (2003) Fifteen, female and stressed: Changing patterns of psychological distress over time. *Journal of Child Psychology and Psychiatry* **44**: 399–411.

Whitaker, A., Johnson, J., Shaffer, D., Rapoport, J., Kalikow, K., Walsh, T., Davies, M., Braiman, S. and Dolinsky, A. (1990) Uncommon troubles in young people: Prevalence estimates of selected psychiatric disorders in a non-referred adolescent population. *Archives of General Psychiatry* **47**: 487–496.

White, M. (1991) *Against unemployment.* Policy Studies Institute: London.

Wight, D., Henderson, M., Raab, G., Abraham, C., Buston, K., Scott, S. and Hart, G. (2000) Extent of regretted sexual intercourse among young teenagers in Scotland. *British Medical Journal* **320**: 1243–1244.

Wikström, P. (2004) *Individual risk, life-style risk and adolescent offending: Findings from the Peterborough Youth Study.* www.scopic.ac.uk [accessed 11 March 2004].

Williams, F. (2004) *Rethinking families.* ESCRC CAVA Research Group. Calouste Gulbenkian Foundation: London.

Williams, R. (1995) (Ed.) *Suicide: The challenge confronted.* Health Education Authority: London.

Williamson, H. (1997) Status zer0 youth and the 'underclass': some considerations. In MacDonald, R. (Ed.), *Youth, the 'underclass' and social exclusion.* Routledge: London.

Willis, P. (1977) *Learning to labour: How working class kids get working class jobs.* Saxon House: London.

Wilson, A., Cairney, A., Jahoda, A. and Stalker, K. (2005) "What's happening?" Young people with learning disabilities and their parents'/carers' understandings of anxiety and depression. The Mental Health Foundation: London.

Window, S., Anderson, L. and Vostanis, P. (2004) A multi-agency service for child behavioural problems. *Community Practitioner* **77**: 180–184.

Young, J. (1999) *The exclusive society.* Sage: London.

Yule, W. (1999) Post-traumatic stress disorder. *Archive of Disease in Childhood* **80**: 107–109.

Zimiles, H. and Lee, V.E. (1991) Adolescent family structure and educational progress. *Developmental Psychology* **27**: 314–320.

Index